The Meaning Makers

The Meaning Makers
Children Learning Language and Using Language to Learn

GORDON WELLS

ONTARIO INSTITUTE
FOR STUDIES IN EDUCATION

Formerly Centre for the Study of Language
and Communication, University of Bristol

Heinemann
Portsmouth, New Hampshire

Heinemann Educational Books, Inc.
70 Court Street   Portsmouth, NH   03801

LONDON   EDINBURGH   MELBOURNE   AUCKLAND
HONG KONG   SINGAPORE   KUALA LUMPUR
NEW DELHI   IBADAN   NAIROBI   JOHANNESBURG
KINGSTON   PORT OF SPAIN

©1986 by Gordon Wells

10 9 8 7 6 5 4 3 2 1

Library of Congress Cataloging-in-Publication Data
Wells, C. Gordon.
  The meaning makers.
  Bibliography: p.
  1. Children—Language. 2. Language acquisition.
3. Literacy. 4. Language arts. I. Title.
LB1139.L3W44 1986   372.6   85-21969
ISBN 0-435-08247-7

Audio cassette ISBN 0-435-08253-1
(See page xv for more details.)

Printed in the United States of America

CONTENTS

Acknowledgments   vii

Introduction   ix

Notes on Transcriptions of Dialogue Extracts and Cassette   xv

O N E ■ THE CHILDREN AND THEIR FAMILIES   1

T W O ■ LEARNING TO TALK: THE PATTERN
OF DEVELOPMENT   19

T H R E E ■ LEARNING TO TALK: THE CONSTRUCTION
OF LANGUAGE   33

F O U R ■ TALKING TO LEARN   53

F I V E ■ FROM HOME TO SCHOOL   67

S I X ■ HELPING CHILDREN TO MAKE KNOWLEDGE
THEIR OWN   103

SEVEN ■ DIFFERENCES BETWEEN CHILDREN
IN LANGUAGE AND LEARNING   125

EIGHT ■ THE CENTRALITY OF LITERACY   147

NINE ■ THE CHILDREN'S ACHIEVEMENTS AT AGE 10   163

TEN ■ THE SENSE OF STORY   193

ELEVEN ■ RELATING PRACTICE TO THEORY   215

Notes   223

ACKNOWLEDGMENTS

Behind this book lie fifteen years of longitudinal research, to which many people contributed. First, the research team, whose work in making, transcribing, and coding the recordings, observing and testing the children, interviewing the parents and teachers, and then analyzing all these different types of data provided the foundation on which this work of interpretation is built. Although they are too numerous to mention individually, I should like to take this opportunity of thanking them for their unflagging commitment to the project and for their enthusiasm and support.

Second, I should like to acknowledge the support received from the various institutions that have funded the research: the Social Science Research Council of Great Britain (now the Economic and Social Research Council), the Nuffield Foundation, the Boots Charitable Trust, the Spencer Foundation (USA), and the Department of Education and Science. I should also like to thank the University of Bristol for providing a home for the project and the many other facilities without which the research could not have been carried out; also the County of Avon Education Authority for allowing us to observe the children in their classrooms.

My greatest debt of gratitude, however, is to the children themselves and to their parents and teachers. Their cooperation over the successive phases of the investigation has been more complete and freely given than I could ever have dared to hope. If any of them recognize themselves, despite the use of pseudonyms, in the pages that follow, I hope they will not be offended by the way in which their words have been presented. To all of them I wish to express my thanks for their patience and generosity.

In illustrating my discussion of different ways of working with children at school, I have made use of quotations from the work of other researchers. These are acknowledged in the notes. However, I should particularly like to thank Harold Rosen for allowing me to quote extensively from *The Language of Primary School Children* and Moira McKenzie, Warden of the Inner London Education Authority's Centre for Language in Primary Education, for letting me use the video recordings that were made under her direction for the *Extending Literacy* ETV series.

In writing this book, I have received help from many people. Discussions with teachers (many of whom are also parents) taking courses with me both in Bristol and Toronto have forced me to clarify my ideas about the broad issues with which it is concerned. I have also benefited from the comments of colleagues who have seen drafts of individual chapters. Two people deserve a special mention: Margaret Spencer, who read the whole of the first draft and helped me to see in what ways it needed revising; and Gen Ling Chang, who acted as a critical reader of the various successive revisions. I am grateful to both of them for their very positive and constructive suggestions. But my most unfailing source of help and encouragement has been my wife, Jan, herself a parent and teacher. It was she who persuaded me to write the book and, in numerous ways, made it possible for me to bring it to completion. In a very important sense, it is our joint creation.

INTRODUCTION

I still remember the excitement I felt when I first read Chomsky's claim that "language is a window on the mind." By studying the underlying regularities of the sentences that a speaker of a language can produce or understand, he suggested, we can discover the nature of the knowledge that he or she must possess, and from that we can draw conclusions about the workings of the mind itself. Heady stuff for someone concerned with the education of young children!

Reading further, I found that these were not merely philosophical speculations. Chomsky believed that his claims were empirically verifiable and that the study of children's language development was one way of carrying out such a test. Fortunately, my younger daughter was of a suitable age and I immediately embarked on an observational study.

According to my understanding of the theory, learning a language was very much a matter of arriving at appropriate rules of various kinds. I say "arriving at" since Chomsky argued that these rules were not taught; neither could they be deduced in any simple way from the sentences that the child might hear. The only possible explanation, therefore, was that they were in some way latent in the structure of the mind. The rules that I decided to investigate were those involved in the formation of questions to which the answer is either yes or no. In abstract, these rules state that a yes/no interrogative sentence can be formed from its associated declarative sentence by taking the first auxiliary element of the verb group in the main clause and permuting it with the subject noun phrase of the same main clause or, in the absence of an auxiliary verb, by adding the auxiliary "do" to the verb group and then permuting as before. This is apparently what every young child who can ask a question knows!

At this stage, Deborah had no auxiliary verbs in her repertoire and her yes/no questions all relied on rising intonation to achieve their effect. For example, when she wanted me to admire her bright new sweater, she said, "Like my new sweater?" Even when asked to repeat my "model" question, she still failed to imitate it correctly, saying instead, "Uh like my new sweater?" Every ten days I recorded her spontaneous speech, waiting for the first well-formed interrogative to appear. But, just in case she knew the rules but wasn't using them, I also tried to elicit interrogatives by such strategies as asking her to go and ask her mother if she wanted a cup of coffee. For several weeks, all her questions continued to be asked with intonation only: "Want a cup of coffee, Mummy?" she asked, as she obligingly relayed my question.

Then one day, in carrying out the same procedure, I heard her say, "Do you want a cup of coffee, Mummy?" and then she came straight back to where I was sitting and asked, "Can I have my little book a moment?" Within five or ten minutes, she had produced several more well-formed interrogative sentences, with "will" and "have" as auxiliaries. And then, after I had switched off the tape recorder, I heard her say to her elder sister, as they were playing on the stairs, "We can climb up the stairs, can't we?"—her first "tag-question," the description of which involved even more complicated rules.

In what sense she could be said to "know the rules" I was not sure, but there was no doubt that, apparently in one step, she had discovered and was making use of a principle of very wide generality. I was hooked. I wanted to know more. Fortunately for me, the opportunity arose a few years later to engage in a larger and more systematic piece of research and, at one level, this book is the story of that investigation.

At the start, the Bristol Study was planned as an investigation of language development in the years before entry to school. The aim was to chart the course of development of a group of British children learning English as their first language and, on the basis of what was discovered, to try to answer the more difficult questions about the causes of development.

As my own informal research had shown, by the age of two the process is well under way. By that age, the majority of children have begun to put words together to form rudimentary sentences, and they can clearly understand a considerable amount of what is said to them. But how do they initially crack the language code and, indeed, how do they discover that there is a code to be cracked?

Parents are delighted when they find that they are able to communicate with their children through words. Together they can now begin to explore the world through talk as well as through action. They also find that they can discover more precisely the needs of their children rather than having to rely on the interpretation of cries, smiles, and other nonverbal gestures. Equally important, parents are no longer dependent on physical means to exert control over their children when this is necessary. As a result, during the next few years children in almost every home engage in a great deal of talk, much of it with their parents or other caregivers. How important is this for their language development? Should parents deliberately set out to teach language, or will their children learn to talk whatever their parents do or do not do?

We were also interested in possible differences between children. In appearance and in rate of physical development, children vary considerably. Is the same true of their linguistic development? Do they all follow the same route, or are there important individual differences? We should probably expect some children to develop more rapidly than others, but how wide is the gap between the fastest and the slowest? What are the causes of this variation, and what are the consequences for progress at school?

Questions concerning consequences cannot be answered from a study of the preschool years alone and, having already carried out the first stage of a longitudinal study, it became clear that we should try to extend it at least into the first stage of schooling. There was a further, and more political, reason for doing so. In the late 1960s and early 1970s, both in Britain and in North America, considerable sums of public money were being spent to try to improve the educational achievement of children from families of lower socioeconomic status (SES). Various explanations were offered for the underachievement of many low-SES children, but most of them attributed at least part of the problem to some form of mismatch between the language of the home and the language of the school. At that time, however, there was little systematic relevant evidence based on observations of the same children at home and at school.

By following some of the children that we had first recorded at the age of 15 months into school, we hoped to be able to provide some much-needed information. If the language of the school is different from that of the home, what is the nature of these differences and do they affect all children equally? It has often been suggested that children from low-SES families are at a particular disadvantage in this respect and that this is a major cause of the relatively lower educational achievement of many of these children. Is there a causal connection between socioeconomic status, language experience in the preschool years, and educational achievement? If so, what are the specific linguistic skills, important for success in school, that are associated with membership of one social group rather than another, and what can be done to give children from all types of family background a more equal opportunity to succeed at school?

Children's language development before they come to school takes place very largely through talk—through the conversation that they have with the members of their immediate family circle. As soon as they enter school, however, they are expected to learn to read and write and, by the time they are seven or eight years old, a substantial part of their learning is dependent on their ability to cope with written language. Some children have little difficulty in mastering these skills and, from the beginning, are keen to explore the possibilities that literacy opens up to them. There are others, however, for whom written language seems to have little meaning; despite much time and effort they are unable to reach the stage of "independence" in communicating through reading and writing and, as a result, their progress in other areas of the curriculum is jeopardized. All too often they come to be seen—and to see themselves—as failures. What is it that is required, then, for children to be able to extend their command of language to include the written mode? Are there preschool experiences that prepare some children more effectively than others to take the learning of writing in their stride? If so, what sort of experiences at school can best help children to make up for what they have missed at home?

In order to try to provide answers to these qustions—insofar as this is possible on the basis of a single study carried out in one particular cultural environment—we followed 32 of the original representative sample of 128 children through to the final year of their elementary education. Using tests, assessments by the teachers, interviews with the parents, the teachers, and the children themselves, as well as direct observations, we tried to identify the major linguistic influences on the children's educational achievement. The information that we obtained provides the basis of the story of language development that this book attempts to tell.

Some readers may be surprised at my use of the word "story." But I have chosen it quite deliberately. Stories are a way of making sense—of giving meaning to observable events by making connections between them. However, for any set of events there is almost always more than one possible interpretation—as a day in any courtroom would amply demonstrate. Carrying out research is, in this respect, like any other form of inquiry based on evidence. Only a certain number of events can be observed and although, like good detectives, researchers have hunches to guide them in choosing what events to observe and what clues to look for, in the last resort they have to go beyond the evidence in order to present a coherent account. The available evidence is given meaning by being embedded in a story in which it makes sense.

Stories, like other language forms, are created in the telling. They are influenced, of course, by other stories—in this case, the work of others who have thought and written about language development and its relation to education. They also have a history in the accumulated experience of the storyteller. But, most important, a story is the expression of the present attempt by the teller to find meaning in those experiences. My purpose in writing this book, therefore, is to make sense of the evidence that was collected during the research project and of the ideas that I have obtained through reading and discussion, and to tell the meaning that I have made to others who share my concerns.

Seen from this perspective, there can be no true stories. The evidence is never so complete or so unambiguous as to rule out alternative interpretations. The important criteria in judging the worth of a story are: does it fit the facts as I have observed them and does it provide a helpful basis for future action? It is my hope that many who are concerned with the care and education of young children—parents, teachers, and educational policy makers—will feel that, on these criteria, the story was worth the telling.

NOTES ON TRANSCRIPTIONS OF DIALOGUE EXTRACTS AND CASSETTE

In order to convey something of the pace and tone of the conversational extracts, I have used the following conventions:

- **Emphasis.** Where a word or syllable is spoken with extra emphasis, it is presented in boldface type.
- **Simultaneous speech.** Where two people speak at once, the overlapping portions of their utterances are underlined.
- **Incompleteness.** Where an utterance is interrupted or otherwise left incomplete, this is indicated by "—." This often occurs within a speaking turn when the speaker stops and makes a fresh start at what he or she wants to say.
- **Pausing.** Both between and within utterances, there are sometimes noticeable pauses. These are indicated by one or a series of dots. Each dot represents approximately one second of silence. Where the pause lasts for 5 seconds or longer, this information is stated in brackets.

Because no transcripts can ever capture all the features of interaction to which a listener responds, we have decided to produce a cassette containing some of the longer extracts quoted in this book. These extracts have been taken from chapters 2, 3, 5, 6, 8, and 10 respectively. This cassette (ISBN 0-435-08253-1) can be purchased from the publishers.

One

———

THE CHILDREN
AND THEIR FAMILIES

———

"It's half past nine. Where's Rosie?"
"She got a knife in her hands, Dad."
"Oh, my God!"

This was our first meeting with Rosie. Up to that point unnoticed, as she sat quietly under the table playing with a knife, she became briefly the focus of attention. Then, the knife removed, she was left once again to her own devices.

■ ROSIE

It was shortly after breakfast on 27 July 1973, and we were making our first observation of Rosie. But an observation with a difference. The only evidence of our interest in Rosie was a slight bulge under her dress at the front and a rather larger hump between her shoulders. This was the bugging device—a pair of miniature microphones and a battery-operated radio transmitter—left in hcr home on the previous afternoon. Her elder brother and sisters were naturally intrigued. A little later, when Rosie had fallen asleep on the sofa, Kelvin (age 8) and his friend Mike took a closer look.

Mike: What's it connected to? Her ears or her mouth?

Mother: Eh? No, she just got it on. She got a square thing over her shoulders and round to the back.

Kelvin: Mike, look at this. There it is—look.

Mother: The round thing there is the microphone.

Mike: How does the noise come out, then, if it ain't in her mouth?

Mother: I don't know. You see there's a wire going over there and a wire going over that side.

Mike: Is there a wire in her mouth?

Mother: No. There's another microphone there. When she speaks it goes on that recorder in there [*pointing to a box in the corner of the room*].

Mike: Can you hear her speak?

Mother: No. They're coming tonight to play it back . . . And if there's anything comes out what we wants rubbed off, they'll rub it off.[1]

Like most of the children, at 15 months Rosie wasn't saying much that we could interpret with confidence. She also slept for quite a lot of the day. But this first recording gave the family an opportunity to get used to having the recorder in their home (there were very few references to the equipment on subsequent recordings). It also gave us our first glimpse of them and of their relationships with each other.

Rosie and her family lived in the inner city in a small terrace house built in the year of Queen Victoria's Jubilee. Father, a laborer, was not regularly employed and spent most of his time around the house. So, with two adults and five children—ranging from Kelvin, age 8, to Donna, only a year older than Rosie—as well as a large dog, there was not much space in the house when all of them were at home. With little money, providing for the children was a fairly constant preoccupation and so, although they were clearly fond of Rosie and concerned for her welfare, her parents did not find time to give her a great deal of individual attention. As she grew older, however, her brother and elder sisters included her in their activities; and by the time she went to school, she and Donna were almost inseparable.

■ ABIGAIL

Abigail, whom we first met a few weeks later, was another child with several older siblings. She, however, lived on the other side of the city center in a spacious four-floor house in a Regency terrace with a large garden. Like Rosie, though, she tended to get overlooked when all the family was at home—at least until she had learned to take part in the conversation. On one occasion, her mother found her in one of her sisters' bedrooms, playing alone with materials for tie-and-dye.

Abigail [asking about the bottles of dye]: What's those?
Mother: Did you take anything out?
Abigail: Yeh.
Mother [under her breath]: Oh, my God . . . Oh, Christ. [*Then, to Abigail*]
Open your mouth.

Fortunately, it was a false alarm. Abigail had not tried to drink the dye.

What both these narrow escapes illustrate (though more dramatically than usual) is just how much of parental speech to the one- to two-year-old is likely to be concerned with the child's safety and welfare, particularly when, with older and more verbal children competing for their attention, parents only notice what the youngest is up to when the damage is done. In fact, for many of the children at this age, controlling utterances, together with exclamations and endearments, provided the majority of the speech addressed to them.

[*While Mother is talking to Rosanna, Abigail has gone into the garden with no shoes on and stepped in a puddle.*]
Abigail: [shouts with glee].
Mother [looking out of the door]: Oh, Abby! For goodness' sake! You've come out in your tights after I've just dressed you. Taken ages to get you ready. [*She picks Abigail up, takes her inside, and returns to her conversation with Rosanna.*]

Notice, though, that such controlling utterances can also provide quite a lot of information about the way things are—or, perhaps, about the way they *should or should not* be. As we eavesdropped on these families, we came to realize very clearly that learning to talk is just one facet (albeit probably the most important one) of learning to be a member of a particular culture, with all the taken-for-granted assumptions of what is important, what is approved or disapproved of, and what that entails. Here is another example.

Abigail, now 21 months old, has been to the supermarket with her mother. On the way home, Abigail has been exploring the box of groceries and has found a packet of stock cubes. She is now sucking one of them. (*Note:* Where an utterance is unintelligible, the number of asterisks corresponds to the number of words judged to have been spoken.)

Abigail: *.
Mother: Oh, yucky! Oh, where's the packet gone, darling?
[*No response, as Abigail continues to suck the cube.*]
It's for cooking, sweetheart. Look, it's for putting in a cooking pot to make a stew.

Abigail's parents, both professional people, were involved in a Franco-British society and, on several of the occasions when we observed her, there were young French people staying in the house. This led to many interesting conversations about places and customs that the visitors had remarked on or that were drawn to their attention. Thanks to her microphone, we were able to eavesdrop on these conversations just as Abigail was. What she made of them we cannot tell, but there is no doubt that, compared with many other children, the range of language to which she was exposed as a listener was extremely wide and varied.

By 24 months, Abigail had acquired sufficient linguistic resources to begin to join in the conversation, provided the other person gave her his or her full attention. In the following extract, she was talking with her father about the jigsaw puzzle that they were doing together.

Abigail [*referring to a figure in the puzzle*]: Mummy.
Father [*confirming*]: That's Mummy. And who's that?
Abigail: Man.
Father: Very good. And who's that?
Abigail: Bike.
Father: Bicycle.
Abigail: Bicycle.
Father: And that?
Abigail: And car.
Father: And a car. Ooh, look!
Abigail: Man.
Father: Lots of men.

Three months later, she was well on her way to mastering the adult language. In the following extract, we find her alone with her mother, engaged in drawing and coloring.

Abigail: There Teddy. There 'tis.
Mother: Is that your teddy?
Abigail: Yes, it is.
Mother: Do you want to draw a teddy?
Abigail [*referring to a crayon*]: I have that one.
Mother: Can I color him in with that one?
Abigail: Yeh.
Mother: Oh no, it won't color. Can I have another color to color him in?
Abigail: Yeh. Have that one [*handing her a crayon*].
Mother: A brown teddy. Oh, that one's nearly gone too [nearly worn out].
Abigail: Green one. Can I have green one? [*Whispers to self*] We haven't done green . . . greeny one. Purple, green. [*Softly*] We haven't got green one. [*Addressing mother again*] Those are too big!

■ GARY

Our first impression of Gary was of a child with a healthy appetite—
perhaps because much of his parents' speech to him during the first
two observations was about food. The following extract comes from
the second, at 18 months.

Gary [crying]: Look [?].
Father: What do you want?
Mother: Come here.
Gary [wanting to look in the cupboard]: Look.
[*Father lifts him up to the cupboard at which he's pointing. Gary takes out
the biscuit (cookie) tin.*]
Father [to Mother, amused]: Hey, Joyce, look! [*To Gary*] That what you
wants?
Gary: Uh [yes].
Father: What d' you want?
Gary [taking a handful of biscuits]: That.
Father: He don't take one [only one].
Mother: He got to take two.
Father [to Mother]: Yes. [*To Gary*] All right?
Gary: Uh.
Father: Get down?
Gary: Uh. [*Father puts him down, the biscuit tin still in reach. Mother and
Father talk together for a minute.*]
Gary: Hey, Dada! Look! [*Gary gives one biscuit each to Mother and Father
and has two left in his hand.*]
Father: Is that one for Sandra? [his sister]
Gary: Hm. [*Makes no attempt to give it to her.*]
Father: How come you got two?
Gary [running off]: Ha!

Gary's sister was just under two years older than he and, like the
other two children we have met, he was often overshadowed by her—
at least to begin with—and there were many minor tiffs. But they also
played happily together, as in the following extract, when Gary was
27 months.

[*Gary and Sandra are pretending to go shopping.*]
Mother: Where is you going?
Gary: Going up the shops.
Mother: All right.
Sandra [to Mother]: I won't be late. [*To Gary*] Right, get in the car then.
Gary: All right.
Sandra [with a sudden change of plan]: We're going to be married now.
Gary: Here comes the bride.

Sandra: Here comes the bride.

[*They continue, shouting together.*]

Gary's father was a diesel engine mechanic and his working hours meant that he was quite often at home during the day. He would spend some of this time in his garage, working on his car or motor bike. Gary often went to "help" him, playing with the tools and "mending" his favorite toys, a tractor and a pedal car. But he also enjoyed helping his mother, as in the following extract, at 33 months, when Mother was doing the ironing.

Gary [*referring to the nylon thread that he is using as his washing line*]: I break it, Mummy.

Mother: No, you won't be able to. It's nylon.

Gary: Why, Mum?

Mother: No, you won't be able to break it, Gary. That's to hang your washing on.

Gary: Oh. [*Asking about what Mother is ironing*] What—what have you got there?

Mother: Mm?

Gary: Hang my washing out. That's my washing line, isn't it? I can put some clothes on there, can't I?

Mother: All right.

Gary: I'm going to put some clothes on there. [*He hangs up some hankies.*] Hang them up. I shall hang them up.

This was the longest conversation that Gary had had up to this point in our observations, and it is significant, I think, that it took place when he was "helping" his mother with the ironing. Parents are busy, most of the day, with the routine business of running the household; only a minority in our study took time to play with their children, joining in the children's activities. From time to time, of course, they would ask about or comment on what the child was doing, or respond to requests for help. But such conversations were, on the whole, brief and undeveloped. When a mother or father had the time and patience to allow the child to become engaged in her or his adult activities, on the other hand, quite long and interesting conversations often occurred.

There are two reasons for this, I suspect. On the one hand, children have a natural desire to try out those adult activities that they understand (as we see in the sort of role play illustrated above in the shopping episode), and talking about them is one of the ways in which they come to understand them better. And, on the other hand, from the adult's point of view, the purposefulness of the task gives purpose to the conversation. Under these conditions, children's questions and observations are more easily understood and hence are more likely to receive more satisfying responses.

■ PENNY

While Gary liked best to help his Dad (when he was allowed to), Penny was from an early age a regular little housewife. Here she is at 24 months. Father, a fireman just returned from work, is having his dinner in the front room, and Penny is running to and fro from the kitchen to serve him.

Penny: I've got more dinner.
Father: Get a piece of bread and butter, please.
Penny: Want some bread and butter?
Father: Yes, to put over these.
Penny [*running into kitchen*]: Me going to get bread.
Mother: He's a nuisance. He ought to have done it hisself. He's lazy.
Penny: I take in Daddy's bread. Daddy wants some tea?
Mother: I expect so. Here you are. Go and give that to Daddy.
[*Penny runs into the front room and gives bread to her father.*]
Father: Thank you.

Of all the children introduced so far, Penny was the most linguistically advanced when we first met her. This was the very first interchange on the tape:

[*Penny is playing with a clock.*]
Mother: Oh-oh-oh! What's that?
Penny: Tick-tock.
Mother: It's a tick-tock.

No child was so obviously into the "naming game" as Penny, as both she and her mother asked and answered the question "What's that?" about household objects and pictures in a mail-order catalogue. At 18 months, looking at a picture book of clocks and watches, her mother encouraged her to count, which she did, somewhat erratically:

Mother: One, two, . . .
Penny: Three.
Mother: Three, four, five . . .
Penny: Six, seven, ten.
Mother [*firmly*]: Seven, **eight** . . .
Penny: Ten.

At the same age, she pretended to read a picture book by herself, while her mother was busy in the kitchen. Surprisingly, though, we never heard anybody read a story to her.

Penny, too, had elder siblings: two brothers, five and six years older

than she. However, her situation was very different from that of the
other children we have so far considered, for the two boys spent much
of their time playing with their friends and were much less frequently
competing with Penny for their parents' attention. Indeed, although
not spoiled, she was quite obviously the whole family's pride and joy,
and they all enjoyed playing and talking with her. The following extract
comes from the recording already quoted above, just after her father
had finished his dinner. Penny is playing with her teddy, which is in
her doll's pram (carriage).

Penny: Teddy isn't * * [two unintelligible words].
Father: Eh? Teddy isn't what?
Penny: Er . . . [*sighs*].
Father: All right now?
Penny: Yeh.
Father: Is he in the pram?
Penny: Yeh.
Father: Good. Put the blanket over him, then.
    [*Penny covers Teddy with the blanket.*]
    Not over his face. He won't be able to see.
Penny: Come on, Teddy.
Father: Want me to do it?
Penny: Yeh.
Father [*whispers*]: All right.
Penny [*shouts to Sam, the dog*]: Stay there!
Father: Shh!
Penny: Shh!
Father [*referring to Teddy*]: He's going night-nights. [*To Penny*] Say "Night-
    night, Teddy."
Penny: Night-night, Teddy.
    [*She wheels the pram into the kitchen.*]
    He asleep, Mummy.
Mother: Who?
Penny: Teddy. He's a bad.
Mother: Bad, is he? Oh, poor Teddy!
Penny: He's got a bad leg.
Mother: Oh, poor Teddy!

The other striking characteristic of Penny's family life was the
constant stream of visitors: relatives, friends, neighbors, and their children. Not a single observation passed without at least one visitor calling
for an hour or two. A friendly, vivacious child, Penny benefited enormously from this wide range of playmates and conversational partners.
In other homes, however, the effect of visitors could be very different.
Some mothers, of course, invited friends with children, in order to

ensure that their own children had friends of the same age to play with, and the adults would keep a watchful eye on them while they drank a cup of tea or coffee, occasionally entering into the children's play. Others, though, were so relieved to have another adult to talk to that they resented any interruption from the child. Already short of adult conversation, Rosie, for example, would be almost completely ignored while a visitor was in the house.

■ ANTHONY

This sometimes seemed to be the case with Anthony, the only child of somewhat older parents. Mother had had a management position in a large company before Anthony was born and, although she was obviously very fond of him, she sometimes seemed to find the continuous company of a young child rather irksome.

[Anthony is playing with the stick used for stirring the bucket of soiled nappies (diapers).]

Mother: Oh, Tony! Don't put that in your mouth. Ugh!
   [Anthony puts the stick down, goes to the socket where the fridge is plugged in, and tries to switch it on and off.]
   Now what are you up to? You know what? You and I are going to have a little chat—

Anthony: ∗ ∗.

Mother: —about plugs, for a start, and not—

Anthony: ∗ ∗.

Mother: —switching them on and off. Right? Especially the one that's plugging in the fridge.

Anthony: ∗. *[Begins to hit his mother.]*

Mother: Who are you thumping?

Anthony: ∗.

Mother *[crossly]*: You sit down there.

An only child—or one with much older brothers and sisters—can put a severe strain on a parent who is at home alone all day. With no other children to play with, such a child is dependent on the adult for company and stimulation as well as for physical care. When the latter proves difficult—for example, when the child is not cooperative—it is not surprising that some parents easily lose their patience.

Mother *[trying to dress Anthony in order to go out]*: Tony! It's very not funny. It's hard. It's difficult. And you're not making it any easier. Stand up! Don't be so stupid!

Anthony: That pom-pom *[swinging it so that he hits his mother's face]*.

Mother *[crossly]*: Don't ever do that again, Tony! *[Still struggling to get his gloves on]* Tony! Concentrate on what I'm trying to do, will you? There's a good boy.

Anthony: Mm.

Mother: There's nothing worse than trying to put gloves on somebody who's not concentrating.

Not all Anthony's conversational experience was like this, of course. There were many more enjoyable exchanges. But there was no doubt that his mother found the toddler stage hard work and perhaps looked forward to the day when he would be able to engage in intellectually more stimulating conversation. Anthony was, in fact, rather slow in learning to talk, and although his mother tried to be patient, she obviously found his limited abilities frustrating on occasion. The following extract comes from the recording made when he was 2½ years old. They were looking at a picture book together, and Mother had asked him to find a mouse in the picture.

Anthony: Where's it gone, Mummy?

Mother: It's sitting on a little boat.

Anthony: Uh?

Mother: Here you are—sitting on a little boat.

Anthony: All gone, Mummy.

Mother: It's on that page right in front of you. [*Anthony still can't see the mouse.*] Ever such a tiny little mouse.

Anthony: Uh?

Mother: Can you see it? [*Trying a new tactic*] Can you see the sheep? See the baby sheep? Well, just in front of the baby sheep is a little tiny mouse.

Anthony: All gone, Mummy.

Mother [*under her breath*]: Oh, God! [*To Anthony*] What's that?

Anthony: Little, Mummy.

Mother: Can you see the baby chicken?

Anthony: Huh?

Mother: Can you see a baby chicken?

Anthony: Ah. All gone, Mummy.

Mother: You look for the baby chicken.

Anthony [*excitedly*]: There it is!

Mother: There it is. A daddy chicken and a mummy chicken and a baby chicken.

[*With a sigh of relief, she moves away, leaving Anthony with the book.*]

■ JONATHAN

Jonathan was also an only child with older-than-average parents. But in his case, family life seemed to a much greater extent to revolve around him. Not that he was spoiled. Rather, it appeared that, from an early age, parents and child enjoyed doing many things together. Jonathan was a great lover of books and stories. On the very first observation, when Jonathan had a cold and an ear infection, Mother produced a book as soon as he had finished breakfast and looked at it with him in order to cheer him up.

[*Jonathan moans.*]

Mother: Shall we look at your book? Come and look at your book? [*Jonathan mumbles.*] Come on then.

Jonathan [*showing interest*]: Doddy [doggy?].

Mother [*checking*]: Who's that? [*Jonathan coughs.*] Dog.

Jonathan: Dog.

Mother: Dog.

Jonathan [*coughs*]: Dog.

Mother [*turning to next picture*]: Baloo [name of the bear in the book]. Bear.

Jonathan: Bear. [*Coughs.*]

Father [*entering the room*]: If that cough gets any worse, take him to the doctor's.

Mother: I *shall*, darling. Honestly, I'm sure you think I'neglect him.

[*Jonathan gives the book to Father.*]

Father: Thank you.

Mother [*to Jonathan*]: Say, "My Mum don't neglect me. She just weighs up which I'm likely to do worse by—sitting in the doctor's surgery [office] getting coughed and spit all over, or being cured at home!"

The significance of books and stories in Jonathan's life can be gauged from the following account of what happened during the day of our second observation, when Jonathan was 18 months old. The timing device on the tape recorder was programmed to switch on for 90 seconds at approximately 20-minute intervals between 9:00 A.M. and 6:00 P.M. From the 24 samples recorded in this way at each observation, 18 were selected for transcription. In Jonathan's case, 9 included some activity involving a book.

9:19 A.M. Mother is ironing. Jonathan points to a book, saying, "There, there," asking to be read to. "Let Mummy just iron the anorak," says Mother. She finishes and starts to read.

9:51 A.M. Jonathan is eating an apple. Mother opens a picture book. "Teddy there," says Jonathan. They continue to look at the book.

10:07 A.M. Mother is putting on Jonathan's shoes. "Find the shoes in the book," says Mother, looking at the Mothercare catalogue.

12:09 P.M.   Jonathan is just waking up from his morning nap. He is sitting on his mother's lap, looking at a picture book with her.

1:03 P.M.   After his lunch, Jonathan is looking at his picture book.

1:17 P.M.   Mother has joined him, and they look at the book together.

2:55 P.M.   Jonathan's nose is blocked and he has difficulty breathing. Mother reads a book to distract him from his discomfort.

3:57 P.M.   "Do you want to look at this new book?" asks Mother. Jonathan, who is sitting on her lap, is eager to do so.

5:59 P.M.   Mother sings nursery rhymes to Jonathan as she gets him ready for bed. He recognizes the figures on a poster by his bed as those he has seen in one of his books.

On these early occasions, the books are almost always picture books, and the "reading" is essentially matching words and pictures. But these are soon replaced by picture storybooks, which, because they are much longer, are more widely spaced through the day. When Jonathan is 36 months old, his mother insists, as she finishes a story, "I told you I'm only reading one book now." On another occasion, she refuses to read him a story because he's just wet his pants instead of asking to go to the toilet.

Because of his work as a motor mechanic maintaining machines in a factory, Jonathan's father was rarely at home during the observations. When he was at home, though, he joined in the story-reading as well, as we found in our observation at 27 months.

However, not all Jonathan's interests were so literary. Our observations show him engaging in many other joint activities with his mother, such as playing with toy bricks, helping with the baking and the cleaning and, of course, just talking.

Jonathan was, in fact, the most advanced of this group of children when we completed the last round of the home observations. At three and a half, he had already mastered the basic grammar of English and had an estimated vocabulary of several thousand words. With these resources, he was able to converse effectively on a wide range of topics, as the following extracts demonstrate. In the first, he is offering his mother some of the imaginary dinner he has just cooked with play dough.

Mother: You're cutting my food up for me, are you? Can't I cut it myself?
Jonathan: There's just a chance because I'm going to have a bit of it before and then a bit of the big one. And then you're going to have a bit of the

little one, then a bit of the big one. But you eat that bit of the little one.

Mother: Oh, that was delicious!

Jonathan: That's my best meal.

Mother: You cooked it beautifully. How did you cook it?

Jonathan: Let me show you. Well . . . I rolled it first, right?

Mother: Yes.

Jonathan: Then, when it was too big, right— ?

Mother: Yes.

Jonathan: When it was dropping—right?—I folded it over again—right?

Mother: Yes.

Jonathan: Then rolled it again.

Mother: And was that how it was so nice—because you kept rolling it?

Jonathan: I rolled it like that—right?—and flattened it again. I rolled it bigger and bigger and bigger and bigger.

Mother: And you put one of those [*indicating a pretend oxo—bullion—cube*] to crumble up, don't you? Because Mummy does.

Jonathan [*uncertainly*]: Well I don't *crumble* it up.

Mother: Crumble it up and make the gravy nice.

Jonathan: Well that is to make it so nice.

Unfortunately, at this moment, the recorder switched off, so we shall never know what other delicacies Jonathan cooked that day. Not many of the conversations that we recorded in these early observations were sustained over so many turns. This in itself is an indication of Jonathan's relative linguistic maturity. But is interesting to note that the majority of extended conversations developed around topics like this, which arose from shared activities to which both participants were giving their full attention.

The last extract also involves play dough, from which Mother has been making a model figure. In its wry humor, this conversation captures another side of the quality of family life in Jonathan's home.

Jonathan: What are you making?

Mother: Wait and see what I'm making.

Jonathan [*after several seconds*]: What are you *making*?

Mother: A man with a cigarette in his mouth. [*Laughs.*]

Jonathan: Make—make his feet. Shall I give you some play dough to make his feet?

Mother: There's his feet—there.

Jonathan: Where is his feet?

Mother: One, two.

Jonathan: Why is he a little man?

Mother: Because he's only tiny. Smoking's stunted his growth.

Jonathan: He'll grow big, won't he?

Mother: If he gives up smoking, yes.

Jonathan: He's giving up smoking.

[*Father coughs loudly in the background.*]

Mother: You'd better take the cigarette out of his mouth then, hadn't you?

Jonathan: I know. Coo! He's growing and coughing.

Mother: Growing and coughing.

Jonathan: Because he shouldn't have a cigarette in his mouth, should he?

Mother: No.

Jonathan: He's a silly man, isn't he?

Father [*kisses Jonathan*]: See you later. [*Father is going to work.*]

Jonathan: See you later. [*Referring to his father*] He's a silly man, too.

■ CHOOSING THE CHILDREN

Rosie, Abigail, Gary, Penny, Anthony, and Jonathan are just 6 of the 32 children that we studied from shortly after their first birthdays until the last year of their primary (elementary) schooling. However, the 32 children were themselves selected from a larger sample of 128, picked from a random sample of more than 1,000 names of preschool children resident in the city of Bristol, England, drawn from Health Department records. Each family was interviewed and, on the basis of the information obtained,[2] the 128 children were picked from those families who agreed to participate (more than 87% of those interviewed). In selecting the children, an equal number of boys and girls at each age were chosen, and season of birth and the full range of family background were equally represented.[3] Half the children were three and a half years old when we first observed them. These children were observed until they were just over five years old. (We shall be meeting some of them in later chapters.) The others were fifteen months old, and it was exactly half of this group who were selected for the full longitudinal investigation.

Observations were made once every three months, ten for each child, so that by the time we had finished this phase of the research we had carried out more than twelve hundred observations and collected a corpus of nearly a quarter of a million child utterances.[4] At each observation, in a playroom at the University, we tested the children's comprehension and their ability to imitate the sentences in a simple story and, when each child was three and a half years old, we interviewed the parents in order to gain further information about the home environment and about the parents' views on bringing up their children. Then, over the next five years, we carried out a variety of analyses of this material in order to try to answer questions about the sequence of language development and about the influences of the home environment on that development. These answers and the conclusions that I believe we can draw from them will be the subject of the following chapters.

However, the material we collected has more to tell us than can be revealed by this sort of quantitative analysis. Learning to talk is more than acquiring a set of linguistic resources; it is also discovering how to use them in conversation with a variety of people and for a variety of purposes. To understand children's language development, therefore, we need to study it in its context of interaction: people talking to each other as they go about their normal business. And it is this embeddedness of conversation in the texture of everyday life that is the strongest impression one gets from listening to the recordings that we made and from reading the resulting transcripts. In the following chapters, I shall quote from them at some length in order to try to convey something of this texture as well as to illustrate the conclusions we arrived at.

Some examples have already been given in the first part of this chapter. From them one gains a strong sense of the individuality of each child's experience and of the enormous variety that is to be found in any representative sample of children. Every child is unique, and so is every family. However, reading through the transcripts also convinces one of the very great degree of similarity that exists between children and families, if not in detail then at least in broad outline. And in trying to explain the universal accomplishment that language learning represents, these similarities are perhaps even more important than the differences.

One of the most striking features that is common to all families is the repetitiveness of the everyday life of a young child. Meals, dressing and undressing, and the performance of bodily functions provide the content of talk in sample after sample. (A whole book could be written on the different approaches to toilet training and on the varied vocabulary involved!) As a result, the same sorts of conversation occurred over and over again, different in small details from family to family but in function essentially the same. In all families, too, there was a concern with safety—both the child's and that of the property of other members of the family: "Don't touch! That's Daddy's." It is not surprising, therefore, that there is great similarity between children in the sorts of utterances that they first produce. For example, the 's marker of possession appears quite early in the speech of almost all the children.[5]

Another striking characteristic is the brevity—not to say the disjointedness—of a large proportion of the conversations. The examples quoted earlier in this chapter are nearly all longer and more coherent than average. In fact, the average length of a conversation was 3.3

sequences (that is to say, about 6 turns) at 18 months and still only 4.0 sequences (or about 8 turns) at 42 months. There are several reasons for this. Perhaps the most obvious is that young children are very limited in what they are able to say (though probably not so limited in the meanings they try to express), and quite a lot of their utterances are uninterpretable, even by their parents, who know them well. Sometimes the adult just doesn't have the time or the patience to discover what the child is trying to say, so the conversation comes to an abortive end. On other occasions the adult may understand all too well but decide that feigning incomprehension or not hearing is easier than having to refuse a request and cope with the consequences. "We'll see" or "When you've done ———" are similar strategies that we observed parents using to avoid confrontation.

A further reason for the brevity and for much of the apparent incoherence is the close relation between what is said and the activity in which the speech is embedded. What to an eavesdropper is incoherent may make perfect sense to the participants, who can see what the speaker is looking at and who have a very good idea what he or she wants them to do or think about it. The following conversation took place between Penny and her mother when Penny was 2½ years old.

Penny: I wants that one.	1
Mother: Mm.	2
Penny: A ball. I get it back.	3
Mother: Yes.	4
Penny: Our ball out there.	5
Mother: Which one do you want?	6
Penny: That one.	7
Get them all there—in there now.	8
Is that yours, Ma?	9
Mother: Yes.	10
Penny: Yes?	11
Mine is hot, Ma.	12

At first sight, this appears almost incomprehensible. In fact, it is two different conversations that are interwoven: the first about the dinner that Mother is serving and the second about the ball that Penny notices in the garden as she looks through the window. Lines 1, 2, 6, and 7 concern Penny's choice of plate; in lines 9–11 she checks that the other plate is her mother's; in line 12 she comments on the heat of her own plate. It is this conversation—and the activity of serving the dinner to which it is related—that is at the focus of the mother's attention. The second conversation, lines 3–5 and 8, are on a topic of Penny's choosing, to which the mother gives only the minimum of attention, in the form of an acknowledgment. Nevertheless, both conversations succeed in achieving their purposes: Mother serves the dinner in a way that meets with Penny's approval (a very important matter—as we discovered from listening to many episodes in which children objected because they hadn't been given the right spoon or because the ketchup was obscuring the picture on the plate, and so on), and Penny shares with her mother her interest in the ball she has noticed. She also appears to recognize—with no words spoken at all—that her intention, "I get it back," will have to be deferred until later. Most conversations involving young children, then, like this one, are rooted in the here and now of perception, intention, and action and so can be inexplicit and even fragmentary, yet still be successful for the purpose at hand.

When more extended conversations did occur, they were likely to be of a more discursive or exploratory nature: recalling past events, discussing what could be seen from the window, explaining how things work, or considering what might happen—to the speakers themselves or to characters in stories or on television. For such conversations to take place, it seems, attention needs to be freed from the pressure of action so that it can be devoted to the attempt to achieve mutual understanding. Young children not only have restricted powers of expression, they also have an understanding of the world that is both limited and naive. If adult and child are to succeed in elaborating a shared meaning over a number of turns, the adult has to make the effort to understand the child's intended meaning and to extend it in terms that the child can understand. This requires a willingness to listen sympathetically and an intuitive ability to pitch what one says at the right level—both intellectually and linguistically. Most parents are able to talk with children in this way, we discovered, but the pressure of other concerns meant that some of them rarely found the time to do so.

These pressures, in some cases, were considerable: family breakdown, shortage of money, ill health, and overcrowded housing, to mention only the most obvious. But in no family did we observe a child for whom the parents did not show love and affection and a concern for his or her well-being—even though the manner in which this was expressed varied considerably and was not always consistent. We were also struck by the amount of humor: parents joking with the children and teasing them in a friendly fashion, and parents joking with each other about their children's annoying characteristics as well as the more obviously endearing ones.

These, then, were the homes in which the children were growing up—enormously varied, yet sharing many common characteristics in their patterns of everyday life and in the conversations that arose from them. This was the experience through which the children learned to talk and, through talk, also learned about the world they lived in. How did they do it? The following chapters offer the beginnings of an answer.

Two

LEARNING TO TALK: THE PATTERN OF DEVELOPMENT

How do children learn to talk? This is a question to which many parents and teachers would like to know the answer, for then they would know better what sort of help they should give. But to ask the question in this way is to assume that all children—or at least the majority of them—are sufficiently similar for one single answer to be possible. From the point of view of the concerned parent or teacher, of course, it would be much easier if that proved to be the case; but it certainly should not be assumed without question.

On the face of it, there are quite strong reasons for expecting the opposite. The evidence of differences between children in rate of learning is overwhelming, as is the evidence for wide divergences between families in the model of language in use that they provide. These differences were clearly apparent just from listening to the recordings we made—as could be seen in the extracts quoted in the previous chapter. When we consider the much greater differences that exist between different cultural groups who happen to speak the same language and the still greater differences between language communities, there are even stronger reasons for wanting evidence that the sequence of learning is essentially the same in all children before assuming that an answer to the question about *how* they learn can be given in a form that applies to all children.[1]

One way of tackling this issue is to compare the sequence of development across a large sample of children who are all learning the same language. To the extent that they all show essentially the same sequence, there will be a basis for continuing to seek a universal explanation of how learning takes place. On the other hand, strong evidence of dissimilarity would be a reason for doubting the feasibility of such an attempt. If similarity were found in one language, the next step would be to make the same sort of comparisons in a number of different languages, for only if there is a common sequence within every language can a universal explanation be considered.[2]

In very general terms, of course, the answer to the question concerning the sequence in which children learn to talk is already known. Children produce what appear to be random vocalizations and babbling before they begin to produce recognizable words; two-word utterances occur before two-clause utterances; direct imperative requests in all situations precede the appropriate matching of the various forms of indirect request to the particular status of the person addressed.[3] But, within this general outline, there is room for considerable individual variation in the detail of the developmental sequence and, at this level, there is much less available information.[4] It was in order to provide this sort of detailed information about the sequence of development in English that we started to analyze the material we had collected.

■ THE SEQUENCE OF DEVELOPMENT

In order to understand what we discovered, a brief explanation of the method we used is probably necessary at this point. This can best be given by means of a particular example. Suppose we take what I shall call a *linguistic system*, such as the personal pronoun system: "I," "me," "you," "he," "she," "it," etc. In the recordings of the speech of any particular child, these words are going to occur for the first time in a particular order. And if these first occurrences are widely separated in time, there will be reasonable grounds for thinking that the order in which they occur corresponds to the order in which they were learned. When we look at the recordings of another child, we shall again find that the pronouns first occur in a particular order. What will be interesting, though, is to *compare* the two children to find out if the order for the second child is the same as that found for the first or whether it is different. This procedure can then be extended until all the children have been included in the comparison and a large number of linguistic systems have been investigated in the same way.[5]

The linguistic systems that we investigated can be divided into three groups: those concerned with the *functions* for which children use language (for example, to make requests, ask questions, give explanations, etc.); those concerned with the *meanings* they express (the states, events, and relationships that they talked about); and those concerned with the *form* of their utterances (that is, with their grammatical structure). Altogether, we investigated some thirty-five linguistic systems.

The results of our analysis can be told very briefly. For each system and for all systems combined, the evidence strongly suggested a single common sequence of development. Despite their differing experiences, therefore, it seemed that all the children were learning in the same sort of way.

Unfortunately, our observations did not begin until after the stage at which most children had begun to produce recognizable words, so we can say nothing about the very early stages of language development. However, we can offer a summary of the main stages through which children pass between their first and their fifth birthdays.[6] To illustrate this sequence, extracts will be presented from the speech of one particular child. Each extract will be followed by a discussion of the main characteristics appearing at that stage. It must be emphasized, of course, that referring to "stages" is nothing more than a convenient way to describe the child's development. In fact, this development is more or less continuous, with no sharp boundaries between successive stages. Not surprisingly, therefore, the extracts that follow contain some examples of characteristics that are more typical of the following stage as well as occasional occurrences of immature forms that are characteristic of earlier stages. In this sense, almost any extract represents a period of transition.

Mark, the child from whose recordings the extracts are taken, was not one of the children in the main study. I started observing him the year before the study began in order to try out the recording techniques. Instead of taking many short samples, the recorder was switched on at a time unknown to his mother and allowed to run continuously for 45 minutes. Most of the recordings took place during the course of the morning—the time, as we later discovered, when the greatest amount of conversation occurs. Mark was the elder of two children (his sister was nine months old at the time when the observations began) and, as it turned out, his development proceeded rather more rapidly than we later found to be the norm. He was also somewhat atypical of the children we observed in having a mother who spent quite long periods of time talking with him (though he was by no means unique in this respect). As a result, I was able to select particularly long stretches of conversation to illustrate the successive stages of development.

■ STAGE I

[*Mark is in the kitchen with his mother and his sister Helen. He is holding a mirror in which he sees reflected now himself and now his mother.*]

Mark: Mummy, Mummy.	1
Mother: What?	2
Mark: There. There Mark.	3
Mother: Is that Mark?	4
Mark: Mark.	5
[*pointing to Mother*] Mummy.	6
Mother [*exaggerated rising intonation*]: Mm.	7
Mark [*pointing to Mother*]: Mummy.	8
Mother [*exaggerated rising intonation*]: Yes, that's Mummy.	9
Mark: Mummy.	10
Mummy.	11
Mummy.	12
Mother: Mm.	13
Mark: There Mummy.	14
Mummy, there—Mark there.	15
[*A minute later, looking out of the window at the birds in the garden*]	
Look-at-that. Birds, Mummy.	16
Mother: Mm.	17
Mark: Jubs [birds].	18
Mother: What are they doing?	19
Mark: Jubs bread [Birds eating bread(?)].	20
Mother: Oh look! They're eating the berries, aren't they?	21
Mark: Yeh.	22
Mother: That's their food. They have berries for dinner.	23
Mark: Oh.	24
[*Some minutes later*]	
Er fwa, Mummy? [Want water.]	25
Mother: What?	26
Mark: Er fwa?	27
Mother: No.	28
Mark: Fwa?	29
Mother: No.	30
Mark: Fwa?	31
Mother: No.	32
Mark: Fwa?	33
Mother [*with rising intonation*]: No.	34
Mark [*with rising intonation*]: No.	35
Fwa?	36
Mother [*with tone of finality*]: No, Mark.	37

One of the characteristics of the early part of Stage I is the use of what have been called *Operators*, such as "there," "look," "that," "want," "more," and "all gone," either alone or in combination with the name of the object referred to. Essentially, what such utterances communicate is what is being referred to (the meaning) and what is to be done about it (the function). Mark provides several examples of this sort of utterance—for example, "There Mark" (line 3) and "Er fwa" (line 25). Although the objects may be very varied, depending on what is of interest or importance to the child, what is to be done about them is more limited. The first three functions to be expressed are almost always *Call* (to obtain somebody's attention), *Ostension* (to direct attention to an object or event), and *Want* (to obtain some object or service). In this extract, Mark clearly distinguishes between calling his mother (line 1) and identifying her (reflection) as the object of his attention (line 6) by using a fall-rise intonation (~) for the Call function and a high fall (↘) for Ostension. In line 3, however, he also uses the operator "There" to convey the same Ostension function and, in line 25, the Want function is also expressed by an operator—the idiosyncratic "Er," pronounced in a very nasal way.[7]

By the end of this stage, two further functions are typically added. In line 20, "Jubs bread," we can see an example of a rudimentary *Statement*, though with the action linking the actor and the acted upon not yet expressed. No example of the other Stage I function, *Request*, is to be found in this extract, however, although later in the same recording, Mark said, "Up" (meaning "Lift me up"). At the same time, we also find the meaning content of utterances beginning to develop beyond the simple naming of the object referred to. Typically, the first types of relationship to appear are those concerned with location. One of these, static object-location, is illustrated in the statement "Mark there" (line 15).

At this stage, Mark still has very limited grammatical resources. As can be seen, his utterances consist either of a single word—the operator alone (line 3) or a word that in adult speech would be classed as a noun (line 18)—or of the two-word Operator + Object structure already discussed above. However, as can be seen from the above extract, when he is talking with someone who knows him well and who is able to interpret his intention from the combination of his utterance and its context, he is successfully able to mean more than he can say.

■ STAGE II

[Mark is in the living room with his Mother. He is standing by a radiator.]
Mark: 'Ot, Mummy?   1

Mother: Hot? Yes, that's the radiator.	2
Mark: Been—burn?	3
Mother: Burn?	4
Mark: Yeh.	5
Mother: Yes, you know it'll burn, don't you?	6
Mark [*putting hand on radiator*] Oh! Ooh!	7
Mother: Take your hand off of it.	8
Mark: Uh?	9
Mother [*asking if he needs his other shoelace tied*]: What about the other shoe?	10
Mark: It all done, Mummy.	11
Mother: Mm?	12
Mark: It done, Mummy.	13
Mother: It's done, is it?	14
Mark: Yeh.	15
Mother: Oh. [*Mark tries to get up to see out of the window.*]	16
Mother: No! Leave the curtain.	17
Mark: Oh, up please.	18
Mother: Leave the curtain, please.	19
Mark: No.	20
Mother: Leave the curtain, Mark.	21
Mark: No. [*Looking out of window, he sees a man digging in his garden.*] A man—a man er—dig—down there.	22 / 23
Mother: A man walked down there?	24
Mark: Yeh.	25
Mother: Oh, yes.	26
Mark: Oh, yes. [*6-second pause*] A man's fire, Mummy.	27 / 28
Mother: Mm?	29
Mark: A man's fire.	30
Mother: Mummy's flower?	31
Mark: No.	32
Mother: What?	33
Mark [*emphasizing each word*]: Mummy, the man . fire.	34
Mother: Man's fire?	35
Mark: Yeh.	36
Mother: Oh, yes, the bonfire.	37
Mark [*imitating*]: Bonfire.	38
Mother: Mm.	39
Mark: Bonfire. Oh, bonfire. Bonfire. Bon—a fire bo—bonfire. Oh, hot, Mummy. Oh, hot. It hot. It hot.	40 / 41
Mother: Mm. It will burn, won't it?	42
Mark: Yeh. Burn. It burn.	43

From a functional point of view, Stage II sees the appearance of questions. To begin with, they are usually limited to "Where" and "What" questions, in which the interrogative pronoun is followed immediately by the entity questioned (for example, "Where ball?" or the naming question, "Wassat?"). Where the question seeks the answer "yes" or "no," it is signalled by rising intonation only, instead of by the presence of an auxiliary verb (for example, "do" or "is") at the beginning. Mark's only question in this extract is of the latter type: " 'Ot, Mummy?" (line 1).

The question "Wassat?" and its answer also illustrate one of the major characteristics of semantic development at this stage: an insatiable concern with naming and classification. The exchange at lines 37–38 concerning the bonfire is an example. Other meanings that appear at this stage have to do with changing location—people "coming" and "going" or getting "down" or "up" (line 18)—and with simple attributes such as "hot" (line 1), "big," or "nice."

At Stage II we also see the clear emergence of grammatical structure, both in the combination of two constituents within the clause—Subject + Verb (line 43, "It burn"), Verb + Object, or Subject + Object/Complement (line 41, "It hot")—and in the various two-word combinations in the noun phrase Article + Noun (line 23, "A man"), Preposition + Noun/Adverb (line 23, "down there"), and the possessive construction (line 28, "man's fire"). In fact, line 28 combines two of these types of noun phrase structure in "A man's fire," and line 23 combines two of the clause combinations to give the three-constituent structure "A man dig down there" with each of the noun phrases having its own internal structure. Typically, such a grammatically complex utterance would not appear until Stage III.

■ STAGE III

[*Mark is in the kitchen with his mother. He is waiting for her to finish washing the dishes so that she can play with him.*]

Mark: Play, Mummy.	1
Shish [finished] wash up, Mummy?	2
Mother: Pardon?	3
Mark: Shish wash up?	4
Mother: Yes.	5
Mark: Oh.	6
Mother: Let me just dry my hands.	7
Mark: All right. In there [*wanting to put towel in laundry basket*].	8
Mother: Here.	9
Mark [*said all as one word as he hands towel to Mother*]: 'Ere-you-are.	10

Mother: Just a minute.   11
    Will you put the top back on the washing basket, please?   12

Mark: Uh? Uh?   13

Mother: Put the **top** back on the washing basket.   14

Mark [*pointing to laundry basket*]: On there, Mummy? On there?   15

Mother: Yes.   16
    [*Mark goes to put the towel in the basket.*]
    No, not the towel in there. The top of the basket on it.   17

Mark: All right. On there? Uh? Uh?   18

Mother: Put the **lid** on top of the **basket**.   19

Mark: Oh. On there?   20

Mother: Yes, please.   21

Mark: All right. [*Command*] You dry hands.   22

Mother: I've dried my hands now.   23

Mark: Put towel in there. [*He wants her to put the towel in the bas-
ket.*]   24

Mother: No, it's not dirty.   25

Mark: It is.   26

Mother: No it isn't.   27

Mark: 'Tis.   28
    Mummy, play. Play, Mummy.   29

Mother: Well, I will play if you put the top on the basket.   30

Mark: All right. [*He finally puts the lid on the basket.*] There. There.   31
    Play, Mummy. Play. Play. Play, Mummy.   32
    Mummy, come on.   33

Mother: All right.   34

Mark: Helen play, please? [*He wants his sister to play with him, too.*]   35
    Helen still in bed, Mummy?   36

Mother [*from the next room*]: Mm?   37

Mark: Helen still—Helen still gone sleep, Mummy?   38

Mother: No. She's up there talking, isn't she?   39

Mark: Yes. Helen come down? [request]   40

Mother: No. Let her rest.   41

Mark: All right. All right, Mummy.   42
    [*Mother finally comes to play with him. A few minutes later,
Mark is playing with a collection of toy cars, running them down
a ramp from the roof of his garage.*]
    [*Referring to one of his toys*] Top of the coach [bus]. Broken.   43

Mother: Who broke the coach?   44

Mark: Mark did.   45

Mother: How?   46

Mark: Out.   47

Mother: How did you break it?   48

Mark: Dunno [I don't know]. [4-second pause]   49
    Mend it, Mummy.   50

Mother: I can't, darling.   51

Mark: All right.   52

Mother: Look, the wheels have gone as well.   53

Mark: Oh! I want Daddy take it to work ⌒ mend it.   54

Mother: [*checking*]: Daddy did?   55

Mark: Daddy take it away—take it to work ⌒ mend it.   56

Mother: You'll have to ask him, won't you?   57

Mark: Yeh. You do it [ask him].   58

By Stage III, questions are well established: Mark asks a whole spate (lines 35, 36, and 38), but they are still signalled only by rising intonation. We also see the more complex expression of wants which, as in line 54, find expression in the first type of grammatically complex sentence: the object of wanting ("Daddy take it to work") is itself a complete embedded clause. This utterance (line 54) is particularly interesting as it also illustrates a strategy that Mark employed on a number of occasions when he wasn't yet quite able to cope with the necessary grammatical structure. Between "work" and "mend" he left a very short gap (indicated by ⌒) but continued the intonation unbroken, as if to indicate that he knew a connecting word was needed at that point even though he wasn't able to produce it.

"Mend" also illustrates a development in the kind of meanings that are expressed: an action somebody carries out that causes a change in the state of the object acted upon. "You dry hands" (line 22) is another example. At this stage, though it is not illustrated in this extract, we also typically find verbs like "listen" and "know" beginning to appear—verbs that refer to people's mental states. By Stage III there are also references to events in the past and, less frequently, to the future. The only example in this extract is line 45, "Mark did," in answer to the question "Who broke it?" However, we do see an example of another aspect of the temporal organization of events. "Shish wash up?" (lines 2 and 4) asks about the *aspectual* state of the action—is it completed or not? The ongoing status of events is also regularly marked by this stage through the use of the *-ing* form of the verb. There are no examples in this extract, but in the same recording we find "Mark doing it," and "Helen still in bed" (line 36) expresses very much the same notion of a continuing state.

Grammatically, development at this stage is seen in three-constituent structures: Subject + Verb + Object/Adjunct (already seen in "A man dig down there" in the previous extract), and Subject + Auxiliary Verb + Verb (*e.g.,* "I am going"). Mark's most complex utterance in this extract, "I want Daddy take it to work ⌒ mend it" (line 54), is, as already noted, even more complex and is more typical of Stage IV. In the noun phrase we might similarly expect to find three-word structures, such as Preposition + Article + Noun (e.g., "in the basket").

■ STAGE IV

[Mark is having lunch with his mother and sister. Mark has just taken a piece of cheese from the refrigerator so that he can have some.]

Mark: Oh, I wan—I want do this [i.e., cut the cheese].	1
Oh, cheese [laughs with excitement].	2
Mother: That's right. Sit up, then!	3
Mark: Look, I'm doing it [cutting the cheese].	4
Can I do it? Can I do it?	5
Mother: Be careful, the knife is sharp!	6
No [that's not right]. Cut it straight, not at an angle.	7
All right [can you manage]?	8
There you are [you have succeeded].	9
[Sister shouts in background. Mark gives the knife to Mother.]	
Thank you.	10
Mark: Shall I cut another one?	11
I want some meat.	12
Mother: All right. Eat your cheese first.	13
Mark: Can I have other piece of meat, Mummy?	14
Mother: Yes.	15

[A little while later, Mark is looking out of the window. He can see traffic going up the hill in the distance. Mother is in another room and cannot see.]

Mark: Why going r-round that bend, Mummy?	16
Mother: Pardon?	17
Mark: Why going round that bend?	18
Mother: Round what bend?	19
Mark: That bend.	20
Mother: What's going round the bend?	21
Mark: Bus.	22
Mother: Oh, you can see a bus down on the hill?	23
Mark: Yes. You go down left—you turn left and go that r—that road and go see traffic lights, see?	24
Mother: Oh, it goes to the traffic lights, does it?	25
Mark: Yes. It goes down there.	26
Mother: Oh.	27
Mark: By traffic lights.	28
See. Down there. There's a ambulance.	29
[Demanding a response] Mummy! Mummy!	30
Mother: Yes.	31
Mark: Yes.	32
Mother: Does it?	33
Mark: Yes.	34

[*A few minutes later, Mark wants a pen to draw with.*]

Mark: Where's the pen what Pappa um gave me? Mummy? 35

Mother: Pardon? 36

Mark: Where's Pappa's pen ⌒ draw on there? [Where's Pappa's pen that
I want to use to draw on there?] 37

Mother: You left it at Clifton, didn't you? 38

Mark: No. I want it. [*Noises to self.*] I want it please, Mummy. 39
Mark—Mark bring it home, think so. 40

Perhaps the most striking development that occurs at Stage IV is
the integration of the auxiliary verb into the structure of the clause,
thus allowing the production of both interrogative and negative sentences. Mark provides several examples of the former (lines 5, 11, 14),
though none of the latter in this extract. With the availability of this
structure comes a diversification of the functions associated with the
control of activity. In line 5 we see him *requesting permission* and in
line 11 taking a more *indirect* route to getting what he wants. At this
stage we also see the first appearance of *explanation* and *request for
explanation.* Usually it is the child who supplies an explanation in
response to somebody else's "Why?" question; here it is Mark who
asks the question (line 16).

Amongst the auxiliary verbs, "do" is the first to appear, followed
by "can" and "will" (or " 'll"). *Can* has two possible meanings ('ability'
and 'permission'), but in the child's world these are closely related:
many of the things he or she is able to do also require permission, such
as, for example, Mark's cutting the cheese for himself.

Two other types of semantic development occur at about this stage
in association with developments in grammar. The first is the appearance of complements to psychological verbs like *know* (e.g., "I know
that you are there"), and the second is the qualification of a noun phrase
by a relative phrase or clause (e.g., "Where's the pen what Pappa gave
me?" [line 35]).[8] Both require one grammatical clause to function within
the structure of another, thus introducing the principle of *recursion.*
With this development, the child is well advanced towards mastery of
the basic grammar of the sentence.

■ STAGE V

[*Mark is playing with his train. His sister is trying to play, too, but she is
not really very welcome.*]

Mark: I can't put my train over—over the bridge, Helen, if you put that
like that. 1
If you have—if you have. If you have, I pu—I can't put my train on
the bridge. 2
[*Helen makes unintelligible response.*]
Here it comes. Here it comes, then. Here it comes. 3
It's coming, like that. It's coming, like that. 4

Put the other bridge there.   5
I want a *.   6
You put that one there, Helen *.   7

Helen: Yes.   8

Mark: Don't do it again.   9
If you do, I'll smack your bottom for you.   10
Here it comes.   11

[*Some time later, Mark is doing a jigsaw puzzle with his mother.*]

Mother: There. Now you've got two Camberwick Green pictures.   12

Mark: Yeh.   13

Mother: One you made, mm? And one on the box.   14

Mark: Mm.   15

Mother [*pointing to the jigsaw puzzle and a set of dominoes*]: Look,
these Camberwick Green men are the same as the dominoes in
Camberwick Green.   16

Mark [*thoughtfully*]: Mm.   17

Mother: Look!   18

Mark: Can I see which is like that one?   19

Mother: There's the policeman.   20

Mark: Yeh.   21
[*4-second pause*]

Mother [*comparing the puzzle with the dominoes*]: I don't think there
is a man with a yellow hat.   22

Mark [*proudly*]: I made this puzzle, didn't I?   23

Mother: Mm.   24

Mark: Shall we do this puzzle again?   25

Mother: Yes. Break it up, then.   26

Mark [*imitating*]: Break it up.   27
[*They break up the puzzle and start again.*]
And I got to start the words of it, haven't I?   28

Mother: Go on, then.   29

Mark: I got to start the word. You got to do—   30
Now what does it say now?   31
[*Pretending to read instructions*] Make the lorry.   32
You make the lorry, Mummy.   33

Mother [*by now getting tired of doing the puzzle*]: Mm.   34

Mark: And make the cars, please.   35
[*Several seconds' pause*]
Have I got to—um—do the most of it?   36

Mother: Well, it would help.   37

By now, Mark can use his linguistic resources for most of the major
functions—giving information, asking and answerering questions of
various kinds, requesting (both directly and indirectly), suggesting,
offering, stating intentions and asking about those of others, and ex-

pressing feelings and attitudes and asking about those of others. In this extract, the new development we notice is the *conditional* or *hypothetical* statement (line 1). In line 10, the same grammatical structure has the function of a *threat* ("If you do, I'll smack your bottom for you"). Another more indirect controlling function is seen in line 30: "I got to start the word. You got to do—." These two utterances *formulate* the action that is required as an alternative way of getting the action performed. Very often, this function has a general applicability: whenever the appropriate conditions apply, you have got to do X.

Along with the appearance of hypothetical events and formulating functions, we find other ways in which utterances go beyond the here and now of present activity, in particular in a more differentiated expression of the time frame within which events occur. As well as general references to past and future, there is the beginning of reference to particular times as points of reference—"before dinner," "when Daddy comes home," "until bedtime." Aspectual distinctions are also made— for example, *habitual* ("Daddy's always late for dinner"), *repetitive* ("He kept on banging the door"), and *inceptive* ("The snow's beginning to melt").

Several of the functional and semantic options that become available at this stage require sentences that contain more than one clause. The first of these was seen in the previous stage, in the asking for and supplying of explanations, using sentences in which clauses were linked by *because, and, to* (*in order to*), etc. However, by Stage V their variety has increased considerably, as can be seen from Mark's speech in lines 1, 10, and 19. A further grammatical development at this stage is the final sorting out of the structure of questions that begin with words like "What" and "When." This is illustrated in line 31: the auxiliary is now inverted with the subject after the question word: "What does it say?"

Whereas almost all aspects of grammatical development up to this point have added to the length of the sentence, there now begin to appear the results of processes that make for greater economy of expression. These processes, collectively referred to as *Cohesion*, relate the present clause back to a preceding one by referring to the whole or a part of it by means of a pro-noun or pro-verb, or simply by ellipsis— taking it for granted. A clear example of this is given in lines 9–10. The words "do it" in line 9 refer back to "You put that one there" in line 7—which Helen is not to do again—and the pro-verb "do" in line 10 refers to "do it again" in line 9. However, Mark's first recorded use of cohesion was seen in his last utterance in the extract given for Stage IV: "so" to refer to the whole of the previous clause, "Mark bring it home" (line 40). At that stage he had clearly grasped the idea of cohesion, but was not yet altogether sure about how to use that particular form.

By the end of Stage V, then, the major linguistic systems are more or less in place and a basic vocabulary of several thousand words has been acquired.[9] There is certainly much more to learn, or course, particularly with respect to the socially appropriate uses of language. But, from this point onwards, what is learned and the order in which it is learned becomes progressively more dependent on experience—on having opportunities to hear the relevant functions, meanings, and structure used appropriately and to use them oneself.[10] At one and the same time, then, this point marks both the end and the beginning: after an almost sheer climb up the face of the cliff, the rest of the mountain lies ahead, but there are many possible routes that may be taken and, in general, the going is somewhat easier.

Three

LEARNING TO TALK:
THE CONSTRUCTION
OF LANGUAGE

The end of the previous chapter saw Mark well advanced towards mastery of the language of his community. By then, the most difficult part of the task had been achieved. However, the real puzzle is: how did he get started? How did he discover that the vocal sounds that people produce are intended to communicate specific meanings and to do so by virtue of the choice of particular sounds and their arrangement in particular temporal sequences?[1] Putting the question in that form, however, may be to overemphasize the apparent arbitrariness of the language system at the expense of its functional significance as a resource in interpersonal communication. Language may be thought of as a code to be cracked, but before the child attempts that task he or she has already become familiar with the code in use. It has been encountered in meaningful interactions that also involve the more "natural" channels of sight, sound, touch, and smell.[2]

■ GETTING STARTED

It has become clear from research over recent decades that the newborn baby is not as helpless as used to be supposed. Human infants are born with a drive to make sense of their experience and with certain effective strategies for doing so. For example, they readily recognize regularities and are able to respond to abstract patterns in their environment. One very interesting experiment shows that, by five months, infants are able to track a moving object behind a screen, anticipate its emergence at the other side, and show surprise if a different object appears.[3] Their sense-making also seems from the beginning to be goal-directed. Everybody is familiar with the older infant who drops toys from his or her highchair or crib in order to get somebody to come and pick them up. But this sort of purposeful exploration and manipulation of the environment can be shown to be present very much earlier—for example, experiments have shown that babies discover that they can bring about changes (switching on lights, bringing pictures into focus) by turning their head or sucking on a dummy (pacifier).

Most important for language development, however, is the infant's inherent sociability. Babies show a clear preference for faces and face-like shapes and show that they distinguish human voices from other sounds. The result of these inborn traits is that they orient to other human beings in a way that parents and other family members find very appealing. They seem to want to communicate. Split-screen film of mothers and infants as young as three months sitting facing each other show quite clearly that the infant's gestures (lip-pursing, frowning, etc.) alternate with the mother's similar gestures and are sometimes also accompanied by vocalization, in what looks to an observer very much like conversation without words. True, the temporal sequencing owes a great deal to the mother's sensitivity in timing her gestures to follow the infant's, but there is no doubt that the infant is interactively involved as well, as can be seen from his or her distress if the mother ceases to respond in a contingently appropriate manner.

By six months, then, a baby and his or her chief caregivers have established the basis for communication: a relationship of mutual attention. The establishment of this relationship and the wordless communication that takes place within it—*protoconversation*, as it has been called—occurs so early and so smoothly that it seems that the human infant must be biologically preadapted to initiate and engage in such interactions.[4]

While that may well be so, there is a further advantage that newborn babies have to help them towards language, and that is the attitude of their parents or other caretakers. Just as babies are strongly predisposed to make sense of their surroundings, so adults are predisposed to treat their behavior as meaningful and potentially communicative. The baby burps, and the mother asks, "Have you got windypops?" The baby smiles, and she is pleased that the baby is happy. The baby looks, and she follows his or her line of regard and tries to see what the baby is interested in. Thus, from the beginning, parents treat their babies as if they had intentions and respond to them in the light of the intentions that they believe their babies to be communicating. And so, by being treated *as if* they already had intentions, babies do in time come to have them, discovering in the process that their behavior can affect the people in their environment—that they can indeed communicate.[5]

However, the parent's interpretations of the baby's behavior have another important function. As mature members of a human culture, parents have quite specific ideas about what sorts of behavior have meaning and so, in interpreting the baby's gestures, noises, and so on, parents assimilate them to behaviors that they themselves find meaningful. The meanings attributed are therefore *cultural* meanings and, in their responses, parents provide culturally appropriate feedback that has the effect of shaping the infant's behavior towards what is culturally acceptable and meaningful.

Finally, we should add that the baby's early environment is highly repetitive. The day is made up of a regular cycle of feeding, sleeping, cleaning, and bathing. And many of the activities that the baby is involved in when awake themselves have a regular structure, involving interaction with the mother or some other regular caregiver. There are thus ample opportunities for the recognition of regularity and for the discovery of the connections that exist between persons, objects, and events. This enables predictions to be made and provides the satisfaction that comes from the recognition of predictions fulfilled. It is from this experience that the infant is already beginning to construct his or her internal model of the world.

By the second half of the first year, then, the infant is well advanced towards recognizably communicative behavior. Through oft-repeated experiences of protoconversation, he or she has discovered the reciprocity of mutual attention: "I know that you are attending to me, and you know that I am attending to you, and we both know that we both know that that is so." This pattern of mutual attention has been given the name *intersubjectivity*.[6] It can be shown diagrammatically as follows:

Adult ◄————————► Infant

Intersubjectivity is the essential foundation of any communication. Within this relationship infants discover, albeit as yet only partially, both their separateness from their communication partners and also their essential similarity to them.[7] In this relationship they also learn to take a more active part in controlling the sequencing of turns that make up an interaction and discover the contingent nature of the relationship between turns, as they notice how their own specific behavior regularly elicits particular types of behavior from their partners, and they begin to produce particular types of behavior themselves in response to specific behavior by others.

The next step occurs when the world outside is drawn into the relationship of intersubjectivity and made the focus of joint attention. Typically, an interesting object will attract the child's attention and the mother will follow the child's line of regard, identify the object, and then either touch it, give it to the child, or in some other way indicate to him or her that she, too, is looking at the same object. Quite quickly the children learn to use looking to signal their attention; they also learn to use the line of regard of another to locate what the other is interested in. And, with the achievement of deliberate engagement in joint attention, the basic triangle of communication is complete: "I am looking at O (an object), and you are looking at O, and we both know that we are both looking at O."

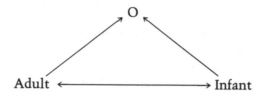

Such occasions of joint attention frequently become incorporated into playful routines, which involve handing an object back and forth, hiding it, and so forth. These routines introduce the child to two further important characteristics of linguistic communication: the basic structure of exchange—one person gives and the other receives, with these roles being reversible—and the way in which utterances are associated with the performance of the actions that make up an exchange. In this way, the child comes to recognize and respond to certain words and phrases in familiar contexts, such as " 'kyou," "bye-bye," "peek-a-boo," and perhaps the names of family pets or favorite objects, such as "teddy." Bruner describes one child's transition from action to speech as follows:

Ann had learned between 8 and 10 months to play a well modulated exchange game involving the handing back and forth of objects. When, at 13 months, the game was well organized, Ann picked up her mother's receiving *Thank you.* She used it both when giving and receiving an object. After two weeks the expression dropped out of the giving position, nothing at first taking its place, but remained in the receiving position. Meanwhile, the demand demonstrative *Look* was appearing in Ann's lexicon, used in referential situations, as when looking at pictures in a book. At the end of the thirteenth month, *Look* was transposed as well into the position at which Ann handed her mother an object. *Look* was later replaced by *There* in the giving-taking format.[8]

But perhaps the most important factor urging children into speech is their desire to communicate their intentions more precisely. Almost all researchers who have studied this stage of development (which occurs around the end of the first year) have noted that the child's earliest utterances are *functional*.[9] In our own study, as noted in the previous chapter, we found that almost all the utterances in the first observations could be described as either calling for attention, expressing a want, indicating something of interest, or expressing feeling (pleasure, surprise, etc.).

To begin with, these functions are often expressed by a combination of gesture and vocalization. But gradually the vocalizations take on a more regular form as distinct "words"—though not necessarily words recognized in the adult language—and the child is able to communicate recognizable intentions, at least to those who know him or her.

One way of describing the stage that the child has now reached is to think of it as a recapitulation of the construction of the communication triangle, but at a higher level. At first, intersubjectivity was achieved entirely through gestures of various kinds; now it can be expressed through words. But, in order to complete the triangle at this second level, it is necessary for the child to be able to engage verbally in joint reference, and to do that he or she has to understand that objects have names.

The naming game is one that all parents play, and they seem to know intuitively when to start doing so. As objects are exchanged in the familiar playful routines, they begin to add the name; they look at picture books and name the pictures or name the parts of the child's body. "What's that?" they ask and, as often as not, also supply the answer. To begin with, the child's attempts to take part involve no more than a vocalization to fill his or her turn in a familiar exchange. But associations are formed and, suddenly, the penny drops. The words the child has learned are labels. Things have names.[10]

When this happens, the triangle is completed at the verbal level. The child has discovered that the words he or she utters enable him or her to communicate both *that* he or she has intentions and *what* these intentions refer to. The majority of utterances may still be restricted to single words, but the child has learned to talk.

■ LEARNING THE LANGUAGE OF THE COMMUNITY

Expressing intentions and indicating what those intentions refer to are only the beginning of learning a language, of course. At this stage, children have clearly discovered the existence of the code; they have also discovered, in some sense, that it is based on an arbitrary but conventional relationship between meanings and sounds. Now they have to figure out how the code works. They have to learn the particular language that is used in their community.

To understand how they do this, it might be helpful to focus attention for a moment on the internalized representation of the world that children have been constructing from their experience of interacting with their environment. As we saw earlier, children seem to be predisposed to pay closer attention to certain aspects of their environment rather than to others. In particular, they notice people and clearly defined objects, especially if those objects can be touched and manipulated or if they move or cause other things to move. As a result, the internal model of the world that they build up is largely organized in terms of movement, appearance and disappearance, and the relationships of cause and effect that bring about those perceptible changes. Summarizing his own research on what he calls the "sensori-motor" stage of development, Piaget described the 18-month-old child as having come "to regard himself as an object among others in a universe that is made up of permanent objects . . . in which there is at work a causality that is both localized in space and objectified in things."[11]

Put rather differently, we could say that the basic categories in terms of which children make sense of their world are those of Agent, Object, Location, State, etc. and the changing relationships that can hold between them. Now these are precisely the sort of categories that are encoded in language, in such sentences as the following:

- Teddy (*object*) is on the bed (*location*).
- Daddy (*agent*) is painting (*change state*) the gate (*object*).
- Mummy (*agent*) put (*change location*) the knife (*object*) in the drawer (*location*).

and in a high proportion of the sentences that children hear addressed to them. Their task, then, is to match the sentences that they hear to the situation to which they apply and to work out how the former encodes the latter.

What makes this very difficult task possible is the context. A very high proportion of the utterances that people address to children are about what they can see and hear—about what is going on. Much of the time, too, these events are already familiar. So the child picks out the one or two words that he or she recognizes and uses them and an interpretation of the context to make a guess at what the speaker means.

There are usually other clues as well: gestures and exaggerated intonation. In the following example (quoted earlier, in chapter 2), Mark wanted his mother to play with him and she agreed, but only on condition that he first replaced the lid on the laundry basket, into which he had just tried to put a towel.

Mother: Put the top back on the washing basket.
Mark: On there, Mummy? On there? . . .
Mother: Put the **lid** on top of the **basket**.

As Mark does not seem to understand the first time, his mother tries again, breaking her utterance into two parts to correspond to the two parts of the action that she wants him to perform. At the same time, by pointing to the lid by gesture and gaze and by emphasizing the word "lid" by heavy stress and rising intonation, she uses several different cues to help him identify the object to be moved. Then, when she sees that he has understood that much, she shifts her gaze to the basket and verbally specifies the place where the lid is to be put, again using heavy stress on "top" and "basket" to help him to pick out the key words in her utterance. The complete utterance can be represented as follows:

Mother: Put the **lid** on **top** of the **basket**.

At last Mark understands and successfully carries out the action, his success being due in part to his mother's helpful guidance but also in part to his strong motivation to succeed so that she would do what he wanted, which was to play with him.

From a parent's point of view, the process of language learning must sometimes seem a painfully slow one. There is so much for children to learn: not just the words, but their pronunciation and the ways of combining them to express the relationships between the objects, attributes, and actions to which they refer. They also have to learn how the more subtle distinctions of intention are expressed— indirect and direct requests, questions of various kinds, and expressions of different attitudes, such as sympathy, anger, apology, and so on— through different selections and orderings of words and structures and the use of different patterns of intonation and facial and bodily gestures.

For each new linguistic distinction to be mastered, children first have to become aware that such a distinction exists in their community's way of interpreting experience; then they have to discover how it is expressed in the language spoken by that community. As has already been suggested, children usually discover the distinctions of meaning first, through nonlinguistic encounters with the environment. They are then on the lookout for ways in which these meanings are expressed in the speech addressed to them. As they acquire greater command of the language, though, they are also able to learn from the conversations going on around them. Words or sentence patterns that they hear and recognize as unfamiliar alert them to possible distinctions of meaning that they have not yet discovered for themselves. A lot of children's learning, then, is dependent on making connections between what they know and what they are able to understand in the speech that they hear.

But they don't learn only by listening. Since the motivation for learning language at all is to be able to communicate, children are constantly using the resources they have already acquired to interact with other people about their needs and interests and about the activities in which they are jointly engaged. On many occasions their resources are just not sufficient to encode the meanings they want to express—distinctions they are aware of in their experience but for which they have not yet discovered the linguistic expression. On such occasions they press into service whatever means they have available, giving rise to the sorts of "error" that adults often find amusing—such as referring to the milkman as "daddy" or to an elephant seen at the zoo as "hosh" (horse)—or to neologisms, such as "boxing" for the action of putting an object into a box, which are indicative of the active nature of their search for meaning and the means for expressing it.[12]

Frequently, however, their attempts are not successful, and their conversational partners do not understand them. However, this too can be helpful, even if only by giving children negative feedback about the adequacy of their utterances. Quite often, though, the partner will probe further, offering alternative interpretations in an attempt to discover what the child means, often in the form of expansions that, as it were, present in full what the child has been trying to say him- or herself. Such negotiations about intended meaning are likely to be particularly informative, as they provide children with evidence about the language at the very moment when they are most disposed to make use of it. Here is an example from Anthony:

Anthony: There ninny car.
Mother: Mini car? Yes.
Anthony: Mini gone.
Mother: Mini car's gone.
Anthony: Daddy gone.
Mother: Yes. Daddy's gone.

In all these ways, then, children gradually add to and modify their representation of the language system and discover how it is used as a resource for communicating with other people. Although the process may sometimes appear slow and laborious to parents who are involved in it, when viewed from outside it appears to happen rapidly, even in more slowly developing children.

■ COPYING OR REINVENTING?

In the previous chapter, we traced the sequence of one child's development in some detail and briefly considered some of the evidence for believing that this sequence is followed quite closely by all children learning English as their first language. The question we must now consider is why there is this substantial uniformity.

In considering possible explanations, there seem to be two very different alternatives. On the one hand, the order of learning may be controlled by the model presented to children in the speech they hear—either in the form of a carefully graded program of instruction, or simply through the effect of frequency, as they hear some words, structures, and so on much more frequently than others. According to this explanation, children simply copy what they hear, and the sequence of learning is determined by characteristics of the model, together with the effect of positive and negative reinforcement.

The alternative explanation, on the other hand, attributes the order of learning to an interaction between the characteristics of the learner and the relative difficulty of what has to be learned. Provided that the speech that the child hears contains examples of what has to be learned, the precise characteristics of the input are of little importance.[13]

Clearly, these are very different explanations, with different implications for those who are concerned with helping children to learn language. We thought it important, therefore, to try to decide which (if either) seemed to square best with the evidence that we had collected. We think the results are reasonably clear.

First, there is very little evidence of deliberate instruction, graded or otherwise. Most parents do teach certain polite expressions, such as "please" and "thank you." They also teach the names of familiar objects and attributes. However, in the case of the polite expressions it is largely a matter of getting children to remember to use them, for the words themselves are very quickly learned. As for vocabulary teaching, this tends to be concentrated into quite a short period towards the end of the second year, when the principle that everything has a name is learned. Thereafter, only a minority of parents continue to teach vocabulary, and even then, this tends to be limited to common nouns and adjectives; verbs, adverbs, and other parts of speech are hardly ever explicitly taught at all. As for grammar, there is barely any evidence at all of deliberate instruction. This is hardly surprising, for the vast majority of parents, although their own speech is entirely grammatical, have no conscious knowledge of the rules of grammar to which their speech conforms.

If not deliberately taught, is what children learn perhaps presented to them with differential frequency? Do they simply learn first what they hear most frequently? At first sight, this does appear quite plausible—all the more so since, in general, we found a strong correspondence between the overall frequency with which particular items (functions, meanings, and structures) occurred in the speech addressed to the children and the actual sequence in which those items were learned. However, there are a number of reasons for rejecting this explanation.

First, although the correspondence was strong for the sample as a whole, it was much more variable in the case of individual children. Second, for one out of the four linguistic systems that we investigated in detail, that of the functions that utterances perform, there was not a significant correspondence at all. Children, for example, learned to answer questions before they asked them, but they heard far more questions than answers. Similarly, at a later stage, they requested permission before they granted permission to others; but in the speech addressed to them, they were granted permission far more often than they were asked for it. These results hardly seem surprising. But what they make clear is the underlying interactional basis of language learning. Children are not learning to talk in order to be able to behave like their parents for the sake of conformity, but rather to be able to communicate with them in collaborative activities in which the roles played are *reciprocal* rather than imitative.

However, since at one time it was thought that children did indeed learn to talk by imitating their parents, it is perhaps worth examining the role of imitation a little more closely. In one sense, of course, language *is* learned through imitation. Without examples of the different items to be learned, children would have no way of knowing how particular meanings were expressed, even though they might have made the necessary conceptual distinctions. But, in the sense of repeating what an adult has just said as a means of learning it, there is no evidence that this is the main way in which children learn. Most children quite rarely imitate in this way; and, when they do, the phrase or sentence they imitate is usually one that they have already used spontaneously on an earlier occasion.

Recently, however, one or two researchers have noticed children who recall whole chunks of utterances they have heard some time earlier and use them in constructing an utterance of their own. Ruth Clark, for example, reports how her son, having just heard his mother say "Do you want to get off?" as he was riding on a roundabout (carousel), replied, "No, I want to get on," meaning he wanted to stay on. On another occasion, he responded to his mother's statement "We're all very mucky" with, "I all very mucky too."[14] This child seemed to be reusing chunks of what he had just heard (and probably understood, at least partially, in context) without analyzing them into their constituent parts. Then, when what he wanted to say taxed his productive ability too greatly, he would insert the stored chunk unmodified into an utterance, the rest of which he constructed for the occasion.

This is indeed a form of imitation. But to have stored and then recalled the chunk in order to combine it with other words on a later occasion shows that this child was doing more than simply repeating what he had heard. As William Labov once put it, the difference between a man and a parrot who both repeat the sentence "I'll meet you downtown" is that it is only in the case of the man that one would be surprised if he didn't show up. Moreover, as far as is known at present, children who use this strategy are in a minority, and even they only use it occasionally.

This is not just a quibble over the meaning of the word *imitation*. What is at issue here is how children use the information about the language they are learning that is presented to them in the speech addressed to them. Those who argue that imitation plays an important role in language learning usually explain the process in terms of acquiring a repertoire of ready-made phrases or routines that are associated with and elicited by particular contextual events. Some phrases, such as "Hello" and "How do you do?", probably are learned in this way. However, most students of child language would agree that this mode of learning is the exception rather than the rule.

For the most part, children seem to analyze the utterances they hear into smaller units. Then they store those units, together with information about how they think they are combined, so that the units can be used on future occasions to produce or comprehend new utterances that contain them. The units may be of varying size, but some are smaller than what we think of as words and some, such as "going to" or "got to," consist of more than one word—although it may be some time before children recognize that this is so.

At any stage, then, children have certain hypotheses about the principles for combining units; and, on the whole, they seem to prefer to work with principles of maximum generalizability—principles that they construct for themselves on the basis of the regularities that they perceive in the speech of others and perhaps also in their own. However, these principles do not always correspond exactly to those that apply in adult speech—hence, such errors as "goed," "foots," and, later, "How could he of done that?"

Most of the time children's hypotheses correspond very closely to the rules that actually underlie adult speech, so it is not possible to tell by what means they have acquired them—whether by passively absorbing the model provided or by some more autonomous process. What is important about such errors, therefore, is that they provide compelling evidence that children *actively construct* their own hypotheses. Since they haven't heard these particular forms in the speech of adults, they must have put them together themselves.[15]

Taking all the available evidence together, then, we can state the situation as follows. Children learn language because they are predisposed to do so. How they set about the task is largely determined by the way they are: seekers after meaning who try to find the underlying principles that will account for the patterns that they recognize in their experiences. At each successive stage, therefore, they are capable of dealing with new evidence of a certain degree of complexity, and they are able to incorporate it into their developing language system. But using that system as a resource for interaction with other people leads to the making of errors and to the recognition of inconsistencies. This, in turn, leads eventually to modifications of the prevailing hypotheses and to some reorganization of the language system. And this then permits evidence relating to more complex items to be considered and resolved.

In this way, children progressively construct a representation of the language of their community. And they do so on the basis of the evidence provided for them in conversation with more mature members of that community. Furthermore, because human beings are similarly endowed as language learners, the sequence in which they construct their internal representations is very similar from one learner to another, and so are the underlying principles in terms of which their representation of the language system is ultimately organized.

■ THE ROLE OF ADULTS IN LANGUAGE DEVELOPMENT

From the description of children as largely autonomous contructors of their own representation of language, it may appear that there is little that adults contribute to this process. But this is very far from being so. In order to proceed with the learning task, children require evidence about language in use. They also need feedback on the effectiveness of their own linguistic behavior so that they can test the hypotheses that they are currently using in the construction of their language system. Or, to put it more simply, in order to learn to talk, they need a considerable amount of experience of conversation.

Sheer quantity is important. In the Bristol Study we found a clear relationship between the children's rate of progress in language learning and the amount of conversation that they experienced with their parents and other members of the family circle. But this can't be the whole story, for although the children who experienced the most conversation enjoyed almost ten times as much as the children who experienced the least, even these latter children continued to make progress, though at a much slower rate.

What seems to be more important is that, to be most helpful, the child's experience of conversation should be in a one-to-one situation in which the adult is talking about matters that are of interest and concern to the child, such as what he or she is doing, has done or plans to do, or about activities in which the child and adult engage together.[16] The reason for this is the fact that, when both child and adult are engaged in a shared activity, the chances are maximized that they will be attending to the same objects and events and interpreting the situation in similar ways. This means that they will each have the best chance of correctly interpreting what the other says and so of being able collaboratively to build up a shared structure of meaning about the topic that is the focus of their intersubjective attention.

Even between mature speakers of the same language, however, there is no guarantee that they will achieve mutual comprehension; hence the frequency of requests for repetition and clarification in most conversations. When the conversation is between two participants who are as unequally matched as adult and child, the chances of mis-understanding are even greater. This therefore places a very great re-sponsibility on the adult to compensate for the child's limitations and to behave in ways that make it as easy as possible for the child to play his or her part effectively.[17]

This means that, as speaker the adult must take into account the limited capabilities of the child—both the internal model of the world and the linguistic resources—and select his or her meanings and adjust the utterances in which they are encoded so that the child is able to make sense of them. In fact adults, particularly parents, seem to be intuitively aware of the need to behave in this way; in the Bristol Study, little difference was found between the children in the extent to which they received speech that was adjusted to their capabilities as listeners—at least as far as the average length and complexity of the adult utterances was concerned.[18]

Similar findings have emerged from several other studies, carried out for the most part on European languages. From them, it seems that, compared wih their behavior when speaking to adults or other chil-dren, parents modify their speech when talking to young children in a number of ways: keeping their utterances short and grammatically simple, using exaggerated intonation to hold the child's attention and to emphasize the key words, limiting the topics talked about to what is familiar to the child, and frequently repeating and paraphrasing what they say.[19]

In modifying their speech in this way, adults not only increase the chances of their children understanding what they say, but they also provide evidence that is particularly clear and easy for their children to use in their task of language construction. The episode, quoted earlier, in which Mark's mother tried to get him to put the lid on the laundry basket is a good example.

Equally important, though, are the special efforts that adults must also make as listeners. With their limited resources as speakers, chil-dren's utterances are often difficult to interpret. The adult therefore needs to make considerable use of contextual clues and knowledge about the individual child's likes and interests in order to make a good guess as to what he or she intends. Amongst researchers, this is known as "making a rich interpretation." And, again, we found that most parents did just that.

However, what was less common was adults' checking to ensure that they had correctly understood the child before making their next move in the conversation. Many early utterances are ambiguous and, unless the adult is alert to this possibility, what he or she says next may not be an appropriate response. In many cases this will simply lead to an abandonment of the topic; however, if the conversation continues, the child will be provided with evidence that is positively unhelpful in the task of matching what is said to the meaning he or she believes is intended.

A good example of an adult who systematically checks her interpretations is Mark's mother, in the extract quoted in chapter 2 to illustrate Stage II of language learning. The extract begins with a successful sequence of exchanges:

Mark: 'Ot, Mummy?
Mother: Hot? [*Checking*] Yes, that's the radiator.
Mark: Been—burn?
Mother: Burn? [*Checking*]
Mark: Yeh.
Mother: Yes, you know it'll burn, don't you?

As well as illustrating the strategy of checking, this short extract also shows very clearly how, with the adult's assistance, a proposition can be jointly constructed that is far more complex than the child is able to express alone. Mark offers the first element: *hot.* Mother confirms the appropriateness of his observation (and, of course, of the way in which he expressed it) and adds the second element: *the radiator.* Mark then adds the third element, *burn,* to complete the complex proposition, *hot radiator burn,* which his mother confirms in the final turn.

Sometimes such checking utterances lead to the recognition that the adult's interpretation is not correct, and a sequence of negotiation over the intended meaning is begun, as in the later episode in the same extract concerning "the man's fire." In addition to making it more likely that the conversational participants will achieve mutual comprehension, such exchanges provide children with valuable feedback on the success with which their utterances have communicated their intentions. Such exchanges may also lead to the presentation of relevant new evidence about how to communicate a given intention more effectively, as when Mark's mother gives him the word for the particular kind of fire he is looking at—a bonfire. Note how, because that is the focus of his interest at that moment, Mark is quick to assimilate the new piece of information and relate it to other relevant knowledge that he already possesses:

Mark: A man's fire, Mummy.
Mother [requesting a repetition]: Mm?
Mark: A man's fire.
Mother [*checking*]: Mummy's flower?
Mark: No . . . the man . fire.
Mother [*checking*]: Man's fire?
Mark: Yeh.
Mother: Oh, yes, the bonfire.
Mark [*imitating*]: Bonfire.
Mother: Mm.
Mark: Bonfire. . . . Oh, hot, Mummy. Oh, hot. It hot. It hot.
Mother: Mm. It will burn, won't it?
Mark: Yeh. Burn. It burn.

By chance, no doubt, but nevertheless very relevantly, the conversation comes full circle to the ideas with which the extract started. What a rich opportunity for learning—both about language and about the world to which the language refers!

As both these examples show very clearly, a really satisfying conversation needs to go beyond a single exchange. And it is in enabling this to happen that an adult can make perhaps the most important contribution to the child's development. As already emphasized, conversation involves the cumulative and collaborative construction of meaning, in which the linguistic links between utterances are like the mortar that holds together the bricks in a wall. For the child to be able to understand the nature of the meaning connections and to discover how the links are made linguistically, it is important that he or she should be able to form expectations about how the building process might proceed. For this to happen, the adult needs to try to adopt the child's perspective and, in his or her next contribution to the conversation, to incorporate some aspect of what the child has just said and to extend it or invite the child to do so him- or herself.

In the first extract from the recordings of Mark, we see very clear examples of these strategies for sustaining and extending Mark's meanings:

Mark [*looking out of the window at the birds in the garden*]: Look at that. Birds, Mummy.
Mother: Mm.
Mark: Jubs [birds].
Mother [*inviting Mark to extend his own meaning*]: What are they doing?
Mark: Jubs bread [Birds eating bread (?)].
Mother [*extending Mark's meaning*]: Oh, look! They're eating the berries, aren't they?

Mark: Yeh.

Mother [*extending and paraphrasing*]: That's their food. They have berries for dinner.

Mark: Oh.

This short sequence of conversation seems an almost ideal example of the way in which parents can most helpfully contribute to their children's language development. In it we see how the mother adjusts her speech to take account of the child's capabilities and helps him to build a conversation with her about a topic that is clearly of interest to him, as it is one that he initiated. In her turns she encourages Mark to extend his initial topic and then takes what he contributes and extends it still further in a number of simple, related sentences that provide evidence for him as to how to express more fully what it is he has invited her to look at with him. Notice, too, how she is also providing him with information about the topic to which they are jointly attending (the O in the triangle of communication), thus simultaneously enabling him to extend his model of the world to which the language refers.

There is one final point to note about this example of collaborative meaning making. Although in the latter part of the sequence it is the mother who is contributing all the new material, the conversation does not become a monologue. Even though Mark may not have fully understood all that his mother is saying, he keeps up his end of the conversation, providing acknowledgments where they are required. He, too, is playing his part in the collaborative enterprise. This is important for, without these minimal but appropriate responses from Mark, his mother would not have felt able to continue to play *her* part.

Mark's responses have another important function. Together with his nonverbal behavior—gestures, facial expressions, and so on—they provide his mother with feedback on the success of her contributions. And, in the light of this, she is able to "tune" her speech fairly closely to his current ability to comprehend. As that ability increases, she increases the complexity of what she says and of the ideas that she tries to communicate. Adults do not need to know about the relative complexity of linguistic items, therefore, in order to provide appropriate evidence for children to learn from. All that is required is that they be responsive to the cues that children provide as to what they are able to understand. Rather than adults teaching children, therefore, it is children who teach adults how to talk in such a way as to make it easy for them to learn.

That only happens, of course, to the extent that the adult is sensitive and alert to the cues that the child offers. Some well-meaning parents, believing that instruction and correction are necessary for language learning, are so concerned with bringing their child's language system and internal model of the world into conformity with their own that they fail to pick up and respond to cues from the child and, as a result, they actually make it more difficult for the child to learn. The next example illustrates how this may happen.[20]

Thomas (age 25 months) has seen a plate of biscuits (cookies) on the table. His first utterance consists of three words, but only the third is intelligible.

Thomas: * * biscuits.

Mother: Those were got specially 'cos we had visitors at the weekend. Who came to see Tommy? Who came in a car?

Thomas: See Grannie Irene uh car.

Mother: Grannie Irene's coming next weekend. But who came last weekend?

Thomas: Auntie Gail in a train.

Mother: Auntie Gail's coming. They're coming on the train, yes.

Thomas: Colin uh Anne a train.

Mother: Colin—Colin and Anne came in the car, didn't they?

Thomas: Colin uh Anne. Colin uh Anne.

Mother: Yes.

Thomas: Colin uh Anne. Colin uh Anne.

Mother: Colin and Anne came in the train.

Thomas: In uh train. Auntie train.

Mother: No, not Auntie train, darling. Auntie Gail and Grannie Irene are coming on the train on Friday.

Thomas: Auntie Gail in uh train.

Mother: That's right.

What was Thomas's original intention? Was he merely expressing an interest in the presence of the biscuits (as his mother decides to assume), or did he perhaps want to eat one of them? We shall never know. For, instead of negotiating to find out what his intended meaning was, his mother launches into what turns out to be a quiz on the topic of which relatives came by which mode of transport on which weekend—a topic that is considerably beyond the level of complexity that a two-year-old can cope with.

Far from being collaborative, this episode is dominated by the mother, who manages the content of the conversation by means of questions and evaluations. It is almost as if she has to assess each of Thomas's utterances to make sure that it is factually accurate and grammatically well-formed before she will allow it into the conversation. The result is that she is so concerned to ensure that Thomas should see the world from her own adult perspective that she fails to pick up his cues, and they are ignored. And, when he does volunteer an idea of his own, using the limited resources at his disposal—"Aunty train" ("Aunty came in the train")—far from being accepted as the basis for collaboration in the construction of a more extended understanding, his utterance is rejected and his mother's "correct" version is substituted.

There are two reasons why conversations of this kind are not helpful to the language learner. First, they fail to recognize the active and autonomous nature of the child's construction of his or her linguistic repertoire. Instead of being cued by Thomas's communicative behavior, his mother tries to impose her own fully developed adult system and, as a result, provides evidence that is far from optimally adjusted to Thomas's current needs.

Second, such conversations are, in themselves, unrewarding: there is none of the satisfaction that comes from achieving a shared understanding of the topic. There is no real meeting of minds. What is more, if this experience is repeated too often, the child may well lose interest in conversing with adults and, as a result, also lose the opportunities for learning that such conversations can provide.

Talking with young children is thus very much like playing ball with them. What the adult has to do for this game to be successful is, first, to ensure that the child is ready, with arms cupped, to catch the ball. Then the ball must be thrown gently and accurately so that it lands squarely in the child's arms. When it is the child's turn to throw, the adult must be prepared to run wherever it goes and bring it back to where the child really intended it to go. Such is the collaboration required in conversation, the adult doing a great deal of supportive work to enable the ball to be kept in play.

Probably all parents want to help their children learn to talk, and some actively seek advice and guidance. I have one very general suggestion to make to any adult involved in caring for children: encourage them to initiate conversation, and make it easy and enjoyable for them to sustain it. The following more specific suggestions should help in achieving that result:

- When the child appears to be trying to communicate, assume he or she has something important to say and treat the attempt accordingly.

- Because the child's utterances are often unclear or ambiguous, be sure you have understood the intended meaning before responding.

- When you reply, take the child's meaning as the basis of what you say next—confirming the intention and extending the topic or inviting the child to do so him- or herself.

- Select and phrase your contributions so that they are at or just beyond the child's ability to comprehend.

In response to a similar parental request for guidance, Roger Brown had this to say:

Believe that your child can understand more than he or she can say, and seek, above all, to communicate. To understand and be understood. To keep your minds fixed on the same target. There is no set of rules of how to talk to a child that can even approach what you unconsciously know. If you concentrate on communicating, everything else will follow.[21]

It could hardly be put better. Children have to work out the way in which language is organized for themselves and, fortunately, they are well equipped to do so. But they can't do it all on their own. They need the collaborative help of interested conversational partners who, in aiming to achieve a shared understanding of the topics that are raised and of the activities that they are engaged in together, provide clear and relevant evidence of how the language works and feedback that enables children to evaluate the appropriateness of their current hypotheses. Above all, children need to feel that conversation is enjoyable and worthwhile and that it enables them to be effective in controlling and understanding their surroundings. This is what provides the motivation to continue to learn.

Learning to talk should thus be thought of as the result of a partnership: a partnership in which parents and other members of the community provide the evidence and then encourage children to work it out for themselves. Andrew Lock sums it all up in a single phrase when he describes the process as "the guided reinvention of language."[22]

Four

TALKING TO LEARN

Conversation is rarely an end in itself, particularly where young children are concerned. They talk in order to achieve other ends: to share their interest in the world around them, to obtain the things they want, to get others to help them, to participate in the activities of the grown-up world, to learn how to do things or why things are as they are, or just to remain in contact. And similar purposes underlie their parents' reasons for talking with them. For most of the time, therefore, conversation is purposeful and goal-directed—aimed at enabling the participants to integrate their behavior in order to achieve the purposes of one or other or both of them. In the process, a great deal of information is called forth, either as a necessary adjunct to the performance of activities or because it is judged to be of interest in itself. In this chapter, we shall consider some examples of spontaneously occurring conversations in which children are not only learning to talk but also, through talk, learning about a great many other things.

■ LEARNING FROM JOINT ACTIVITIES

Children love to help with jobs that their parents are engaged in. When they are allowed to help, these shared activities can provide particularly rich opportunities to learn—about the activities themselves and about the words by which to refer to them and also about the way in which language functions to guide action. Consider the following example.

[*Simon, age 4 years 9 months, is helping his mother to make a cake.*]

Simon [*wanting to grate a lemon*]: Can I do that?

Mother: Well, you can try. But it's not very easy. You can tear your finger if you're not careful.

Simon: What do you mean "tear"?

Mother: Well, if your finger gets too close to the grater, and you're going too fast, you can catch it on the sharp part and scrape the skin off.

Simon: I'll be very careful.

Mother: Hold it like that [*she puts the grater in Simon's hand and then gives him the lemon*].

[*Five seconds of concentrated effort follow, at which point the lemon slips out of Simon's hand into the bowl.*]

Simon: Oh dear!

Mother [*mock anger*]: Oh deary me! Whatever shall we do?

[*Mother hands back lemon; Simon continues to grate.*]

Simon: Look, it's coming off.

Mother: Yes. You have to turn it [the lemon] round. Because when you've got it [the rind] all off one part, you have to turn it round to get the rest off. Let me show you.

Simon: No. I can do it. [*He tries to turn the grater around.*]

Mother: No. You turn the lemon round, not the grater. You see, you've got it off there, so you've got to take it off another part now.

[*Ten seconds of grating*]

Simon: You do it now.

Mother: Thank you. That was a help.

Here Simon is not only learning to cook and testing the limits of his own competence, he is also learning how to talk about some of the activities involved.

In the next example, Jacqueline thinks she is helping: her mother takes a different view.

[*Jackie is playing with the clothes that her mother has tipped out on the floor from the laundry bag in preparation for the weekly wash.*]

Jackie [*putting the clothes back in the laundry bag*]: I'm putting them in.

Mother [*sharply*]: No, no, no. Leave Mummy's washing alone. Mummy's got to wash all that.

Jackie: I want to put those things in, Mum.

Mother: Yes, when they're washed you can. Not before.

Although Jackie's desire to help is unwelcome to her mother on this occasion, notice how her mother deals with the situation: as well as firmly telling Jackie to desist, she explains her prohibition in a way that recognizes her daughter's interest and desire to help and then presents a sequence of later events in which Jackie's intended activity will indeed be helpful. But from this conversation Jackie is not only learning about the sequence of stages in doing the laundry—she is also learning that, even though there may sometimes be a conflict of purposes, language provides a means for negotiating a solution that is mutually acceptable.

Later, within the same short sample, there is another episode in which Jackie and her mother have to reconcile a difference, but this time it arises from Jackie's difficulty in expressing her intended meaning in a form that her mother can understand. (Because intonation plays an important role in the negotiation of the meaning that was finally agreed, both the main, stressed, syllables and the direction of pitch movement have been marked.)

Jackie: **Lin**da bought you **socks**, **Mum**.	1
Mother: **Yes**, Linda bought you **socks**.	2
They're **dir**ty. They've got to be **washed**.	3
Jackie [*trying to repeat Mother's words*]: Did Linda bought you—me got. **washed**? [Have the socks that Linda bought me got to be washed?] [intonation unclear]	4
Mother: **Par**don?	5
Jackie: **Lin**da wa—**wash** them.	6
Mother: **No**. **Mum**my's going to wash them.	7
Jackie: **Lin**da wash them.	8
Mother: **No**. Linda's **not** going to wash them.	9
Jackie: **Lin**da's not going to **wash** them.	10
Mother: **No**. **Mum**my wash them.	11

Jackie has seen a pair of her socks waiting to be washed, which she recalls were given to her by her Aunty Linda. She tries to share all this information with her mother, but has difficulty in organizing the form of her utterance to encode her intended meaning with the right information focus—that is to say, with the emphasis on the right words (line 4). Following a request for repetition, Jackie attempts to express her meaning in a simpler form but, as the hiatus suggests, she still has difficulty (line 6). The arrangement of the components "Linda," "wash," and "them" (socks) suggests that Linda is the agent of the action of washing. But this does not correspond with the situation nor, as far as one can judge, with Jackie's intention. The problem seems to result from a conflict between two intentions: to ask for confirmation of the proposition that the socks are to be washed and to focus attention on the fact that it was Aunty Linda who gave her this particular pair of socks. In line 7, Mother rejects Jackie's utterance as inaccurate and, using marked tonic stress placement on "Mummy," offers a contrasting true statement, which matches the surface form of Jackie's utterance. Jackie seems unable to accept this way of stating things and in line 8 reaffirms her original assertion, placing contrastive stress on "Linda." Mother again rejects Jackie's statement, this time explicitly contradicting it: "Linda's *not* going to wash them." In line 10, Jackie repeats her mother's utterance but places marked tonic stress on "Linda" to indicate her understanding that it is not Linda who is going to wash the socks and signals her wish for confirmation of this interpretation. Finally, in line 11, her mother confirms the correctness of Jackie's negative statement and, picking up the contrastive implication of the stress on "Linda," restates the relationship positively with "Mummy" as agent. Jackie's silence can be taken as agreement with this final version.

I have analyzed this short extract in such detail because it is such a clear example of how a misunderstanding with respect to intended meaning can be quite literally *negotiated* until a collaborative resolution is achieved. At the same time, one can almost see Jackie working on the evidence supplied by the discrepancies between her own utterances, her mother's utterances, and the situation to find the appropriate linguistic devices to express her original meaning. Given her inability, at this stage, to make use of a relative clause, she works on her growing control of intonation to help her resolve the problem.

Jackie was only 2 years 3 months old. By 3½, Jonathan has much more fully developed linguistic resources and, as is seen in the next example, some skill in arguing his point of view.

[*Jonathan is helping his mother with the housework by polishing his wardrobe.*]

Jonathan: Do you think this is lovely?

Mother: I think it's a bit smeary.

Jonathan: Why do you think it's a bit smeary?

Mother: Because you put far too much polish on it. Right. Now you can put the things back on there [on the dresser]. And I'll put the carpet sweeper over the room.

Jonathan: Well, why can't I put the carpet sweeper over the room?

Mother: Because that's my job, O.K.?

Jonathan: What is my job?

Mother: You've done your job. You've polished the furniture.

[*A few minutes later.*]

Jonathan: It doesn't matter if that polish goes in your eyes, does it?

Mother: Oh it does, yes. It makes them sting.

Jonathan: * [unintelligible].

Mother: It makes them sting very badly.

Jonathan: Well, just now some of that polish waved in my eye.

Mother: Did it?

Jonathan: Yes.

Mother: Do they [your eyes] sting? Or did it miss? Don't rub them with the duster, darling. The duster's all dirty.

Jonathan [referring to polish]: Well, how can that get out, Mummy?

Mother: Why don't you go and wipe it with the flannel [facecloth] in the bathroom?

Jonathan [goes to bathroom]: No, I think I'll get it out with the towel. Mummy, I just have to see if I can get it out with this towel.

Mother: All right.

■ QUESTIONS AND ANSWERS

In all these examples, the children were learning about how language is used for various interpersonal purposes. But, because the conversations arose from activities that had their own internal structure, through talking in order to participate in them, they were also learning about the activities themselves and their organization. This sort of learning about the world through talk is perhaps even more evident in the following examples, in which the events themselves become the focus of the child's attention.

[Abigail, age 3, is helping her mother change the bed linen.]

Mother [referring to Abigail's nightdress]: Why not take that and put it under your pillow? I'll just put new pillows on our bed.

Abigail: Mummy, why you putting the new pillow in those? Because the other one's broken?

Mother: No. Going to have clean ones because I want it all to look pretty and in the same color to look nice when Daddy comes home. So that's done. Now we must find a bottom sheet and some other pillowcases.

Abigail: Oh, yes. [*Referring to her nightdress*] Shall I put and wrap it up and put it in my pillow?

Mother: Hurry up. Let's see what we can find for washing.

To begin with, children's questions tend to be incidental to the activity in which they are engaged: "Where's my ball?", "Which one shall I take?", "Why can't I go out in the garden?" What is being asked for is information that will guide or facilitate action or, as in the above example, a justification for Mother's stated plan of action. A simple answer is all that is usually called for, as the child's attention is focused on the action rather than on the explanation.

As they get older, though, their questions show a developing interest in getting to the bottom of things. Their questions seem to arise more frequently from a sense of puzzlement—from a desire to make sense and to get things straight in their own minds. As before, it is frequently the activity in which they are engaged, or one in which they observe someone else engaged, that sparks off the question, but they are no longer satisfied with the straightforward answer. They seek explanations rather than justifications. Here is an example from the observation of Anthony at 3½ and three examples from recordings of the older group of children.

[*Anthony's mother is painting the bathroom. Anthony is standing watching.*]
Anthony: You're painting.
Mother: Oh, yes. Dreadful stuff, paint. It gets everywhere.
Anthony: What it do?
Mother: Gets on everything—
Anthony [*acknowledging*]: Mm.
Mother: —and everywhere, when it's wet.
Anthony: Oh, God! Does it get over me and my Daddy?
Mother: No. Mind, out the way, sweetheart.
Anthony: Would Daddy get it on him?
Mother: When he does painting, it does, yes.
Anthony: He does, doesn't he? He gets it on his hair.
Mother: Does he?
Anthony: Yes. And he gets it on his jacket.
Mother: I don't think Daddy would paint with his jacket on, darling.
Anthony: With his coat on, he do.

[*Mother is making a jelly (Jell-o, in cubes) and Deirdre, age 4 years 6 months, is stirring the jelly cubes in boiling water.*]
Mother: The jelly's melting, look.
Deirdre: Why's it starting to melt?
Mother: 'Cause the water's very hot. And it makes jelly melt when it's very hot.
   [*6-second pause*]
Deirdre: Why's it making jelly melt—when it's very hot? Why does it?
Mother: Well, because it does. That's why. Butter melts when it's very hot.
[*8-second pause. Mother adds cold water to the jelly.*]
Deirdre: It's very cold now, isn't it?
Mother: It's cooler.

[*Elizabeth, age 4, is watching her mother shovel wood ash from the grate into a bucket.*]

Elizabeth: What are you doing that for?

Mother: I'm gathering it up and putting it outside so that Daddy can put it on the garden.

Elizabeth: Why does he have to put it on the garden?

Mother: To make the compost right.

Elizabeth: Does that make the grass grow?

Mother: Yes.

Elizabeth: Why does it?

Mother: You know how I tell you that you need to eat different things like eggs and cabbage and rice pudding to make you grow into a big girl.

Elizabeth: Yes.

Mother: Well, plants need different foods, too. And ash is one of the things that's good for them.

[*James, age 5, comes into the kitchen just as his mother has taken some cakes out of the oven. There is a loud, metallic "Crack."*]

James: Who did that?

Mother: I expect it was that tin contracting.

James: Which tin?

Mother: The one with your pastry in.

James: Why did it make that noise?

Mother: Well, when it was in the oven, it got very hot and stretched a bit. I've just taken it out of the oven, and it's cooling down very quickly, you see, and that noise happens when it gets smaller again and goes back to its ordinary shape.

James: Oh! Was it a different shape in the oven?

Mother: Not very different. Just a little bigger.

James: Naughty little tin. You might get smacked—if you do it again.

By four years of age, most children are great askers of questions, and parents are often hard put to find appropriate answers. There is so much they do not yet know that it is difficult to know where to start. But when, as in these examples, children are encouraged to bring their knowledge to the shared construction of an answer, there is a good chance thay they will be able to assimilate some of the information that is offered and, as a result, will be able to add to and, if necessary, modify their internal model of the world.

Parents' answers are not always as full or as helpful as those in the examples quoted above. Sometimes they simply do not know the answer, or they misunderstand the question. On other occasions they are simply too busy to stop and give the question the time and attention it deserves.[1] Nevertheless, because they are such active seekers after meaning, children do not give up and, in the absence of the necessary information, they will find an answer of their own. It is for this reason that some of the things they say seem so amusingly bizarre to adults.

However, as Barbara Tizard and Martin Hughes point out after recording and observing four-year-olds at home, children do not have a problem only with gaps in knowledge; "it is rather that they have an imperfect grasp of a vast range of concepts which an older child or adult takes for granted." The children they observed seemed, in their words, "in some sense aware that their conceptual framework was not yet substantial enough to cope with their experiences, and engaged themselves actively in the process of improving their intellectual scaffolding."[2] Children *need* to be persistent questioners, therefore, and provided their parents attempt on most occasions to provide an answer, they will continue to ask—using others as a resource for making sense of their experience.

■ INCIDENTAL LEARNING: THE WORLD'S AN INTERESTING PLACE

Questions are not the only source of information, however. As we have seen, a simple expression of interest by the child will often prompt a parent to offer information that fills in a little more of the picture and extends the child's understanding of the topic that aroused his or her interest. Here is another example, which starts with a child's interested observation of a bird.

[*James, age 3½, has been playing in the garden. His mother wants to get him to take his muddy shoes and socks off but, as he comes inside, he sees a bird.*]

Mother: There we are. There—one slipper on.

James: I can see a bird.

Mother: A what, love?

James: See a bird.

Mother [*whispering*]: Is there? Outside?

James [*pointing and whispering*]: Yes. See.

[*Both continue to whisper.*]

Mother: Is he eating anything?

James: No.

Mother: Where? Oh yes. He's getting— Do you know what he's doing?

James: No.

Mother: He's going to the—the paper sack to try and pick out some pieces—
Oh, he's got some food there. And I expect he'll pick out some pieces of thread from the sack to go and make his nest up underneath the roof, James. Wait a minute and I'll—

[James now wants to go out to see more closely, but at that moment the bird flies away.]

James: That bird's gone.

Mother [speaking at normal volume again]: Has it gone now?

James: Yeh.

There are countless examples of this kind, not all so dramatic as this whispered accompaniment to their jointly focused attention, perhaps, but all in their different ways helping the child to make fuller sense of an experience. It is in this way, of course, that the child gradually comes to take on the adult way of interpreting the world— not through deliberate and systematic instruction, but through shared interest and involvement in the events that make up everyday life.[3] Other situations that are particularly likely to give rise to collaborative meaning making are looking out of the window, recalling past events and planning or speculating about future ones, watching television together, or reading a story.[4]

Since television is often considered to have an almost entirely negative influence, it is worth quoting several examples to show that it need not always be harmful. In the first, James (at 3 years 3 months) is watching a nature program about deer. (*Note:* underlining indicates words spoken simultaneously.)

Mother: That one's got horns in the front.

James: Yes, but—

Mother: In front of its head it's got two horns.

James: Yes, but it—but it looks like a deer.

Mother: Mm.

James: But it looks like a little deer.

Mother: Look! What a nice face it's got.

James: Yes. Got any eyes?

Mother: Yes they have, my love. Look, there's their eyes—little black marks—there you are. That's a baby one.
[James climbs onto his mother's lap.]
There's a good boy.

James: Lovely deer they are.

[10-second pause, while they watch. The voice of the commentator can be heard in the background.]

Mother: Some more.

James: What are they playing * *?

Mother: Well, they were just playing— I expect what they were doing is they talk to one another. They were going like this [*rubs noses and giggles*].

[James chuckles.]

As in the earlier extract when they looked at the bird together, what James's mother is doing here is helping him to observe more closely as she provides a framework for interpreting what he sees. Without this help, we found, children of this age were able to get very little from watching television. Certainly, in some homes the television set was switched on for much of the day, but it was part of the background and almost totally ignored by the children until their parents sat down to watch with them.

The second example involves Rosie at the age of 5. With her mother, she is watching a program about making pots.

Rosie [*referring to the potter's wheel*]: Mum, what—what's making it go round?

Mother: Er—well, like a clock.

Rosie: What clock?

[*Mother does not reply. 30-second pause.*]

Mother: They're digging.

Rosie: Why they dig—?

Mother: That's for the boilers.

Rosie: Why's the boy—?

Mother: Tipping it into a machine.

Rosie: Why they tipping it into the 'chine—machine?

Mother: They'll tell you now.
   [*Commentator explains what is happening.*]
   Oh, that's clay.
   [*Picture shows molds being made.*]
   There it is. Look, they're saucepans—not saucepans. What do you call them? Basins. And that's a cup.

Rosie: Is there toilet rolls?

Mother: No * * *.

Rosie: Why they trying to do that for?

Mother: Making cups, you see. That's the mold to shape the cup. He'll get that board and put them on there.

Rosie: Why? Why's he putting them on there for?

Mother: 'Cos he's got to go somewhere else.

Rosie: Might fall in the fishpond.

If this does not seem as successful as the previous example, that is probably due partly to the fact that the content of the program is much more difficult for a young child to understand. But for all its limitations, it is worth noting how the mother's attention to the program is helping Rosie to look more closely than she would otherwise have done and encouraging her to test her interpretation against her mother's understanding.

Television programs, like stories, can also be the stimulus that leads to a consideration of personal experience. In the following extract, at 3 years 6 months, Jonathan and his mother were watching a program about gardening. (*Note:* underlining indicates words spoken simultaneously.)

Jonathan: Planting cabbages here. Why's his Mummy with him?
Mother: Didn't you do that with Grampy—with Gran the other day?
Jonathan: Yes.
Mother: Plant cabbages?
Jonathan: Yes, I did.
Mother: Yes, I thought you did.
Jonathan: I helped to * *.
Mother: <u>What</u> did you do? Did you make the holes? Or did you put the cabbages in the holes that Gran made?
Jonathan [*getting the words "holes" and "cabbages" mixed up*]: Gran made the cabbages, and I helped to put the holes in.
Mother: Can you remember how many you planted? Did you count them or not?
Jonathan: No, we forgot to count.
Mother: Oh. Perhaps when we go up next week we can count them. We'll see how many you planted, eh?
Jonathan: Mm. They're for the winter.
Mother: Yes, they grow in the winter, don't they? And then we can have nice cabbages.

■ EXPLORING THE WORLD OF THE IMAGINATION

Nowhere is this willingness to explore the world through words more apparent than in imaginary and fantasy play. Most children readily engage in "pretend" games alone or with other children. They also enjoy playing in this way with adults who are able to enter into the spirit of the game. Some parents find it quite difficult to join in physically, but simply to adopt the imaginary frame of reference may be sufficient to enable the play to continue, as in the following example.

[*Ann, age 2 years 6 months, is playing with her teddy bear.*]
Ann: Don't wake Teddy up, will you, Daddy?
Father: No, I won't. What's Teddy doing?
Ann: My teddy's not very well.
Father: Isn't he? What's the matter?
Ann: Got a—Teddy's got to have some Abidec [a vitamin preparation].
Father: Has he?
Ann: And some aspirin.

Father: What are you going to give the aspirins to Teddy for?
Ann: 'Cos . . . my teddy's not very comfy.

But what a vivid and exciting world is created when the adult joins in completely. As James (at 3 years 9 months) and his mother drive off in their steam train in the following example, you can almost see the green fields, the cows, and the waving farmer.

[James is playing trains with his mother on the sofa. He is sitting astride the arm, as driver.]
Mother: There we are. I'll sit at the side. Right. Are you ready? All set?
  Right. Off with the brake.
James: I'll start it up.
Mother: Oh, sorry! Right.
James: Mum! You don't steer it yet.
Mother: Oh. Well.
  [James makes a noise, pretending to start the engine.]
  Oh! That was a quick-starting engine. Very good! Got enough coal at the back? Have you shoveled enough coal on, James?
James: Yes.
Mother: Good. Away we go, then. Wave good-bye to your friends.
  Right.
  [Engine noises accelerate. James chuckles and makes a noise for the engine whistle.]
  We're going very fast now, James. Can you feel the carriages swaying?
James: Yeh.
Mother: Can you?
James: Yeh.
Mother: Oh, they're rolling me about. Oh—all my breakfast is rumbling in my tummy. Oh—oh—oh!
  [Engine noises.]
  I think we'll have to slow down, don't you?
James [agreeing]: Mm.
Mother: I think we're going a bit too fast. . . . That's better. That's easier now, isn't it?
James [agreeing]: Mm.
Mother [hums a bit, then says]: Look at the cows in the field, James.
James: Mm.
Mother: And there's a farmer, look. The farmer's waving to you.

■ FROM DIALOGUE TO REFLECTIVE THOUGHT

As this variety of examples shows, almost every situation provides an opportunity for learning if children are purposefully engaged and there are adults around who encourage their attempts to do and to understand

and, in collaboration with them, provide a resource of skills and information on which they can draw. In such situations, language provides a means not only for acting in the world but also for reflecting on that action in an attempt to understand it.

Initially, such reflection takes place through conversation—through dialogue with another, more knowledgeable person. But gradually, if children have many positive experiences of this kind, they begin to be able to manage both roles for themselves. They come to be able to frame questions and interrogate their own experience in the search for an answer. The dialogue begins to be carried on internally. In this way, language becomes a tool for thinking.

In the following example, Simon (age 4 years 9 months) seems already to be moving in that direction. He has just eaten an apple and is left with the pips. He is explaining to his mother what he might do with them.

Simon: A pip is a secd. So he can grow. And we might be able to grow some now. Got some apple seeds— apple pip seeds—and if I put even more, Daddy and me might go out one day, which isn't a rainy day, and we might be able to plant the seeds. Or I could plant them tomorrow.

All the examples quoted in this chapter have been taken from recordings of naturally occurring conversations in children's homes. From them we see how parents spontaneously and intuitively provide opportunities for learning as they talk with their children about the many events that occur during the course of a normal day. These parents do not feel under any pressure to instruct, but they are sensitive to their children's desire to learn—to acquire skill, understanding, and control. And so, whenever possible, they encourage their children's interests and help them to extend and develop them.

In learning through talk—as in learning to talk—children are active constructors of their own knowledge. What they need is evidence, guidance, and support. Parents who treat their children as equal partners in conversation, following their lead and negotiating meanings and purposes, are not only helping their children to talk, they are also enabling them to discover how to learn *through* talk.

Five

FROM HOME TO SCHOOL

In the preschool years, as we have seen, talking and learning go hand in hand. Children talk about the things that interest them and try to increase their understanding; and, for much of the time, their adult conversational partners sustain and support their efforts, seeking, where appropriate, "to add a pebble to the pile."[1] What is characteristic of such learning is that it is spontaneous and unplanned and, because it arises out of activities in which one or both of the participants are engaged, it is focused and given meaning by the context in which it occurs.

This is both a strength and a limitation. It is a strength because the child's purpose in the activity sustains his or her motivation to understand, and the context provides support for the new concepts to be grasped and the new connections to be made. But it is also a limitation because such learning is sporadic and, for the most part, unsystematic: while some areas of experience are gradually illuminated from a variety of perspectives, others are encountered only rarely, and many not at all.

One of the most important functions of schooling, therefore, is to broaden the range of children's experiences and to help them to develop the sustained and deliberate attention to a topic or activity that makes more systematic learning possible. Above all, they need to be helped to become more reflectively aware of what they already know and still need to know, so that they can gradually take over more and more responsibility for their own learning.[2]

It is often assumed that such aims require a sharp break with the incidental style of learning experienced at home. But this is neither desirable nor necessary. The strategies that children have developed for actively making sense of their experience have served them well up to this point; they should now be extended and developed, not suppressed by the imposition of routine learning tasks for which they can see neither a purpose nor a connection with what they already know and can do. Similarly, the adult strategies that supported their talking and learning do not lose their effectiveness just because the children are now in a classroom rather than a home. Adult guidance is certainly necessary, and skill in providing it should be expected of every teacher; but knowledge still has to be "reinvented" by each individual child, building on what he or she brings from previous experience.

Continuity between home and school is important for social and emotional reasons, too. If children are to make the transition confidently and easily, it is important that they experience the new environment of school as an exciting and challenging one, in which the majority of their endeavors are successful and where they are given individual recognition for who they are and what they can do. First impressions—on both sides—can distort subsequent experiences. Children who feel, or who are made to feel, unaccepted and incompetent may be slow to recover their self-confidence and, as a result, their ability to benefit from the enlarged opportunities for learning that school provides may be diminished or even, in extreme cases, irrevocably damaged.

Fortunately, as we have seen, by the time children come to school, they have already acquired a considerable degree of competence as purposeful actors and as effective communicators. There is therefore a solid foundation on which to build. Certainly they differ considerably in the range and level of skills and knowledge that they have mastered, but there are very few children indeed who, in the familiar surroundings of their own homes, cannot successfully plan and carry out quite complex activities and communicate with others to seek or offer assistance, exchange information, and express feelings and respond to those of others. Each child, too, through his or her interactions with other people, has internalized a model of the world of considerable power and complexity that enables him or her to act effectively in the social and physical environment of home and its immediate surroundings.

As far as learning is concerned, therefore, entry into school should not be thought of as a beginning, but as a transition to a more broadly based community and to a wider ranger of opportunities for meaning-making and mastery. *Every* child has competencies, and these provide a positive base from which to start. The teacher's responsibility is to discover what they are and to help each child to extend and develop them.

■ A TYPICAL MORNING AT HOME AND AT SCHOOL

How is the transition from home to school actually experienced by the majority of children? And how well do the tasks that they are given at school enable them to capitalize on the competencies they have already developed?

One difficulty that is often mentioned by teachers, particularly in schools serving areas of predominantly public housing, is the high proportion of children who are perceived to suffer from what, in Britain, is referred to as "linguistic disadvantage." What is meant by this term varies. In some cases, the children are perceived to be essentially without language; in other cases, the problem is thought of as a lack of the specific linguistic resources necessary to succeed in school.[3] But are there many such children? If so, what is the nature of their disadvantage, and how far does it impede these children from adjusting easily to school?

The continuation of our longitudinal study gave us an opportunity to investigate these questions by looking more closely at the transition from home to school as it was experienced by the 32 children that we studied most intensively. For all these children, we had recordings from 15 months to 42 months. In the weeks before they started school we made another recording of each child and then repeated the procedure in their classrooms after they had been in school for about six weeks.

In both settings, nine 5-minute samples were recorded at approximately 20-minute intervals between 9:00 A.M. and 12:00 noon. The recording in the home was made in exactly the same way as on the earlier occasions: no observer was present, and the family was unaware of the times at which the tape recorder would be switched on. The same principle applied in the classroom, except that it was necessary to have an observer, as no class teacher could be expected to remember what a particular child had been doing at every moment throughout a morning. Having once decided that it would be necessary to have an observer, there seemed no reason not to have a mechanical observer as well, in the form of a video camera. This was mounted on a trolley and remained in a fixed position throughout the observation.

At the beginning of each session in school, the video equipment was demonstrated to the children, and each child in the class saw him- or herself on the screen in close-up and—perhaps more important— was seen by his or her friends. The children were then asked to forget about the equipment and, as our video recordings show, this is exactly what happened. As for the teachers, they no doubt continued to be intermittently aware of the camera and perhaps, therefore, not entirely relaxed. But, if this was so, any bias that was introduced was presumably in the direction of what they considered to be good teaching—though perhaps the presence of the camera inhibited them somewhat and kept them from being as adventurous as they might otherwise have been. With these small reservations, however, it can be said with considerable confidence that both home and school observations contain representative samples of naturally occurring behavior.

Before making a detailed comparison of the language used in the two settings, however, it may be helpful to describe the activities in which the children were engaged: what they were doing and who they were doing it with.

As might be expected, there was much greater similarity between children's experiences at school than there was at home. Almost all of them spent some part of the morning on activities associated with reading and writing, and a considerable number of them spent time on activities involving numbers and counting. In most classrooms there were periods when all the children were expected to be involved together in the same activity: a story, "news-time" (or "show and tell"), a TV broadcast, a discussion. In many classrooms, too, the morning began with all the children assembled around the teacher while she called the register, collected the dinner money, and dealt with other administrative matters. Typically, though, such activities occupied only a relatively small part of the morning. For the most part, the children worked, either individually or in small groups, on tasks assigned by the teacher or engaged in self-chosen activities with the teacher's approval.

As for the teachers, the greater part of their time was spent in discussing the work of individual pupils while simultaneously monitoring the whole classroom to try to ensure that every child was profitably engaged, to forestall possible problems, and to check any unacceptable behavior. There were, of course, quite substantial differences between the teachers in their emphases, in the proportion of time they involved the whole class in the same activity, and in their personal styles of classroom management. But there was also a very considerable degree of similarity between them in the way in which they organized the day and in what they considered it important for children to do.

To attempt a similar characterization of the children's experiences at home would be quite impossible, as they were much more varied. One important influence was the time of year at which the recordings were made. In summer, the children tended to spend a great deal of time out of doors, playing in the garden. In winter, they were confined to the house and so were more likely to play with small toys—cars, dolls, etc. However, probably the most important factor in deciding how the children spent their time was whether or not there was a sibling or friend present in the home. As most of the recordings were made on the morning of a school day when older brothers and sisters were at school, it was only those with younger siblings who had another child to play with throughout the day. The majority of the children, therefore, spent a considerable part of the day with a parent as their only companion.

In most homes, a parent (usually the mother) engaged for a part of the morning in some shared activity with the child—reading to him or her, playing a game, cooking, or performing some other household task. But for the most part the children occupied themselves, with a parent becoming involved only intermittently, either when called upon or when, between one job and another, he or she paused to talk with the child. However, the range of such impromptu conversations could be very broad, as will be seen in the examples below.

The children's activities at home, then, were much more varied than at school. But quite a number of the children voluntarily engaged in activities that were not unlike those that they would soon be doing at school—drawing, coloring, cutting out, building with bricks and construction toys, making models, listening to a story. For these children it would seem that, in this respect at least, the transition from home to school should not have been experienced as too great a discontinuity. However, for other children, there was much less similarity between the activities they performed in the two settings.

To illustrate the range of activities and the language associated with them, let us look at two of the children who were introduced in chapter 1 to see what they were doing in each of the comparable 5-minute periods at home and at school.

Like all the children, Gary was almost 5 years old when we recorded him on 5 January 1977. As it was during Christmas vacation, his older sister Tracey was also at home. In the first sample, made at around 10:00 A.M. on this occasion, Gary was playing alone with his toy bricks, making a squirrel. While he was doing this, his mother came into the room.

Mother: What are you making, Gary?
Gary: Er—I'm making a—I'm making a squirrel.
Mother: A squirrel, are you?
Gary: I can make squirrels.
Mother: Can you?
Gary: 'Cos they got—he's going to have—he's going to have a head * * [two unintelligible words].
Mother: Is it?
Gary: This one—

Mother: You're going to make a squirrel?

Gary: It's—it's going to go—

Mother: Know what a squirrel is?

Gary: Yes. I makes them in school. [Gary attends the nursery school.]

Mother: What do they do?

Gary: They climb up trees and gets nuts and acorns.

Mother [*Surprised he knows so much*]: That's right!

Gary: And they get other different things. 'Cos I—they live in trees in a hole.

Mother: That's right.

Gary: 'Cos I knows.

Mother: And they collect them up for the winter.

Gary: Yeh.

Mother: 'Cos they hibernate in the winter.

Gary: Yeh. 'Cos I knows.

Mother [*agreeing*]: Mm. Who told you that?

Gary: No one. Er—I knows how to make a—

Mother: Yeh. But who told you about the squirrels? Your teacher?

Gary: No.

Mother: Who did?

Gary: We knows how to paint the squirrel. Sometimes we paint squirrels in school—in nursery.

Mother: Do you?

Gary: Yeh. In holes. And I—and I can do it. 'Cos I don't need this one. [*Referring to bricks*] I got this body. Break this one.

Mother: Jolly good!

The most striking quality about this episode is Gary's confidence—both that he can make the model squirrel and that he knows about the animal itself. His mother's initial reaction is one of mild interest in what he is doing (signaled by a number of tag-question acknowledgments), but she becomes really involved and invites him to tell her more. With some surprise at the extent of his knowledge, she confirms his account ("That's right!") and then adds further information to the description that they jointly construct. Her final comment ("Jolly good!") once again reaffirms her positive evaluation of Gary's competence.

In the next sample, Gary brings some dirty ashtrays to his mother, who is washing the dishes. He then briefly watches Tracey, who is combing her doll's hair. Finally, he joins with both mother and sister in singing a Christmas rhyme.

Mother: What has Santa in his sack
That he carries on his back?

Tracey: He has presents bright and gay
   All to give on Christmas Day.
Gary: Here's a lovely bouncy ball
   To play with by the garden wall.
   Here a furry—
   What has Santa in his sack
   That he carries on his back?

At 10:40 A.M., Mother is making a cake and Gary and Tracey both want to lick the beaters from the cake mixer. They talk about the cheese and potato pie Mother is making for the midday meal (*note:* underlining indicates words spoken simultaneously):

Gary: What's that?
Tracey: Have you done cheese and potato together?
Mother: Cheese and potato pie.
Gary: Cheese and potato pie.
Mother: That's right.
Tracey: Is it lovely?
Mother: Yes. I'll cook it in the oven, then I'll take it out. Sprinkle some cheese on top and put it under the grill.
Tracey: Sprinkle some peas?
Mother: Cheese.
Tracey: We've had it at home before, haven't we?
Mother: Yes.
Gary: We had it in school and I ate the lot. That's yummy.
Tracey: Mummy.
Mother: What?
Tracey: Remember when we used to have those potatoes still with skins on? They were lovely.
Mother: Yes. I'll do some of them.
Tracey: When?
Mother: Well, not today.
Tracey: Might be next week.
Mother: I'll do some tomorrow.
Tracey: Ooh! They're lovely, aren't they?

There is nothing remarkable about this extract, except perhaps the ease with which the three of them manage to integrate their various perspectives. Gary has less to say than his sister, but he's clearly involved and probably incidentally learning about making cheese and potato pie.

In the next sample, Gary tells about another child in his nursery class who is "scared to ask for her milk." Mother is just taking the cake out of the oven, and Gary touches it.

Gary: Touch that. It's nice and warm. Not hot. Tracey, come and touch this.

Tracey: Yes, I touched it. It's lovely and warm. It's not too hot.

The ideal opportunity, one might say, for learning—or testing—the distinction between *hot* and *warm*.

At 11:40 A.M., Gary is playing alone, pretending that the radio-microphone (now worn on a belt around his waist) makes him the "electric man." Mother and Tracey are watching a television program together, but Gary is more interested in his own game.

At 12:00 noon, they sit down to dinner. During the meal, Mother explains to Gary why he must not waste his food.

Mother: They [starving children] don't even know what fish fingers taste like, because they've never had 'em.

Tracey: Why?

Gary: Well, it's because—

Mother: [*emphasizing what she has just said*]: No.

Gary: Do you know—

Mother: Or corned beef or anything like that.

Tracey: Or boiled eggs.

Mother: All they have is rice. And sometimes they don't even have that.

Tracey: Sometimes they don't have nothing?

Mother: They don't have nothing.

Gary: Mum, you could go up the shop. If you went there, you could have gone up shop to buy them, couldn't you?

Mother: That's no good. I can't buy it and send it to them. That's why it's wasteful when you don't eat your food. [This is aimed particularly at Gary, who is fussy about his food.] You think of the little children who are starving who would love to eat that.

Tracey: I've got to eat it, so it's not wasted.

Gary: Do you—don't they—do they have this?

Mother: No.

Gary: What I'm eating?

Mother: No. Nor bread and butter.

Gary: Nor butter?

Mother: No.

Tracey: Stale bread with no butter on it.

Mother: No cakes or sponges or sausage rolls or cheese flans.

Tracey: They don't ever have a party, do they?

Mother: Or crisps [chips]. It's a luxury to them.

Gary: Yeh. We can help * * *.

Mother: They haven't got the money.

Gary: It's not their mummy and father.

Mother: It's just a poor country, and that's it.

Gary: Mm.

Tracey: Just a poor family. We're not a poor family. We're a very lucky family.

Gary: Yes, 'cos we—we got enough food. We know what it tastes like, don't we?

Mother: Yeh. Well, eat it, then, don't waste it.

This is a difficult idea for a 5-year-old to grasp, but Gary's questions and suggestions indicate that, although he doesn't fully understand, he is entering into the starving children's predicament and is trying to think of ways to help them. Tracey is quicker to see the implication for herself: "I've got to eat it, so it's not wasted."

In the next sample, there is not much talk. Gary is eating sweets after dinner, and his speech is not very distinct. In the final sample, he is playing with the dog, putting tissues on its head.

Gary: Tracey, look!

Tracey: That's funny.

Gary: He can't see that.

Tracey: If Daddy was here, he wouldn't do that.

Mother: I'll get that stick in a minute.

Gary persists, however, and Mother gets really cross with him.

Mother: You stop bloody tormenting that dog! You horrible thing, you are.

Gary [*crying*]: Oh, Mummy.

Mother: You'll get something you don't want in a minute.
[*Gary cries.*] Come here. [*Holding him*] How would you like me to do that to you? You wouldn't like it, would you? [*Gary does not answer.*] Would you? [*Still no answer.*] Well, neither does the dog.

These are only short samples taken at intervals from a complete morning, but there is good reason to believe that they are representative of Gary's experience of language at home. In 6 out of the 8 samples, he engages in talk with his mother or sister about some matter that is of significance to him and, in 2 of the 8, the topic is treated in some depth. The last sample ends in a scolding, but here, too, the mother tries to get Gary to understand why his behavior is unacceptable. At home, then, Gary is appreciated for what he knows and can do, and he is helped to think about the implications of his behavior.

Let us look next at Penny. The recording cited below was made a month earlier than Gary's—in early December—and her elder brothers were at school. As in Penny's earlier recordings, several adult visitors called during the course of the morning.

At 9:10 A.M., her parents are talking to a friend, and Penny is playing with the dog and singing. At the end of the sample, she remembers she has to feed the fish.

At 9:36 she is writing and talking to herself as she writes:

Penny [to self]: Monday, Tuesday, Wednesday, *. *[Singing to self]* When you've got a freezer—Jane said she'd be up with the writing pad. *[To Mother]* Mum, Jane said she'd be up with the writing pad.

Mother: That'll be dinnertime she'll come.

Penny: Oh.

Mother: Where's all your writing pads?

Penny: I haven't got none.

Mother: In Paul's room. Here. You can put those in here for now.

Penny: It's going to be like keeper. All right? Finders keepers.

Father: Finders keepers, losers weepers. That doesn't always go, my girl.

Penny continues to write and sing. A few minutes later (*note:* number of dots refers to number of seconds of pause):

Penny [writing]: I wants to do A first. What's that for? A . . for . . apple. A round and a little B for . balloon.

Mother: For ball.

At that moment, the tape recorder switched off.

At 10:02, Penny is watching her mother do the washing. The (top-loading) washing machine is operating.

Penny: It ain't hot—look. The froth ain't.

Mother [referring to the water in the machine]: It is hot.

Penny: The froth ain't.

Mother: No, not the froth.

Penny: It's not froth, it's suds.

Mother: It's suds, it is.

Penny [sings]: Roundy roundy roundy roundy. Still it goes. *[She puts her hand in the machine.]* Ma, it ain't hurting me—look.

Mother: No. It's not going, that's why.

Penny [thinking Mother is going to start the machine]: Ah, you dare! *[Half a minute later]*

Mother: Will you do me a favor?

Penny: Yes.

Mother: Go upstairs and take the sheets off Paul's bed.

Penny: All right. *[She goes upstairs.]* And bring them down?

Clearly, Penny still likes to help, and her competence is appreciated.

During the next four samples, from 10:28 until nearly noon, Penny is engaged in making Christmas cards. At various points, both her mother and her father join in. The following extract is taken from the third of these samples.

Penny [to self, quietly]: I must stick that. ∗ ∗ ∗. There's a little bit.

Mother: No more. You don't have no glue left.

Penny: I'm just pressing it down. That's baby Lord Jesus. Ma, shall I make a photo? Baby Lord Jesus.

Mother [engaged in making her own card and not giving her full attention]: Don't know.

Penny: I knows how to make 'em. Just cut 'em out in a square. [*To self, as she cuts*] Come on and be straight. [*Singing*] Baby Lord Jesus looked down where she lay. La la la la, Baby Lord Jesus, Baby Lord Jesus. [*Then, to Mother*] Shall I have glue on there?

Mother [telling her where to put the glue]: On the other side.

Penny: What is it?

Mother [reading]: Best wishes for Christmas and the New Year.

Penny: Can I do that?

Mother: Put that one on its top first.

Penny: Oh! I drawed it. Whoops!

Mother: Don't squeeze it no more.

Penny: Whoops! Right.

Mother: No, no, no, no!

Penny: I know how it goes now.

Mother: Look, you've got a load on there.

Penny: Enough like that?

Mother: Yes. You're just spreading it over, not, er—squeezing the jar.

Penny: It's not a jar!

Mother: Well, the bottle.

Penny: Bottle.

Mother: That's it. Bottle.

Penny: It's not plastic.

Mother: It is a plastic one.

Penny: Hang on a minute.

Mother: Yeh.

Penny: No, on there.

Mother: No. You've only got to have it thin, Penny.

Penny: Mum, there's a photo.

Mother: It's upside down.

Penny: It's not.

Mother: Look, some stars.

Penny: Can I have four?

Mother: Flatten it down.

Penny: I've done Happy Christmas there. In here, look.
Mother: Let's see. Oh, yes.
Penny: I've got to stick the stars. Where's the stars?
Mother: In the—in the window in, er—your room, I think.
Penny: In my room or in Vince's?
Mother: Yours or Vince's.
Penny: Try Paul's first. [*Whispers to self*] It must be our Paul's room. [*She goes upstairs.*]

The above represents over an hour of sustained effort, and it was obviously productive. If some of the talk is difficult to follow, this is because it is fully embedded in the context of the joint activity. When both speaker and hearer are working together on the same task, there is no need to be more explicit.

In the final sample, Penny has been locked in the house by a visiting family friend. All treat it as a great joke and there is much shouting and joking. "Oy! I want a word with you!" she shouts, laughing, at the culprit.

Penny's morning was a happy and interesting one, in which she spent almost half the time single-mindedly on one activity. Like Gary, she enjoyed sustained interaction with her parents, talking about the activities in which she and they were engaged, and benefiting from her parents' support and assistance. In neither case is there the slightest sign of the "verbal deprivation" that is so often assumed to be characteristic of lower-SES homes.

Some weeks later, we recorded both of them in their classrooms. Both had settled in without difficulty and were actively participating in the activities that their teachers provided for them. Let us look first at Gary who, as we saw, had already been attending a nursery school.

At 9:15, having finished marking the register, Gary's teacher was settling the children into groups for their first activity of the day. In his case, this was picture-matching Bingo, with cards depicting characters from a Dick Bruna story about a circus. At this point, however, Gary was more interested in a friend's model car.

Gary: Can I have that car?
Darren: No.
Gary: Can I have a look at it? Just have a look at it.
Darren: * * *.
Gary: I just want to have a look at it.
Darren: I'll show you.
Gary: All right. [*Referring to part of the car*] Is it just that that opens up?
Darren: Look. See that? That's the engine. And that is broken now.
Gary: It's only cheap. Are you allowed to keep it?

Darren does not reply to this disparaging comment and they go on to talk about the microphone that Gary is wearing. Meanwhile, the teacher is distributing the picture cards for the game.

Teacher: Right, then. How many carrots have we got, Nicola? How many?
Nicola: Two.
Teacher [*handing the cards to Nicola*]: Have you got them? Ah! Here's a little girl with a pretty ribbon in her hair. Anyone got this one?
Gary: No.
Teacher: What color's the ribbon in her hair?
Gary [*to friend*]: She's not seen that one.
Teacher: And we've got a little chicken.
Anne: I've got that.
Teacher [*gives her the card*]: What color is it, Anne? [*Anne does not reply.*]
Gary: [*pointing to another child's card*]: Hey! There's a chicken. And there's the same chicken.
Teacher: Where?
Gary: You've got a chicken like that one.
Teacher: But my chicken's coming out of an egg. That one isn't, is it? Now, who's got the little bunny rabbits?
Gary: No, not us.
Child: Not us.
Teacher: Who's got the clown? [*Gary raises his hand to claim the card.*] What's he doing?
Gary: He's—he's lifting up his hand. [*Raises hands to illustrate. Teacher gives Gary the card to put on his board.*]

The game continues in this way for another fifteen minutes, with Gary becoming more and more eager for Darren and him to complete their card and win the game. Two of the girls win, however, and at 9:35, the teacher tells the children to go and drink their milk. Gary and his friend have some difficulty getting their straws into the bottles and, in the process, the milk spills all over Gary.

Gary: That's naughty.
Darren: There's a towel.
Gary [*wiping his face on the towel*]: Go wipe the floor with it.
Darren: Ugh! You've got some on your face.
Gary: Is it? [*Wipes his face for half a minute.*] It's off.
Darren: Anyway, I've got a packet of crisps in my drawer.
Gary: I got a packet of biscuits. Me and my sister got a packet of biscuits. [*Calls to observer*] You've seen my sister, didn't you? Her name's Tracey. [*To Darren*] You don't know which—When they phones up the police it's 999.

After they have had their milk, the teacher tells them to fetch their writing books and pencils and get ready to write a story. But before they start, she reads them the story of a circus, which contains the pictures that they have just been matching. As the teacher reads, Gary keeps shouting out, "We had that!", meaning that he and Darren had had that picture during the game. When it comes to the clown, he is so excited that he repeats, "That was on mine," several times but, for whatever reason, the teacher ignores him and continues with the story. He obviously enjoys the story and relates it to a previous family visit to a circus, but this is not picked up by the teacher.

At 9:50, Gary is drawing pictures of circus animals but is more interested in chatting with Darren. When he has finished, his picture is discussed by the teacher in a rather perfunctory manner and he quickly completes his writing, though his copying of the teacher's caption is done very neatly with well-formed letters. When he shows his work to the teacher, she asks him to write one part again and, that completed, he is told to choose what he would like to do. For a few minutes, he plays with the stickle bricks and then wanders around the room to see what is going on in other groups. He joins in several of them briefly but does not settle on anything.

At 10:25, it was time to get his coat on to go out to play. While they waited in the line, the teacher distributed apples to those who had paid for them. Gary did not get an apple, as he had brought biscuits from home. After the play period, Gary goes to the cloakoom to take his coat off. He notices his friend's clothes.

Gary: Likes your brand new trouser suit jumper. That's nice. And the shirt. I got one of they shirts.

Friend: Can I see it?

Gary: No. I haven't got it on. It's at home. This is my vest. I'm wearing my vest.

[*At this point, the teacher comes to investigate.*]

Teacher [*to Gary*]: Come and line up. Can I have the boys in a straight line, please?

Organizing the line takes several minutes, during which Gary continues to chat with his friends. Finally, the children go into the school hall for the school assembly.

By the time of the next sample, at 11:10, the children are back in the classroom and Gary has gone to join the teaching assistant, who is supervising modeling in clay. Gary spends the next half hour working in this group. The following extract comes from the beginning of the session, after Gary and the others have put on aprons.

Assistant: What are you going to make?

Gary [*referring to models that other children have made*]: I can't make
   things on there.

Assistant: I'll help you. [*Giving Gary a ball of clay*] You make that into a
   nice—nice, smooth ball. You feel it.

Gary [*rolling clay on table*]: Ugh! It's a bit soft.

Assistant [*to the group*]: Look. [*Showing models that other children have
   made*] Here's a hedgehog. And there's another one.

Gary [*to Assistant*]: I want a hedgehog. Would you make a he—help me to
   make a hedgehog?

Assistant: You make the ball, and then I'll help you. [*Gary does so.*]

Gary: I'm a—I made it.

Assistant: I—I don't think you need paint brushes to do the clay, really.

Gary [*rolling ball on table*]: I made it into a ball.
   [*Some 20 minutes later, Gary is making an owl, using a pencil to draw
   the face. He shows it to the Assistant.*] I done another owl.

Assistant: Did you do that?

Gary: Yeh. On my own.

Assistant: Oh, that's good.

Gary: I knows how to do my name, I do. [*He tries to write his name on the
   bottom of the owl. Then, not entirely satisfied*] Could you do my
   name?

Assistant: Well, I thought you were going to try.

Gary: I nearly done it.

Assistant: You nearly did it, didn't you?

Gary: Yeh.

Assistant: You're clever at making owls, aren't you?

Gary [*pleased to have his efforts recognized*]: Yeh.

The morning ends in a group activity with the teacher, counting
various objects in sevens and eights. Gary seems able to carry out the
task successfully, but his attention easily wanders to what other children are doing, so he doesn't always give the right answer.

Looking back over the morning, the observer wrote the following
comments:

Gary is a very outgoing child, full of energy and enthusiasm. He talks a lot
to the teacher, the teaching assistant, and to the other children, often in a
competitive way. He is very aware of what *he* can do, what *he* possesses,
etc. He seems to be well liked by the other children, although the head
teacher, perhaps influenced by an episode in the nursery school, describes
him as "moody," but from "a caring home, specially for that neighborhood."
However, there was no sign of moodiness on this occasion. Instead, he was
like a rather assertive ray of sunshine.

Gary quickly tires of an activity and looks for something more interesting to move on to. The teacher did not seem to make any effort to help him
to persevere with a task and failed to engage with him on any of the occa-

sions when he was enthusiastic about what he was doing. The absence of response was particularly noticeable when he took his completed writing for her to see. Of course, she had many other children to think about, but from Gary's point of view, although there were a number of activities organized for him to engage in, there was a lack of thematic unity, which meant that the activities were less meaningful than they might have been. The teaching assistant, on the other hand, was considerably more successful in helping Gary to complete the clay models to their joint satisfaction.

In sum, Gary has much enthusiasm and interest, but little perseverance. He needs to be encouraged to discipline his interest, but at present he is being given little help.

Penny seemed better able than Gary to harness her enthusiasm to the tasks that her teacher had organized. The day started with quite a long period in which the teacher dealt with administrative matters. This finished with her saying "Good morning" to each child in turn. During this time, Penny sat quietly observing. Starting at 9:10, the full 5-minute sample was occupied in this way. A total of 116 utterances were spoken, to which Penny contributed one: "Good morning, Miss Evans."

In the second sample, the teacher was reading—or, rather, retelling—a story to the whole class. This was followed by questions to check the children's understanding and recall of the main events. During this time, Penny spoke only twice, first to gain the teacher's attention and then to give her answer, which was accepted.

At 9:55, Penny was engaged on a number task, threading colored beads on a string to match the number shown on a card.

Penny: Miss Evans, I'm winning.
Teacher: I'll come and see if they're right.
Penny: One, two, three, four, five, six, seven.
Teacher: That's right. What's after seven?
Penny: Eight.
Teacher: Eight. [*Shows her a card with numbers on it.*] Can you find a number eight?
Penny: Can you see a eight?
Teacher: I can see one, two, three, four number eights.
[*Penny picks up the card and starts to thread eight beads on a string.*] :

Fifteen minutes later, Penny is at the teacher's desk:

Teacher: You did that five nicely, didn't you? How did you do your eight?
Penny: Er—
Teacher: Come on. You go and get a pencil and we'll try the eight, shall we? [*Guiding Penny's hand*] Round that way and then back again. Right. Good girl. [*Sending Penny away to write*] Let's do one with a nine, shall we?
[*Penny sings as she works.*]

After playtime, the children listen to music on a record player and sing nursery rhymes. Then, at 10:30 they go into the school hall for a school assembly at which the Local Education Authority music advisor leads various activities with instruments, voices, and hand-clapping to help children focus on pitch and rhythm.

At 11:10, back in the classroom again, Penny is sent to join the teaching assistant, who has a collection of cardboard circles and cylinders prepared for the children to make a collage. The assistant is talking to the whole group.

Assistant: Would you like to run your finger round [a section of toilet-paper roll]? What can you tell me about the round?

Penny [feeling it]: Giddy.

Assistant: Your finger goes giddy. Put your finger all round it. Has it got any sharp corners like a square? Put your finger round. No, it hasn't got corners like a square. It just goes all the way round, doesn't it? David, will you watch please? Scissors have got nothing to do with a round. It goes all the way round, doesn't it? [*Pointing to sections from an egg container*] What are those?

Penny: Egg box.

Assistant: Egg box. They're round, aren't they? [*Demonstrating*] They're round that way and they're round that way. Do you know what these are?

Child: Biscuits.

Assistant: Not biscuits, but cakes. They're out of a cake tin. They're all stuck together like that, and the cakes are all put in. They're all round. They're round that way and they're round that way, aren't they? They go all the way round.

[*20 minutes later, having drawn and cut out circles of various sizes, they are grading the shapes by size.*]

What sort of a pattern do you think we could make? Shall I get rid of those? [*Removing those that are not immediately needed*] We don't want those, do we? We've got those, look. That's the biggest ones. David, will you come and watch, please? [*Crossly*] David! [*Starts to grade the shapes, as the children watch.*] Those are tall ones, aren't they? Those are smaller. They're about the same, aren't they, so—and those are bigger round, aren't they, than that—bigger all the way round. We want to make a nice pattern with all these different things. So roll your sleeves up ready to do some gluing.

And so it continues, with Penny and the other children obediently gluing and then placing the pieces where they are directed. By 11:50, the master plan is almost completed. David, who has once again wandered off, is shouted at to "come and stick some circles on." Then the children wash their hands in preparation for dinner.

At the end of Penny's morning, the observer noted that she appeared to be confident and independent, liked by both adults and children and able to talk freely with them. Reading through the transcript confirms this impression—at least in part. Relative to her peers, she was indeed confident and competent, joining in all the activities and receiving positive feedback. In many respects, it was a useful and busy morning for her.

Compared with her morning at home, though, was this an improvement? There was no doubt about the sense of purposefulness in the classroom. The activities themselves were carefully thought out and well organized and, with a few exceptions such as David, the children were swept along by the brisk efficiency. But what opportunity was there for the children to share in the planning of their activities or to reflect on what they were doing in the sort of exploratory talk that we saw in both the home recordings? Was there time and opportunity for Penny and the other children to try out *their own* ideas in words?

■ THE LANGUAGE OF HOME AND SCHOOL:
A SYSTEMATIC COMPARISON

A comparison of just two children's experience of language use in the two settings of home and school cannot be claimed to be representative, although it does give a flavor of what we observed. To gain a more systematic impression, therefore, we need to look at the results of the quantitative analysis, based on the various assessments of the children as well as on the transcribed recordings.

It will be recalled that one of the reasons for extending the original study beyond the age of 5 was to find out just how much the language demands of the classroom were different from those at home. For example, it has been suggested that some children would not have been used at home to hearing indirect forms of request, such as "I think it would be a good idea if you didn't use that bottle as a hammer" or "Who's not put away their crayons yet?" and would therefore have difficulty recognizing them as commands. Or, for similar reasons, they would not know how to answer a "display" question appropriately—for example, "Can you see what's in this picture?" or, following the reading of a story, "What sort of elephant was Elmer?" It has also been suggested that the nonstandard dialect spoken by some children might impede successful communication at school.

The parallel recordings made it possible to attempt an answer to these questions, by comparing the forms and functions of utterances addressed to and produced by individual children in each of the two settings. Although the task of making the comparisons was itself quite time-consuming, the results can be stated quite briefly.

First, as far as dialect differences were concerned, for this sample of native speakers of English, there was no sign of teachers failing to understand children who spoke a nonstandard dialect or of the children failing to understand their teachers. Nor, when the teachers were asked to rate the children with respect to dialect, was there a relationship between their general level of attainment at the age of 7 years and the extent to which their teachers had rated their dialect at age 5 as diverging from Standard English.[4]

Indirect requests did not appear to cause a problem, either. In the first place, all the children had received commands addressed to them that were to varying degrees indirect and, indeed, they were making indirect requests themselves, both at home and in the classroom.[5] Furthermore, even if some of the teachers' commands used modes of indirectness that were not familiar, all the children were quite familiar, and had been for several years, with the general conversational principle that if an utterance refers to an action that you are or are not performing and there is reason to believe that the speaker would like you to perform or not to perform it, you should interpret the utterance as a request to do so or not to do so. If on occasion, therefore, a child did not respond to an indirect request in what the teacher considered an appropriate manner, the explanation was more likely to be that the child did not recognize the utterance as applying to him or her or did not see it as an appropriate action to perform in the context, rather than the form of the utterance itself being a problem.

With display questions, too, neither the form nor the function was unfamiliar to any of the children. All of them had taken part in rounds of the naming game when they were very young:

Adult: What's that?
Child: Pussy.
Adult: That's right [and so forth].

If they had difficulty with particular display questions, therefore, the difficulty was in identifying what frame of reference to use in searching for an appropriate answer rather than in the recognition of the function of the utterance itself.

In general, therefore, it did not seem to be the case that the children differed in their ability to recognize the major categories of function or form that were regularly used in the classroom. There is no doubt that, for all children, there was a change in the relative frequency with which certain functional types of utterance were addressed to them as they went from home to school, and the change was more marked for some children than for others.[6] However, this does not seem to be the explanation for the apparent incompetence of quite a number of children on entry to school. To account for that, we need to look at other aspects of the total conversational context.

With this aim, we selected 7 of the 9 five-minute samples from each child's recordings at home and at school[7] and analyzed all conversation in which an adult was involved. We looked at the contexts in which the utterances occurred, who spoke, and to whom the utterances were addressed. We classified them according to the functions they performed, the meanings they expressed, and their grammatical structure. For utterances spoken by adults, we also noted how they were related to the utterances by the child that immediately preceded.[8]

From all this analysis came a clear and consistent picture, which showed that children's experience of language in use in the classroom did differ significantly in emphasis from their experience at home. Table 5-1 shows some of the most important differences.

The fact that children speak to an adult more often at home than at school is not surprising. Quite simply, with a ratio of one adult to 30 children in the classroom, there is not the same opportunity. In the light of this, it *is* surprising, therefore, that there is not a greater difference in the number of times the child is spoken to by an adult in the two settings. Part of the explanation is that the classroom total includes utterances addressed to the whole class or group to which the

TABLE 5-1   **Children's Experience of Language Use at Home and at School**

Feature of Language Use	Home	School
Absolute Values		
No. of child utterances to an adult	122.0*	45.0*
No. of adult utterances to the child	153.0	129.0
No. of child speaking turns per conversation	4.1*	2.5*
No. of different types of meaning expressed by child	15.5*	7.9*
No. of grammatical constituents per child utterance	3.1*	2.4*
Proportions (Child)	**(Percent)**	**(Percent)**
Initiates conversation	63.6*	23.0*
Questions	12.7*	4.0*
Requests	14.3*	10.4*
Elliptical utterances; fragments	29.4*	49.4*
References to nonpresent events	9.1*	6.4*
Proportions (Adult)	**(Percent)**	**(Percent)**
Questions	14.3*	20.2*
Display questions	2.1*	14.2*
Requests	22.5*	34.1*
Extends child's meaning	33.5*	17.1*
Develops adult's meaning	19.1*	38.6*

Note: Figures are averaged over all 32 children in the study.

*Statistically significant differences.

child was expected to listen. However, this still represents a considerable imbalance: three teacher utterances on average for every one by the child. In the home, the distribution was much more nearly equal.

But not only do the children speak less with an adult at school. In those conversations they do have, they get fewer turns, express a narrower range of meanings, and, in general, use grammatically less complex utterances. They also ask fewer questions, make fewer requests, and initiate a much smaller proportion of conversations. Why should this be so? The answer is to be found by looking at the other side of the equation. Teachers initiate a much higher proportion of conversations than parents do and, of course, it is the initiator who chooses the topic. Furthermore, in their turns, teachers make a higher proportion of requests and ask a higher proportion of questions, particularly of display questions. The result is that, at school, children are reduced for a much greater part of the time to the more passive role of respondent, trying to answer the teacher's many questions and carrying out his or her requests. This is what accounts for the narrower range of meanings that they express and for the high proportion of utterances that are elliptical and fragmentary.

Most significant of all in explaining the generally reduced level of competence that children show at school is the much more dominating role that teachers play in conversation. Compared with parents, it is only half as often that they incorporate the meanings offered in the children's utterances, either by extending those meanings or by inviting the children to extend them themselves. By contrast, teachers are twice as likely as parents to develop the meanings that they themselves have introduced into the conversation. Small wonder that some children have little to say or even appear to be lacking in conversational skills altogether. As repeatedly emphasized, conversation is a reciprocal activity: the more one participant dominates, the more the opportunities for the other participant to make his or her own personal contribution are reduced and constrained.

As with other researchers who have compared the language experiences of younger children at home and in the nursery or preschool play group, what we have found is that, compared with homes, schools are not providing an environment that fosters language development. For *no* child was the language experience of the classroom richer than that of the home—not even for those believed to be "linguistically deprived." The most similar research is the study by Barbara Tizard and colleagues, who observed 30 girls, half middle-class and half working-class, in their nursery classes in the morning and in their homes in the afternoon. Their results corroborate the Bristol findings, almost point for point, as can be seen from the following quotation:

The most striking finding in the present analysis was that, for the majority of variables considered, home–school differences were very large and social class differences at home small or absent. . . .That is, at home, conversations were more frequent, longer and more equally balanced between adult and child; further, children of both social classes asked questions at home much more frequently than they did at school, and answered adults more often.[9]

A very similar picture emerged from another study of the language used in preschool play groups and nursery classes, carried out by David Wood and colleagues. They also noted the generally passive interactional role assigned to children and the frequency of terse, even monosyllabic replies to adult questions. "Indeed," they comment, "the tendency to ignore children, talk over them, and generally dominate the proceedings, was the single most striking feature of the recordings that our 24 practitioners responded to when they read their own transcripts."[10]

This point can be made most forcibly by looking at some further examples.

Here is Lee at school. He has found a horse chestnut and brings it to his teacher to show her.

Lee: I want to show you! Isn't it big?

Teacher: It is big, isn't it? What is it?

Lee: A conker.

Teacher: Yes.

Lee: Then that'll need opening up.

Teacher: It needs opening up. What does it need opening up for?

Lee: 'Cos the seed's inside.

Teacher: Yes, very good. What will the seed grow into?

Lee: A conker.

Teacher: No, it won't grow into a conker. It'll grow into a sort of tree, won't it? Can you remember the—

Lee: Horse chestnut.

Teacher: Horse chestnut—good. Put your conker on the nature table, then.

In many ways, the teacher's intention here is praiseworthy—to help Lee extend his interest more reflectively, to make the connection between the conker and the tree that it came from and will grow into. But what a price has to be paid. Lee's topic is appropriated by the teacher as she imposes her perspective as the basis for her questions— questions to which she, of course, already knows the answers. Under the constraints that she thus imposes, Lee's utterances decrease in length and complexity; from offering information about what he is planning to do with the conker, he is reduced to providing a simple labeling response to a question on a topic that he hadn't wanted to talk about at all.

The objection to this and to many other similar conversations that start with something in which the child is interested is not that teachers try to extend children's knowledge, but that they try so hard to do so that they never really discover what it is about the child's experience that he or she finds sufficiently interesting to want to share in the first place. Thus are children's enthusiasms dampened and their impulses to question and explore suppressed.

The problem is one that we have encountered before. Meaning making in conversation should be a collaborative activity. But where there is a considerable disparity between the participants in their mental models and their linguistic resources, the more mature participant has to make adjustments in order to make collaboration possible. Unfortunately, teachers often forget how different from the child's is their own model of the world, after nearly twenty years of education. Their goal is, rightly, that children should come to see the world from a similarly mature perspective but, in the way that they engage in conversation, they fail to recognize that their perspective cannot be transmitted directly but must be constructed by children for themselves, through a process of building on what they already know and gradually elaborating the framework within which they know it.

Nowhere was this lack of reciprocity so apparent as in some of the situations we observed in which the teacher talked with the whole class following the reading of a story or when introducing or reviewing a topic. Such "discussions" form an integral part of almost every infant class's day, being seen as a means of fostering a sense of group identity and an opportunity to create shared experiences.[11] In addition, many teachers see them as being particularly important in extending children's thinking and in developing their ability to express their thoughts in language. However, in practice, quite other lessons may be what children actually learn.

In the following example, Stella's class of 5- to 7-year-olds were engaged in a discussion about a visit they had made a few days previously to Berkeley Castle. They had seen many interesting things, including suits of armor, several pieces of antique furniture, and the dungeon in which Edward II met a very unpleasant end. However, they were not invited to talk about what they had found most interesting. Instead, as the topic for discussion, the teacher had decided to focus on a four-poster bed that they had seen, and she had assembled a number of illustrated books on the subject. Her intention was to get the children to think about why such a bed was needed in olden-day castles. In reading the text of the discussion, it is worth thinking about what the children might have been learning, both about the need for four-poster beds and about strategies for learning.

Teacher [holding up a picture of a four-poster bed]: Can anyone tell me **why** the bed's called a four-poster?

Child [*putting hand up and answering immediately*]: Because it's cold.

Teacher: Put up—wait a minute. Put your hand up and I'll ask you. Stephen?

Stephen: Because it's got four posts.

Teacher: Four po— **Why** has it got four posts? Can anyone—Put your hand up if you want to say. **Why** has it got four posts? I want all the little ones to try and think.
[*Several children put their hands up.*]
Why has it got four posts? Where's Sean?

Sean: Here. [*Sean has not got his hand up.*]

Teacher: Why has it got four—Why has it got the four posts, do you think? [*To Sean*] Can you think? [*To whole class*] Think hard inside your heads everybody and—

Child 2: I know. Because it—

Teacher: Wait a minute. Wait a minute. Wait a minute.

Child 3: I know.

Teacher: I want the little ones to try and answer. Try and think hard. Linda, can **you** think why it's got four posts? [*Linda stares, then shakes her head.*] Think hard inside your head. Can you, Stella? [*Stella shakes her head.*] Think. Can you, Karen? [*Shows Karen the picture of the bed.*]

Karen: Um—

Child 4: I know.

Teacher: All right. I know the **big** ones probably know. Let's see if the little ones have got an answer first.

Child: Angela's got her hand up. [*Angela is one of the "little ones."*]

Teacher: Well, I know Angela has. But—We'll ask Angela if nobody else can say . . . why it had four posts. [*Looking at Stephen*] Have you got any ideas why it might have four posts? [*Stephen shakes his head.*] Let's come back to Angela, then. [*Holds book up in front of Angela.*]

Angela: 'Cause it's got curtains. [*The children laugh.*]

Teacher: Yes, it's got to hold the curtains, hasn't it? What else has it got that needs four posts? [*Some children put their hands up; she selects one.*] Paula?

Paula: To hold it [*pointing to roof of bed in picture*].

Teacher: Yes, it's got a—a sort of roof—flat roof to it, hasn't it? Now, let's think why the bed—might have a roof on it. Do you have a roof on your bed?

Children [*scornfully, with laughter*]: No.

Teacher: I wonder why.

Child: I dunno.

Teacher: I wonder why some of these four-poster beds had roofs on top of them—why they would need a roof.

Ian: I got a bunk bed.

Teacher: Can the little ones think? Can you think why they might have needed a roof on their bed?

Ian: I got a bunk bed.

Teacher: You've got a bunk—Well, you have got a roof on yours then, haven't you? Are you on the top bunk or the lower bunk?

Ian: No, I'm on the bottom.

Teacher: Well then you've got a roof, haven't you?

Children [*variously*]: I'm on the top. I'm on the bottom.

Teacher: Neville. Why—why do you think they might need a roof on top of their bed?

Neville: Because there wasn't any fires in those days.

Teacher: In—Where wasn't there any fires?

Neville: In the country. [*The children laugh.*]

Teacher: Yes, but—

Child: There wasn't any matches.

Neville: * cold, and they need um wood.

Teacher: Well, they might have had wood to make a fire, mightn't they?

Child: They had no matches.

Teacher: As a matter of fact, I think they did have—um—fires in this castle—some beautiful fireplaces [*holding up a picture of one of the castle rooms and pointing*]. There's one there.

Children [*in chorus*]: Oh.

Teacher [*pointing to another picture*]: And there's one—there.

Angela: Yes, and one in the cooking room.

Teacher: Was there one in the bedroom?

Angela: No—I don't expect there was.

Teacher: Well, there may have been. There were sometimes. You can't see one there. But then you can't see the whole room, can you?

Angela: No.

Teacher: But they did have fireplaces. And they did have large pieces of wood on the fire to keep them warm. So why do you think they needed a roof on their bed? Joanna?

Joanna: So when they went to sleep they wouldn't get cold on top of their—um—faces. [*The children laugh.*]

Teacher [*rather surprised*]: That's right. Yes, that's quite right. Um—can you think of the castle? Close your eyes and think of what the castle was like. [*Short silence; some children shut their eyes.*]
Was it the same as your house?

Children: No.

Teacher: In what way were the rooms different from your house? David?

David: 'Cos they had no central heating.

Teacher: No. But when I was a little girl I didn't have central heating. And I didn't have a roof on my bed either.

Child: I did.

Children: * * *.

Child: There's a nice * through there.

Teacher: Is there? Um—well—You're nearly there. You're nearly there.

What were the rooms like? What were—What do you have on your walls?

Child: Wallpaper.

Teacher: Wallpaper or—plaster, don't you? And what do they have on the castle walls?

Child 1: Paint.

Child 2: Paint.

Child 3: I have paint on— [*The children laugh.*]

Neville: I have—

Teacher [*looking through the pictures in the book*]: They have plaster on some of the castle walls.

Neville: I have pictures on my walls.

Teacher: Yes, they did have plaster, didn't they? Um, what—how about the size? How about the size of the rooms in the castle?

Angela: They weren't very big. [*The children laugh.*]

Child: [*shouting*]: They **were**!

Children: They **were**!

Teacher: They were. What about the height? What about the height of the rooms?

Child 1: Oh.

Child 2: Very big.

Children: They were very big.

Teacher: Not very big, very—?

Child: Tall.

Children: Tall.

Teacher: Well, high. I would use the word "high." They were very high and they were very wide, weren't they? They were very large rooms. And the little tiny fireplace probably didn't give enough heat. So people had a roof to their beds and they drew their curtains round them and it was like being in a little—like a little tent, yes.

I have quoted this example in full because it was one of the most successful discussions we observed; many were much less coherent. The teacher was well prepared, she sustained the children's involvement—as group members, even if not in every case as active participants—and she kept the discussion tightly focused.

But the very qualities that made it successful from the teacher's point of view are what rendered it so counterproductive from the point of view of the individual pupils in their attempts to make sense of what they had seen through collaborative, exploratory talk. The "correct" answer was present in the teacher's mind from the beginning (note her remark, "You're nearly there"); and, although several pupils provided very acceptable answers on the way, it was only when she had formulated it in her own words, as she indicated by her intonation and her posture at the end, that the question was satisfactorily answered.

But if not successful as a discussion, it may be argued, surely the teacher was successful in fulfilling her intention of getting the children to think about why a four-poster bed would have been needed. However, such a conclusion is only warranted if we look at the discussion from the teacher's informed perspective. Clearly this was not shared by the majority of the children. And although several of them were able, from their own experience, to make appropriate connections, there were others whose answers showed that they were not being helped at all by the teacher's questions (for example, Ian's "I got a bunk bed" or Neville's "We have pictures on our walls"). And the silence of the remainder gave no indication at all as to what sense they were able to make of the whole affair.

It would seem, therefore, that if teachers wish to help young children to extend their thinking, to develop their ability to express their ideas fluently and coherently, and to listen carefully and critically to the contributions of others, they should not attempt to do so through large-group discussion. Instead, they should try to plan one-to-one or, at most, small-group situations, in which more equal interaction is possible and in which children can try out their ideas in a tentative manner, free from the constraints felt by both children and teacher in the large-group situation.

But, some may argue, this emphasis on one-to-one interaction is unrealistic when there are 30 or more children in the class, all needing individual attention. In any case, they may add, although an individualized, child-focused style of teaching may, ideally, be desirable, it is not really necessary, as the majority of children make satisfactory progress without it. Although understandable, these arguments are, I believe, mistaken.

In the first place, although it is undoubtedly true that some children appear to prosper under the more traditional, whole-class instructional regime, their success is only relative, being judged by comparison with those who are less successful. What progress might they have made under more supportive conditions?

The infant school, with its carefully planned resources and curricular objectives, is a place where children are encouraged, many for the first time, to reflect on what they know and how they learn. It is here that they establish strategies and expectations for learning that will influence the rest of their careers at school, and even beyond. It is worth stopping to consider, therefore, what they may be learning about learning from the sort of teacher-dominated experiences that we have been considering. What are the messages that they receive from the conversations and discussion that they have with their teachers? Are these messages what their teachers believe they are teaching, or are children more likely to internalize the following:

■ That the only valid learning is that which takes place when they are engaged in teacher-prescribed tasks.

- That personal experience, particularly that gained outside the classroom, is unlikely to be relevant for learning at school.
- That taking the initiative is unwise; as thinking things out for oneself frequently leads to unacceptable answers, it is better to play safe—to follow only the steps laid down by the teacher.

Following such precepts may be successful in the short term, leading to satisfactory scores on tests and to the ability to reproduce prepackaged answers to preformulated problems. But they do not lead to the ultimate goals that define a worthwhile education. Both from the individual's and from society's point of view, our aim should rather be to help children to become creative thinkers, confident in their ability to recognize problems and find ways of solving them, either alone or in collaboration with other people.

■ ROSIE: A LEARNING-DISABLED CHILD?

If the more confident children are restricted by the style of teacher-pupil interaction that was so typical of the classrooms we observed, what must be the effect on the less confident and less able? What sense do they manage to make of this sort of classroom talk? The second argument against accepting the continuation of this style of interaction, therefore, is the positive harm that it can do to a minority of children. To gain more insight into their plight, let us look at the experience of Rosie as she made the transition from home to school.

Rosie, whom we first met in chapter 1, is in many ways representative of a substantial minority in our schools—children from poor inner-city areas whose lives are impoverished, both materially and intellectually. Rosie is the last child in a family of five. Her father has been unemployed since she was born, and her mother has not worked since the birth of her eldest child. The terraced house they lived in (they have since been rehoused in one of the city's large housing developments) was dilapidated in the extreme—plaster was falling off the walls and the house was inadequately furnished and overcrowded, with seven people in three small bedrooms. All this does not mean that Rosie was not loved, of course. On the contrary, her mother, a large ebullient woman, gave Rosie plenty of physical affection, and she got on well with her elder brother and sisters. Indeed, she was particularly close to her one-year-older sister, Donna; at school they were practically inseparable.

By comparison with the other children we studied, however, Rosie was a slow developer, both socially and linguistically. She was, in fact, the lowest-scoring child on almost all the developmental measures we used. Nevertheless, at the point of entry to school (at age 5), she was very far from being nonverbal, as the following extract demonstrates.

[Mother is doing the housework, and Rosie is eager to help.]

Mother: I've got to do the front room now, Rosie.

Rosie: Can I do the front room? Can I? [She goes off into the front room with the carpet sweeper, whispering to herself.] I taking this in here to surprise Daddy. Surprise Daddy.
[After about a minute she returns.]
Mum. Mum, I've picked it all up there.

Mother: Have you?

Rosie: Yes.

Mother: There's a good girl.

Rose: All—there ain't no bits in there.

Mother: We got to make the beds later on.

Rosie: Uh?

Mother: Make the beds.

Rosie: Come on, then.

Mother: Not yet.

Rosie: What, in a minute?

Mother: Yeh, in a minute.

Rosie: What—what time clock have we got to do it?

Mother: I don't know—I'll see how—we got to wash up first. What's the time by the clock?

Rosie: Uh?

Mother: What's the time? [Points to position of hands on clock.] Yeh, what number's that?

Rosie: Number two.

Mother: No it's not. What is it? It's a one and a nought.

Rosie: Nought—one and a nought.

Mother: Yeh. What's one and a nought? What is it?

Rosie: There's one.

Mother: Yeh, what is it?

Rosie: One—one and a nought.

Mother: What's one and a nought?

Rosie: Um—that.

Mother: A ten.

Rosie: Ten.

Mother: Ten to ten.

Rosie: Ten to ten. [Referring to face and hands of the clock] Well, shall we wash them because they're not clean enough?
[Mother shakes her head in disagreement.]
They're not. Inside he ain't.

Mother: Well, you can't wash them inside, he'd break.
Rosie: Would he?
Mother: Mm.
Rosie: And if—if we wash in—inside, would—would—wouldn't—would—
would that thing won't go round? On the numbers?

This is certainly not what we would consider to be an ideal conversational experience, but it demonstrates that Rosie is a reasonably competent user of English. She may not be able to tell the time, and her mother's method of teaching her may not be very effective, but there is no doubt that Rosie understands the function of her mother's display question and that she can negotiate quite complex ideas through equally complex language: "Shall we wash them because they're not clean enough?" "If we wash inside, . . . wouldn't . . . that thing . . . go round?" This latter idea, in particular, with its negative consequences of a possible but not-to-be-performed action, is as complex as anything that a child said in the recordings that we made at school.

A few weeks after this recording, Rosie started school. Although she had been attending a nursery class, this was her first experience of formal schooling. She was placed in the same vertically grouped class as her sister and some 40 other children housed in a purpose-built cooperative unit (a unit containing one large classroom with a number of smaller adjoining workrooms) in the charge of two teachers. The following extract is taken from our observation of her when she was working in the largest of the adjoining rooms, making a calendar from one of the previous year's Christmas cards. The picture on the card showed Father Christmas skiing down a snowy mountainside. While Rosie worked, one of the teachers (Teacher A) tried to engage her in talk about this picture, although, initally, her attention was somewhat distracted by another child, who had already finished her calendar.

Child: Miss, I done it.
Teacher [to Rosie]: Will you put it at the top?
Child: Miss, I done it, look.
   [*Several seconds' pause*]
Teacher [to Rosie, pointing with finger at card]: What are those things?
Child: Miss, I done it.
   Miss, I done it.
   [*Rosie drops something, then picks it up.*]
Teacher [to Rosie]: What are those things?
Child: Miss, I done it.
Teacher [referring to skis in picture]: D'you know what they're called?
   [*Rosie shakes her head.*]
   What d'you think he uses them for? [*Rosie looks at the card. The teacher turns to the other child's calendar.*]

It's very nice. After play, we'll put some ribbons at the top.

Child: What?

Teacher: Ribbon at the top to hang them up by. Would you put all the cards together now? Put the cards together.

Child: Oh.

Teacher: [*to Rosie, pointing at the skis on the card*]: What's—what are those?
[*Rosie looks blank.*]
What d'you think he uses them for?

Rosie [*rubbing one eye with the back of her hand*]: Go down.

Teacher: Go down—yes, you're right; go on.
[*Rosie rubs both of her eyes with the backs of her hands.*]
What's the rest of it? [*Puts down card*] You have a little think and I'll get—er, get the little calendar for you. I think you're sitting on—.
Right. [*Points to calendar*] Could you put some glue on the back there?
[*Rosie takes the calendar from the teacher.*] He uses those to go down—[*5-second pause*]—Is it a hill or a mountain?

Rosie: A hill.

Teacher: A hill, yes. And what's on the hill?

Rosie: Ice.

Teacher: Yes. Ice. They're called skis.

Child: Miss—

[*The teacher leaves to deal with the other children. When she returns, Rosie has finished her calendar.*]

Teacher: That's lovely, and afterwards we'll put some ribbon—What d'you think the ribbon's for? [*Points to calendar with pencil and looks at Rosie. Six-second pause.*]

Rosie: For Father Christmas.

Teacher [*bending closer to Rosie, looking into her face*]: Sorry?

Rosie [*looking away from teacher*]: For Father Christmas.

Teacher: For Father Christmas? [*Straightens slightly from bending position and looks at the card, pointing at it again with hand*] If you want to put it up on the wall, you have a little piece of ribbon long enough to hang it up by.

The whole episode, excluding the interruption, lasted more than four minutes. In that time, Rosie appeared to understand rather little of what the teacher said and only produced five utterances herself, the last following a request for clarification. None of them consisted of more than a simple phase. With this evidence to go on, the teacher could perhaps be forgiven for thinking that Rosie was one of those "linguistically deprived" children that are believed to be so common in the sort of area that the school served.

When she had finally finished making her calendar and been out to play, Rosie went to the other teacher (Teacher B) to do her reading. The book she was reading was one of a series designed for beginning readers, in which the sentence frame remained the same from page to page, with only a single word changing—that word cued by the accompanying illustration. This book was called *I Am Tall*. As she read, the teacher pointed to the words with a pencil. She had reached the page showing a picture of a chimney.

Rosie: I am tall said the—tower.

Teacher [*correcting her*]: Chimney.

Rosie: Chimbley.

Teacher [*pointing at picture*]: It's a big factory chimney, isn't it?

Rosie: I don't like—

Teacher [*pointing at illustration with pencil*]: There's a lot of smoke coming out of the top.

Rosie [*pointing at picture of chimney*]: I don't like that one.

Teacher: You don't like it? [*Rosie shakes her head.*] Why not?

Rosie: I only likes little ones.

Teacher: Have you got a chimney in your house? [*Rosie nods emphatically.*]

Child: And me.

Teacher [*to Rosie*]: D'you have smoke coming out of the top? [*Rosie nods emphatically.*] Mm?
[*Rosie nods her head again. The teacher turns the page, then closes the book.*]
What's underneath the chimney, then, that makes the smoke come out?

Child: I know, fire.

Teacher [*to Rosie*]: Mm?

Rosie: Fire.

Teacher: Is it? Have you got a fire then?

Child: Miss, can I have this one?

Teacher [*to Rosie*]: Which room's the fire in? [*Shifts gaze to other child*] Yes. [*Looks back to Rosie.*]

Rosie: In the front one.

Teacher: Is it? So it keeps you warm? Lovely.

Rosie: And I got a bed.

Teacher: Where's your bed?

Rosie: E's upstairs.

Teacher: Anybody else got a bed in your room?

Rosie [*very softly*]: Carol got a bed—and Kelvin and Carol.

Teacher: Uh-huh. What about Donna?

Rosie: Donna—we're sharing it.

Teacher: You're sharing with Donna, are you? [*Rosie nods her head emphatically.*] D'you have a cuddle at night?

Rosie: Yeh, and I—when I gets up I creeps in Mummy's bed.

Teacher: For another cuddle? [*Rosie nods.*] Oh that's nice! It's nice in the morning when you cuddle.

Here Rosie's use of language is strikingly different. In fact, if we had not been there to see, we might have thought it was a different child we were listening to. She was alert and vivacious, responding to the teacher's questions and volunteering information unasked. On the basis of this evidence, there was no reason to think of her as nonverbal. Yet it was the same child as the one who had, only a little earlier, appeared to be quite unable to converse.

However, since it *was* the same child in the same classroom on the same morning, the difference that we observed could not be attributed to Rosie herself. It could only be due to the different contexts in which she found herself—to the different communication triangles in which the two teachers attempted to engage her.

On the face of it, one might have expected Rosie to cope more easily with the first situation. She was actively involved in the calendar-making task, and the topic in which the teacher tried to engage her was the subject of a picture she had chosen herself. In the second situation, by contrast, she was engaged in the much more abstract task of getting meaning from print—an activity that was still very new to her. But to look at the two episodes in these terms alone is to ignore the totality of the situation and, in particular, the way in which the two teachers engaged with Rosie in relation to the different topics.

Teacher A was intent on getting Rosie to talk, and she used the picture as a prop. To her, the picture was quite straightforward, and her questions were asked to get Rosie to display her ability to describe the simple scene. To Rosie, the questions were obviously not straightforward. Had it not been for the episode involving telling the time at home, we might have thought that she did not understand the function of the questions. But that seems most unlikely. More probably she did not fully understand the significance of the picture. After all, her limited experience had never involved skiing; perhaps she had not even seen skis before. In any event, she was unable to answer. The teacher, however, repeated her question, then tried an alternative, apparently oblivious to Rosie's obvious discomfort as she rubbed first one eye with the back of her hand and then both of them, backing away from the teacher. What was intended to be a friendly conversation had become an interrogation.

Teacher B's objective was initially rather different—to listen to Rosie read and to give feedback on the accuracy of her attempt to get meaning from the text and pictures. In this case, however, Rosie made a meaningful connection with her own experience and offered an affective response: "I don't like that one." Although this may have seemed somewhat irrelevant to the reading task, the teacher invited Rosie to tell her more and, from that point onwards, Rosie took over the leading role in the conversation, providing information about her own home— a topic on which she was undoubtedly the expert. When provided with the support of a listener who was interested in what *she* had to say, Rosie was no longer incompetent.

The similarity of this comparison to the one made between the two mothers in chapter 3 will probably have already been noticed. Here the difference between the strategies adopted by the two adults is even more striking, as is the effect on the child with whom they were talking. When adults are determined at all costs to develop the meaning that *they* see in the situation, there is little chance of achieving that collaboration in meaning making which is so essential for successful conversation. Also, there is little chance for the child to learn through talking. As we saw earlier, young children need to be helped to participate in conversation, and this means listening in order to discover what meaning they can contribute to the topic and then helping them to sustain and develop it. Teacher B intuitively recognized the value of the lead that Rosie gave her. Perhaps Teacher A would have been more successful if she had started by inviting Rosie to tell her why she liked the picture enough to choose it for her calendar!

To some, these arguments may seem to be urging an easygoing permissiveness—a failure to present an adequate challenge to children. How can it be justifiable to follow the leads that children offer when they are so often irrelevant? But the vital question, I would argue, is: irrelevant to whom? An instructional program or scheme of work may be coherent and meaningful to an adult, carefully structured in terms of the logic and consistency of the topic as the adult perceives it, and yet still fail to engage with the children's understanding of the world— or at least be only partly meaningful to them. In such cases, their answers to an adult's questions may appear wrong and their questions, comments, and suggestions misguided or irrelevant. Yet, unless they are deliberately trying to be awkward (and that in itself implies other unresolved problems), their contributions spring from their attempts to understand and are an indication of the way they are making connections between their existing model of the world and the information that is being presented to them.

From his study of young secondary school pupils, Douglas Barnes quotes the following extract from a chemistry lesson. The teacher was explaining that milk is an example of a suspension of solids in a liquid.

Teacher: You get the white . . . what we call casein . . . that's er . . . protein . . . which is good for you . . . it'll help to build bones . . . and the white is mainly the casein and so it's not actually a solution . . . it's a suspension of very fine particles together with water and various other things which are dissolved in water . . .

Pupil 1: Sir, at my old school I shook my bottle of milk up and when I looked at it again all the side was covered with . . . er . . . like particles and . . . er . . . could they be the white particles in the milk . . . ?

Pupil 2: Yes, and gradually they would sediment out, wouldn't they, to the bottom . . . ?

Pupil 3: When milk goes sour though it smells like cheese, doesn't it?

Pupil 4: Well, it is cheese, isn't it, if you leave it long enough?

Teacher: Anyway can we get on? . . . We'll leave a few questions for later.[12]

As in so many other teaching situations, the teacher was so preoccupied with the development of the topic—as he perceived it—that he failed to recognize the importance of the pupil's proffered example. It may have been wrong or irrelevant to the teacher, but the pupil believed it to be relevant, and the others were keen to take up and develop the suggestion. It was evidence of their attempt at active meaning making and, treated as such, could have formed the basis for a discussion that would not only have helped those pupils to approach the teacher's understanding of the topic, but would probably have been helpful to the other members of the class as well.

■ LEARNING: THE ACTIVE MAKING OF MEANING

Whether it be in the primary school or the secondary school, the essential principles are the same. Unless bludgeoned into an unthinking form of rote learning or forced to play the game of attempting to guess what the teacher wants to hear, children are active learners, attempting to construe what is new in terms of what they already know. In order to help them to learn, it is not sufficient—or indeed even necessarily helpful—to specify in advance the sequence their learning shall take, for that is to ignore what the learner can contribute to the task. It is to render passive what should be an active process.

However unequal the balance of knowledge between teacher and learner, there is no way in which the knowledge of the teacher can be transmitted directly to the learner. Indeed, the greater the disparity, the more inappropriate such a conception of teaching becomes. Teaching is essentially a matter of facilitating learning, and where that learning depends on communication between the teacher and the learner, the same principles apply as in any successful conversation. The aim must be the *collaborative* construction of meaning, with negotiation to ensure that meanings are mutually understood.

In early education, it is an oft-repeated slogan that one should "start where the child is"—not where a child of a given age from a given background can be expected to be, but where each individual child—Gary, Penny, Ian, Rosie—is. And what better way of knowing where they are than by *listening* to what they have to say; by attending, in the tasks that they engage in, to the meanings that they make.

Of course, this is not the end of effective teaching; but it is an essential beginning—and not only at the beginning of the year, but in each new interaction. Only on this basis is it possible to negotiate challenges that will extend children's control and understanding on terms that are *mutually* relevant.

Six

HELPING CHILDREN TO MAKE KNOWLEDGE THEIR OWN

The previous chapter, with its rather disturbing results from the comparison of children's language experiences at home and at school, may have given the impression that classrooms are uniformly unsatisfactory in the opportunities they provide for learning through language. This is certainly not the case, as will be clear from the extracts to be considered below. In them, in their different ways, the teachers have found ways of enabling their children to engage in that collaborative meaning making which, as we have seen, is the basis of the most effective learning in the preschool years at home.

However, there are classrooms in which, despite the teachers' good intentions and obvious dedication, such opportunities rarely occur. In a later section, we shall attempt to find reasons for this mismatch between intentions and achievement and consider ways in which the two can be brought more into line. First, though, let us look at some examples of more successful interaction.

The first comes from an observation of Jacqueline, one of the children in the pilot study, during her first term in school. The teacher was preparing the children to listen to a poem about Jack Frost and wanted them to think about their experiences of frost.

Teacher: When I woke up this morning— I don't know— Who looked out of the window when they woke up this morning?

[*Some children raise their hands.*]
Only—only one, two, three—oh, four of you. Now who can put their hand up and tell me what they **saw** out of the window this morning? Jackie?

Jackie: Ice.

Teacher: Ice. Ice—Whereabouts was the ice? [*Another child answers but cannot be heard clearly.*]

Child: On the grass.

Jackie: On the grass and—and on our car.

Teacher: That's right. It's not—it's ice. But what do we call it? It's little tiny bits of ice.

Child 1: I call it—I call it Jack Frost.

Teacher: Frost really, isn't it? Frost. [*Waving her hands expressively*] What does it make the grass look like?

Jackie: White.

Teacher: White. All white, or was there some green as well?

Child 1: Some green.

Jackie: White and green.

Teacher: White and green.

Child 2: Mine—mine was all over the—

Teacher: The leaves were white. [*To Child 2*] Yours was all over the grass, was it?

Child 4: So was mine.

Teacher: So was yours?

Ian: I had—I had a taste of grass.

Teacher [*about to continue but then deciding to extend Ian's contribution*]: And—Did you? [*She holds up her finger to indicate that they should concentrate on Ian's contribution.*] Ian said he had a little taste of it. [*To Ian*] Did it taste of anything?
[*Ian does not answer.*]

Jackie: Yeh.

Teacher: What did it taste of?

Jackie: Tastes cold.

Teacher: Tastes cold. Who knows what ice is? [*Pressing fingers of both hands together*] It's something that's frozen. Ice is made up of something that's frozen.

Child 2: Well, I have that in my drink at home.

Jackie: Cold.

Teacher: That's right. You have it in your drink at home. And how does Mummy make it?

Children: By water.

Teacher: That's right! [*Pressing fingers together*] Ice is **water** that's frozen hard. That's why it wouldn't really taste of anything. You're right, Jackie, it would taste—? [*Jackie does not answer.*] Cold, wouldn't it? [*Touching her lip*] Cold. And you said you had it on your window. Is that right?

Child: <u>And me</u>.

Teacher: <u>What does it</u> do on the windows of the car?

Jackie: Didn't do nothing.

Teacher: It didn't do anything.

Child 5: You couldn't see out the back window.

Jackie: No.

Teacher: You couldn't see out of the window, no.

Jackie: It's very dangerous. Out of the back window you couldn't. 'Cos there is a wire at the back window.

Teacher: Oh, and it makes—It heats up the back window so the frost disappears?

Jackie: Yeh.

Teacher: Well, then. [*Picking up book*] This is a little poem about a man called Mister Jack Frost.

As with the discussion of the four-poster bed in the previous chapter, the teacher here has a clear aim: to elicit the children's observations and experiences on the subject of frost and ice in preparation for the reading of the poem. But her initial question is much more open in the invitation it offers and, once Jackie's initial response has been refined in order to establish the general topic for discussion, she follows up the children's suggestions in ways that recognize their validity and, at the same time, uses them to build up a clearer understanding of the relationship between water, freezing, and ice. Although her repetition of the children's contributions to confirm their acceptability simultaneously emphasizes her control over the discussion and so, to some extent, belies the apparent openness of the initial question, her attitude throughout makes it clear that their out-of-school experience is relevant to the business of the classroom, and her ready acceptance gives them confidence to volunteer further suggestions.

The second example is taken from Connie and Harold Rosen's book, *The Language of Primary School Children*.[1] The conversation took place in a class of six- and seven-year-olds in a dockland area of London. By chance a bird had built its nest under the school roof and, day by day, everyone had watched the building of the nest and the hatching of the chicks.

The discussion lasts for a considerable period of time and so cannot be quoted in full. At the point where we pick it up, they have already talked about the number of birds in the nest, their appearance, and their feeding habits. Now the teacher attempts to direct their attention to a new matter: the siting of the nest and its relative immunity from certain kinds of danger.

Teacher: I am going to ask you a question. Here's something for you to think about. Do you think the bird was clever to choose that place to build a nest?

Children [*several answering*]: Yes. It was a good place, etc., etc.

Teacher: Why is it?

Child: Because the cats can't get at it . . . Because it is too edgery to go along . . . It's too narrow to go across, and because they've got small feet . . . Well, they wouldn't be able to get on . . . and they would just fall off.

Teacher: You don't think the cat could balance along there? And somebody said it's out of the rain, yes? What's another good reason why the bird would build a nest there?

Child: Not a very good reason . . . Because Mark—He was trying to get—He had a big—He had a big cage and he was climbing up to get the bird down.

Teacher: Well, I'm afraid we've got one or two boys who've done unkind things like that, but most children have been very nice. John?

John: Sometimes they build their nests under shelter to keep out the snow.

Teacher: They do. If they were going to build their nests in the winter time they would, wouldn't they? We haven't had any snow since that nest was built, have we? . . . Who else can think of a good thing about that nest? Why do you think the bird made the nest in that place? Tony?

Tony: In my garden . . . when I came home from school . . . when I looked out of the window . . . when I looked on the ground . . . there was a broken egg . . . And when I looked up in the gutter, the mother bird was up there . . . and the babies was sitting up in turn . . . em . . . One of the babies was . . . was chewing a worm.

Teacher: Well. Our nest is safe from cats and safe from rain and safe from . . . ?

Children [*together*]: Snow.

Teacher: Snow . . . and safe from . . . ?

Child: The sun.

Teacher: The sun, yes . . . and . . .

Child: When I was going swimming Terry Booker was playing out in the street . . . and he looked in the gutter and he saw this little baby sparrow . . . It wasn't one of them like in the nest . . . It was just growing its feathers . . . It'd fell out of the nest . . . and it had all green on his wing. He took it in and gave it some crumbs.

Teacher: To look after it.

Child: Mmmm.

Teacher: That was good . . . Michael?

Michael: You know, I saw the bird . . . flying out of its nest.

Teacher: You saw the bird, did you . . . falling out of its nest?

Michael: Flying!

Teacher: Oh, good! You mean our bird downstairs?

Michael: Mmmm.

Teacher: Yes . . . Well, I expect that was the mother bird going to fetch . . . Terry?

Terry: I had this bird . . . In the roof was this nest and this baby bird, he fell out of it . . . And he was on this window sill . . . So my daddy put it back up . . . and it fell down . . . And the cat had it.

Teacher: Oh . . . what a shame. Another thing about this nest downstairs . . . it's also safe from . . . ?

Children [variously]: Wind. Dust. Children.

Teacher: People—children and people.

Gary: I got that.

Teacher: You did Gary . . . That was very sensible because nobody can climb up there, can they?

Child: No.

Here, more than in the previous extract, the children are contributing freely from their own experience. And as they narrate those experiences to others they are, perhaps for the first time, discovering their significance for themselves. These are the conditions that foster language development: when one has something important to say, and other people are interested in hearing it. It is then that language and thinking most fully interpenetrate in the struggle to make meanings that capture what one has observed and understood and communicate that understanding to others.

The success of the discussion above owes much to the teacher's support and guidance. Her questions help to maintain the focus of attention, but without imposing too tight a control over the direction it takes. She recognizes the relevance of the stories that the children tell for a consideration of the advantages of the site chosen for the nest and, sensitive to the affective and moral charge that their stories carry, she endorses their implicit evaluations of the events that they recount. As the Rosens comment: "The conversation is particularly revealing in showing what happens when teacher and children have shared an experience of this kind. The teacher is not merely instructor and one who knows all the answers before they begin the conversation, but has found something new not only in what occurred but also in the children's comments on it."[2]

A discussion with the whole class almost inevitably involves the majority of the children as listeners only. In the Jack Frost extract, for example, there were more than 20 children who remained silent throughout—though this does not mean, of course, that they were not participating actively as listeners. But if, as was suggested above, it is the art of formulating one's thoughts and feelings in order to communicate them to others that is the strongest spur to actively seeking to understand them, then opportunities need to be found for one-to-one or at least for small-group interaction.

The third example is of just such a situation, which arose in the course of the morning's activities in a class of seven-year-olds in another London school. The class was being filmed over a number of weeks in order to provide material for a series of educational videotapes, and Colin had become so interested in the cameras that he had decided to make a model of one, which he had fashioned out of some pieces of balsa wood. He has just started to plan the construction of his tripod, and he has come to the teacher to discuss it.[3] (*Note*: number of dots refers to number of seconds of pause.)

Teacher: Colin, are you having a problem?

Colin: Just trying to . . think out . . something. Just trying to think out how high I want the pole.

Teacher [*to two girls with whom she had been talking*]: Could you work there a while? I'll just help Colin. [*To Colin*] How * do you need it?

Colin [*using a meter rule and a smaller ruler, trying to read off the height of the tripod he is planning to make*]: One meter and—

Teacher: Can you imagine for a minute that you're taking a photograph? How—how high would be comfortable?

Colin: Er, this—this is what I done—trying to find that out. I put this [the model camera] like that and held it and just pretend that I was looking through, and I thought I'd have it about that high 'cos that includes the camera on top and that's how—how far I want it—one meter and [*counting on small ruler while teacher talks to another child*] thirteen—One meter and thirteen centimeters.

Teacher: Is that going to be the <u>height of</u> your tripod?

Colin: <u>Yes</u>, of the pole.

Teacher: Is each—is each pole going to be that height?

Colin: I'm go—I'm only going to have three. Um—yes. I mean—The other two are going to be a bit longer.

Teacher: Can you show me how you're going to do your plan? [*They go to Colin's table.*]

Colin: I've got—

Teacher: Sit yourself down . . You sit down.

Colin: I've got a lump of wood—

Teacher: Pardon?

Colin: I've got some wood—and [*indicating plan*] that's what it's going to look like. It's going to have those bits of, er—so I can put, um, something around it to hold the camera on, and—I'm going to try and get something that can—a round shape that could slide around inside the hole, that could hold on to, um, legs, which is going to be rather hard.

Teacher: Have you looked in the camera book to see if it shows a diagram that would help you?

Colin: Er—I have looked in one * * * .

Teacher: <u>Did you no</u>tice that there was another one there today?

Colin: No. Yes, there is.

Teacher: Perhaps in a moment you'd like to look at that—that might be helpful.

Colin: Yes.

Teacher: What else will you need?

Colin: Um. Yes. A sharp tool that I can make the ends of them rather sharp so they can dig in the ground—or I could have blunt ones that just stand out to keep it steady.

Teacher: And how will you set your tripod up?

Colin [*laughing*]: It's going to always be set up. Just all I'm going to have to do is just take it outside or something—like that.

Teacher: How do you think that's going to improve your photography?

Colin: It's going to keep it much stiller and .. the pictures—the pictures will be much better 'cos they won't go blurry through movement.

With the teacher as listener and occasional prompter, Colin is helped here to think through the requirements of the task he has set himself, using language to consider alternative courses of action and to evaluate their consequences before he actually undertakes the activity. This example also shows how, in order to carry out his task more effectively, he is led quite naturally to consult reference books and to represent his proposed solution in another symbolic form—that of the plan he is drawing.

At this point it is interesting to recall the four principles that were suggested in chapter 3 (p. 50) for helping children to learn through participation in conversation. Colin's teacher illustrates how each one of them applies equally validly to conversation in a deliberately educational context:

- She takes Colin's perceived problem seriously.
- She listens carefully to make sure that she understands his intentions.
- Her questions and suggestions are based on *his* intentions and are designed to help him to extend his thinking about them.
- Although they are quite challenging, these questions and suggestions are couched in terms that Colin is able to understand—as he shows by his full and informative responses.

Having helped Colin to resolve his problem and suggested that he might look at the other reference book (a suggestion that he takes up), the teacher leaves him to work with his friend, Alan, while she attends to the needs of the other children. Later in the day, she returns to see how they have been getting on. (*Note:* number of dots refers to number of seconds of pause.)

Teacher: All right. How've you got on since I was here?

Colin: We wrote about it. I'm doing stages and we've done stages.

Alan: We've got to use another page.

Teacher: What do you mean, "stages"?

Colin: We've got to do one bit and then another bit. Like a two-stage rocket—like a rocket. It's got stages. It doesn't just have one great big lump. When it—say—when it's used one bit it lets it go—

Teacher [*pointing to diagram*]: What kind of stages are they, though?

Colin: Stages of, oh—things you've got to do.

Teacher: I see. And you're going to do your stages, are you?

Colin: Yeh.

Teacher: Would you like to tell me how it's going to work with your camera [the tripod]? [*Turning to Alan*] Have you seen his model? [*Alan nods. Then, to Colin*] You show us.

Alan: It turns round—that thing.

Colin: It goes—I'm going to lay this on the top of my tripod—

Teacher: Yes.

Colin: —which will keep it steady. Near the edge so I can go like that [*demonstrating*]. And then that'll practically be it.

Alan: He should draw a sort of square on there, so that—you know—they'll think it's—

Colin: I'm going to cut that out.

Teacher: What would that be for then, Alan?

Alan: The—the thing to look through.

Colin: Viewfinder.

Teacher [*to Alan*]: Did you do that on your clay one? Would you like to show me?

Alan: I didn't cut it out. I only done the lines.

Teacher [*to Colin*]: Look at that. It's nice, isn't it? Have you seen his model?

Colin: Yeh.

Alan [*pointing to his model*]: The clicker's coming off.

Colin: He could always make another one—out of plasticene [a modeling substance] or something. Can I make another model of mine, a camera model out of plasticene, maybe?

Teacher: That would be nice. Would you like first of all to show me the front of yours? Explain to me what you've been doing.

Colin: Here I've got the dials. The other picture dials are coming off. I've got to try and get those.

Teacher: They're not very clear, are they?

Colin: No.

Teacher: Can you explain to me what they are?

Alan: They're the weather things and the numbers on the thing—

Colin: I've forgotten now, but I'm going to do much better, after.

Alan: Yes. He can draw a picture of—round—

Teacher: Do you remember in your seed diagram you drew little sketches?

Colin: Umm.

Teacher: Could that be helpful when you're drawing on your dial?

Colin: I could always take this off and turn it inside out. Look, I didn't glue it on or anything. But it can come off.

Teacher: I should think you'll think of a way of doing that clearer, won't you?

Colin: Yes. * * *.

Teacher: Well, if you look at the real camera and look at the sorts of pictures they've got on that—

Colin: That's—I copied from it.

Teacher: Did you?

Colin: Yeh.

Alan: Yeh. They've got clouds, dark clouds and light—

Colin: It's got hazy, thunder, and seaside. Guess what the difference between seaside and just a normal bright sun is. Because seaside you get the water reflecting up light so it's got its own dial, and you put it on seaside whenever you're taking a picture near water.

Teacher: Do you think there's anywhere near here that we might need to put it on the seaside dial?

Colin [*pointing*]: The pond up there.

Teacher: Do you think there would be enough light reflected off it to have that effect?

Colin: I think there might.

Alan: Yeah, if he was in the shade.

Colin: And if you want sun and half misty sun, you put it in between the dials . . and that gets it.

Teacher: You do?

Colin: Yeh.

Here the emphasis is on what has been done: reporting, explaining, and evaluating. As before, language provides the means for reflecting on action—not only actions that have been performed, but also those that might be performed, such as taking a photograph by the nearby pond. In this way, Colin is helped to establish connections between different aspects of his experience, using the power of language as a system of symbols to represent objects and events that are absent or no more than hypothetical possibilities.

Language always has this potential, of course, but most of the time we don't exploit it. As Edward Sapir, the American linguist and anthropologist, put it when making exactly this point, "It is somewhat as though a dynamo capable of generating enough power to run an elevator were operated almost exclusively to operate an electric doorbell."[4] One way of helping children to harness the dynamo of language to power their own thinking is through such exploratory talk. Lev Vygotsky refers to this sort of collaborative exploration at the limits of the child's ability as working in "the zone of proximal development," suggesting that this is one of the most important contributions that a teacher can make to a child's development. What the child is able to do today in conversation with a supportive adult, he or she will tomorrow be able to manage alone in that interior dialogue that he called "inner speech."[5]

Some might argue that such positive conversations are only possible in classrooms with the most able children. And there is little doubt that Colin is an able child; he is certainly very fluent for his age. Indeed, if one were to make any criticism of the teacher's contributions it would be that they weren't challenging enough. Given his interest in photography and his obvious understanding of some of the principles involved, she might well have suggested that he try to make a real camera, of the simple pinhole variety. This could have led to some very interesting practical observations of the images produced and to attempts, both through experiment and discussion, to explain them.

But less able children also benefit from the opportunity to try out their ideas in conversation that is purposeful, yet collaborative and nonthreatening. In the previous extract, Alan was clearly gaining both in confidence and in fluency from working with Colin and from being included by the teacher in the discussion of their model cameras. The same is happening for Matthew in the following extract, recorded earlier the same morning, when the teacher included Amanda and Maxine as she discussed the clay model of a diver that Matthew was making. (*Note:* number of dots refers to number of seconds of pause.)

Amanda: Mrs. M., if he put this bit in the belt and this bit in the back with the oxygen, it might look like a real diver.

Matthew: That's what I'm going to do.

Teacher: Do you think it looks like a real diver at the moment?

Matthew: No.

Amanda: No.

Maxine: Not much. It hasn't got the equipment on it.

Amanda: Yes, but if you put the feet too small, it could easily fall down.

Teacher: How do you know about a real diver, Matthew?

Matthew: I read a lot about it.

Maxine: Why? Have you got a book about divers?

Matthew: Two. Two great big annuals of divers at home and I read 'em . . . every night 'fore I go to bed. But I'm in—I'm in the middle book one and in book two it tells you about deep-sea divers. In book one it tells you about frogmen.

Maxine: How to make it?

Matthew: Not how to make 'em.

Teacher: What's the difference between frogmen and deep-sea divers?

Matthew: 'Cos deep-sea divers aren't like frogmen—deep-sea divers haven't got flippers and—

Teacher [*turning to answer a child in another part of the room, then turning back to Matthew*]: Sorry!

Matthew: —and they have different kinds of—Frogmen don't have helmets, but deep-sea divers do. [*Pause, while teacher answers another child.*] So frogmen are quite different, 'cos they haven't got helmets.

Perhaps what is most striking about this teacher is the quality of her listening. It is noticeable, in the above text, that even when she has to break off for a moment to respond to another child, she keeps her arm around Matthew, thereby signaling to him that it is only a temporary interruption; and, on both occasions, when she turns back, Matthew continues where he had left off.

By listening attentively in this way, giving the children her full attention, she indicates that what they have to say is important—that they have expertise that is of value. When she asks questions, it is in order to be further informed, not to check that the child's answer is in conformity with her knowledge about the topic. And by inviting other children to listen and ask questions in the same way, she builds up in each child a feeling of self-respect and confidence in what he or she knows and can do and, at the same time, a feeling of respect for others as well.

Most of this teacher's time is spent with individual children or with very small groups, helping them to plan their activities and to evaluate the outcomes in the sort of interactions illustrated above. From time to time, however, she brings a group together in order to introduce a new topic, such as the following example. Here, her purpose is to teach the children how to use reference books—consulting tables of contents, using indexes, and so forth. To this end, she has assembled on the table a variety of twigs gathered from trees on the neighboring common and has prepared some reference books, including one entitled *Trees and Leaves.* The children begin by examining the twigs.

Yelshea: Miss, why has—why has it gone all furry? Most plants that I see— wild plants—are not furry. But is there anything that's meant to—why it's meant to be furry?

Teacher: What do you other children—[*to Richard*] what do you think?

Richard: 'Cos, er—it—er—protects it.

Colin: It's a warm coat . . that keeps it warm if it opens up too early.

Yelshea: It could be, because I can see the green—little bit of green inside and—I see green there . . sort of protecting it.

Donna: Like my plant—

Teacher: I beg your pardon?

Donna: It's like my plant. Mine's all furry.

Teacher: Which plant is this?

Donna: I don't know which—which one I've planted, though. Might be the oak one.

Teacher: Why do you think that needs protecting?

Colin: Protecting from the cold so's it doesn't die.

Yelshea: No, or protecting from the sticky bud. It might get up and stick all around it.

Teacher: Do you know how we—how we could find out about why it needs protecting?

Yelshea: I know. Just watch it.

Richard: From a book.

Colin: Just study and . . . find out.

Teacher: Which book would you look in, Richard?

Richard [*turning to get one from the shelf*]: I'd look in, um, this book.

Teacher: Yes. It's not over there. I know which one you mean.

Richard: That big book [*Trees and Leaves*].

Teacher: This one?

Richard: Yes.

Teacher: You have a little look through that while Nicola says what she was going to say.

Nicola: Miss, you know this bit here? It looks like—You know them sweet lollies and things? Well it looks like that. And this bit here, it's different from the other bit. Or is it another plant? [*She fingers the leaf of the horse chestnut.*] Because look . .

Teacher: Bring it closer to yourself.

Colin: I think it's the same—it's the same plant, except the sticky bud is still underneath it . . if you can see it. All round this side. You can see it, can't you?
[*The teacher speaks to another child who has just entered the room.*]

Richard [*indicating a picture in the book*]: Is this the sticky bud? Is this the one? This one here?

Teacher: Hang on. [*Taking book*] Can I show you this book, which Richard's seen before?

Colin [*reading*]: Trees and Leaves.

Yelshea: Trees and Leaves.

Richard: Miss, was that it what I just showed you—sticky bud?

Teacher: Yes. I know that you've looked in this book. I saw you looking the other day.

Donna: ✳ ✳ ✳ ✳ .

Colin: Is it—is it wild? Is it a wild book or just a plain book that you usually see?

Teacher: What do you mean?

Yelshea: Sort of . . like wild plants . . and stuff like in the common.

Colin: Does it have just normal everyday trees, or does it have great big wild trees?

Teacher [*handing book to Colin*]: Well, would you like to see?

Yelshea: Um, would it, um, be like the things in the common there? If they found out about that and wild things and all things that grow in different places.

Nicola: Miss, those * look like—

Teacher: Do you know where you'd look in the book to find out whether it tells you about trees that you'd find on the common? Where—where would you look in the book?

Donna: On the <u>tree</u> page.

Yelshea: <u>Miss</u> .. the wildlife, wildlife.

Teacher: Shall I show you? If you look in this book with Richard.

Colin: That's got the contents.

Teacher: Yes Right in the front it's got what's called the "contents."

Colin: Which has got a list of everything that's in it. It's got little pages or <u>little—or a few pages about</u> whatever it says, like—
[*Several children speak at the same time.*]

Donna: The fruit ones.

Colin [*reading*]: "What to look for on a tree." That's one.

Teacher: If you wanted to find out about these horse chestnuts, Nicola, what would you look for in the Contents? What would you look for? [*She passes the book to Nicola.*] Have a little read through it and see if you can find the part that will help you.

And so the lesson continues: the children using the book to enrich their observation, and their observation to elucidate the text of the book. As the children themselves observed earlier, in answer to the teacher's question "Do you know how we can find out about . . . ?", direct observation and consultation of reference material are complementary ways of obtaining information, each illuminating the other.

However, what is understood in either case depends on what the observer/reader brings to the situation. Prior knowledge is often insufficient or inappropriate, as was the case with Colin's somewhat idiosyncratic classification of trees into the two classes "wild" and "everyday" (or the other boy's suggestion of sour milk as an example of the suspension of solids in a liquid, in the previous chapter). When the teacher is supportive and the topic is treated in an exploratory fashion, as in the example above, children are willing to volunteer their suggestions or ask questions and so reveal to the teacher the framework they are using to interpret the new information. The teacher can then take this into account by building on it or clarifying it, as appropriate.

A teacher's manner of interacting with the children is thus at the heart of his or her style of teaching, for it is the collaborative approach— a willingness to negotiate meanings—that encourages children to explore their understanding of a topic and gives them the confidence to try out their ideas without the fear of being wrong. Risk-taking is necessary in any enterprise that aims to move beyond the status quo, and this is particularly true of learning in school, where errors as well as successes can be productive.

Central to this style of teaching is the recognition that knowledge cannot be transmitted to students in a prepackaged form in the hope that it will be assimilated in the form in which it is transmitted. Knowledge has to be constructed afresh by each individual knower, through an interaction between the evidence (which is obtained through observation, listening, reading, and the use of reference materials of all kinds) and what the learner can bring to bear on it. The teacher arranges the situations—or encourages those that the children themselves have set up—and so has considerable control over the evidence that the learners encounter. But teachers cannot control the interpretations the children will make. On the other hand, teachers can provide guidance by drawing attention to additional evidence, clarifying misunderstandings, and asking questions that point the learner in directions for further exploration. To be most beneficial, however, these strategies need to be embedded in a style of interaction that, like the one used for helping children to learn to talk, is supportive and collaborative.

When presented with these arguments, most teachers express their agreement with them, for they are confirmed by their own experience. Nevertheless, in many cases—as our observations showed—their practice is not guided by the principles that they claim to espouse. In the remainder of this chapter, we shall explore some of the reasons for this mismatch between theory and practice and consider some practical suggestions for bringing the two more closely into line.

■ SCHOOLS AS ENVIRONMENTS FOR LEARNING

The first and most obvious cause of the impoverished interaction that so often occurs between teachers and pupils is the number of children involved—30 or more in the average class, with only a single adult. All of these children have to be kept profitably occupied on tasks that stimulate their interest and promote their learning. The demands on teachers in terms of management, safety, and control are therefore enormous, so it is not surprising to find that there is little sustained interaction.[6] Added to this, at the outset, is the inexperience of children entering school for the first time. They have to learn to behave according to the norms of the classroom, wait while others take their conversational turns, and discuss the shared topic rather than changing the subject at will. The classroom thus suffers from organizational problems that can militate against children's spontaneity and restrict the opportunities for sustained adult-child interaction of the kind experienced in many homes. As a result, the more intellectually stimulating uses of language get submerged under the demands of the sheer number of children to be attended to and the tasks that have to be done in each day.

A second contributory factor seems, more and more, to be the curriculum itself—or, rather, the increasing emphasis on standardization in the interests of accountability with respect to the mastery of the "basic skills." Clearly, it is highly desirable that every pupil should become both literate and numerate and be conversant with certain facts about his or her social and physical environment. But these skills are only of value when they are integrated with the purposes and interests that the pupil brings from outside the classroom. As Barnes puts it, to be useful, school knowledge must be converted into action knowledge.[7]

Too often, though, the concern with the curriculum takes little account of what individual pupils bring to the tasks that they are required to engage in. Instead, curriculum planners concentrate on breaking down what has to be learned into smaller and smaller, relatively self-contained steps, so that they can be arranged into linear sequences for the purposes of instruction. This has led to an exaggerated belief in the efficacy of finely graded, structured programs of work. The problem with this approach, however, is that, while certain types of learning *can* be promoted in this way, it is certainly not the case that children only learn—or even learn most effectively—when all the tasks in which they engage are imposed on them by others in the interests of ensuring a uniform progression through a predetermined sequence. Furthermore, it takes little account of the fact that learning takes place in individual children, each of whom has different interests and abilities; and that, in any class, children proceed at different rates, learning quickly and effectively when they are personally motivated and emotionally stable but more slowly and with greater difficulty when the task seems irrelevant or their personal motivation is low. This is not in any way to suggest that children should not be encouraged to engage in tasks that stretch them, that demand effort and application. But it is to suggest that the commitment that such tasks demand is only likely to be forthcoming if children perceive these tasks to be meaningful and relevant to them.

A further disadvantage of centrally controlled curriculum planning is that the curriculum becomes fragmented into isolated bodies of subject matter, and children are discouraged from making connections between the various topics and types of learning in which they are engaged. In addition, under the pressures that are induced by the perceived need to "cover the curriculum" that is imposed from above, teachers are likely to adopt a didactic style of teaching in which the roles of teacher and pupil are sharply differentiated, with the result that opportunities are seriously reduced for the sort of open-ended, exploratory interaction that encourages children to take some share in the responsibility for planning and pursuing their own learning.

But perhaps the most serious impediment to a more collaborative relationship between teacher and pupil is the mechanistic model of education that is implicit in so much of the discussion about account-ability. To talk of the curriculum, or of individual units of work, in terms of "input" and "output" is not only inappropriate in its implicit assimilation of education to the organizational principles and ethics of industrial mass production,[8] but it is also misguided in its simple assumption that well-prepared "input" is all that is needed to guarantee effective learning.

It is not simply that, as has already been stressed, children bring different aptitudes and experiences to each learning task—important though it is to recognize this diversity—but that the learning itself involves an *active reconstruction* of the knowledge or skill that is presented, on the basis of the learner's existing internal model of the world. The process is therefore essentially *interactional* in nature, both within the learner and between the learner and the teacher, and calls for the *negotiation* of meaning, not its unidirectional transmission.

To recognize this essential characteristic of learning is to see in a new light the significance of that well-known precept "Start where the child is." All too often this is interpreted in practice to mean "Ad-minister a test or some other form of assessment in order to decide which ability group to place the child in or which reading primer or worksheet to give him or her." But this is not discovering where the child is—what his or her mental model of the world is like or what his or her current needs and interests are. Instead, it is discovering into which of the places that are prepared in advance the child can most easily be slotted. Really to discover where a child is and, hence, how we can most helpfully contribute to his or her further learning, it is necessary to listen to what he or she has to say—to try to understand the world as he or she sees it. Only then can the teacher's contribution have that quality of contingent responsiveness that we have seen from the preschool years to be essential in helping the child to develop his or her understanding.

The pressure of numbers, the constraints of accountability, and the prevailing mechanistic model of education, then, all tend to reduce the opportunities for a collaborative style of teaching. But perhaps the most insidious influence of all is our own previous experience. Most of us have had many years of being talked *at*, first as pupils and students and, later, during our professional education, both pre-service and in-service. As as result, we have probably unconsciously absorbed the belief that a teacher is only doing his or her job properly when he or she is talking—telling, commanding, questioning, or evaluating. And, in many cases, that is what we see when we look to our colleagues for a model of successful teaching. Despite the lip service that is paid to the "student-centered"conception of education, actual practice tends on the whole to be "teacher-centered," based on a predetermined curriculum at every level from kindergarten to university. It is not surprising, therefore, if, under pressure, teachers tend to fall back on the traditional transmission model of education without realizing how poorly it enables them to fulfill their best intentions.

How, then, can this situation be changed? How can teachers bring their practice more closely into line with the theories to which they probably already subscribe?

There is no simple panacea, of course. But there are a number of changes—some of which every teacher is in a position to make—that are likely to lead towards the style of teaching that has here been described as collaborative.

■ TOWARDS A COLLABORATIVE STYLE OF LEARNING AND TEACHING

For many teachers, the first question is, quite naturally: "Will it work?" Of course, the only convincing answer is that of experience—and personal experience, at that. However, there is already the testimony of individual teachers, teaching in many different school systems in countries all over the world. They all say that, having taken the plunge and tried the collaborative style, they would never want to return to their old ways of doing things.

But for those who are still undecided, hesitating because of the risks that they perceive to be involved, there is a simple step that will probably be sufficient to convince them that some sort of change is necessary: they could record themselves at work. Before making the recording, they should set down in writing what they hope will be achieved, in particular what types of learning the children will engage in and how their own behavior will contribute. Then, afterwards, they should listen to the tape, noting how far these aims were achieved and, where they were not, asking what were the probable reasons. More specific questions that one might ask are: What are the most frequently occurring patterns of teacher-pupil exchange? Who initiates the interaction, and in which contexts? What sorts of questions are asked, by whom, and for what purpose? Most teachers who undertake this form of self-assessment find that they talk too much, repeat themselves unnecessarily, and give children too little time to respond; they also ask too many questions that restrict children's participation to providing minimal answers requiring only the lowest level of intellectual activity.

If, after making and listening critically to such a recording, it seems desirable to attempt to change, then there are a number of aspects of the total classroom situation that are worth thinking about. First, there is the interactive style itself. Most teachers find that they vary their strategies from one context to another, so it is worth trying to identify those contexts which allow them most readily to engage in genuine collaborative interaction. These can then be developed and the same strategies extended to other contexts. A general principle that almost all teachers find to be rewarding—although initially extremely difficult—is to talk less and to listen more, in particular allowing pupils a longer time to think out what they want to say and giving them time to say it without interruption. It may also be worth thinking about the sorts of questions the teacher asks and about ways of encouraging pupils to ask more questions themselves.

But to focus on language alone may be self-defeating, in the same way that a millipede would probably not be helped by being advised to think about how it was moving one of its legs. More important is for teachers to think about where they are going and which route is likely to be most satisfactory. That means reconsidering what it means to be a teacher in the light of what is known about how children learn and about how others, both adults and other children, can facilitate that learning.

From observations outside school, we know that children are innately predisposed to make sense of their experience, to pose problems for themselves, and actively to search for and achieve solutions. There is every reason to believe, therefore, that, given the opportunity, they will continue to bring these characteristics to bear inside the school as well, provided that the tasks that they engage in are ones that they have been able to make their own. All of us—adults and children alike—function most effectively when we are working on a task or problem to which we have a personal commitment, either because the goal is one that we are determined to achieve (balancing the family budget, repairing a machine) or because the activity is one that we find intrinsically satisfying (writing a poem, building a model), or both. In these circumstances, as the extracts concerning Colin and his model camera show, discussion with someone more skilled or knowledgeable takes on real purpose and significance, as progress to date is reviewed and alternative plans for further work are considered in terms of their feasibility and appropriateness. This is perhaps the teacher's most vital contribution: as a master providing guidance to an apprentice, who utilizes that guidance in the pursuit of his or her chosen goal, the value of which is appreciated by both of them.

For children to achieve this active involvement in their own learning, it is important to find ways of enabling them to share in the responsibility for deciding what tasks to undertake and how to set about them. This does not mean that the teacher should abnegate responsibility or tolerate a free-for-all in which children do exactly as they choose when they choose. Few children can work productively without the support of an understood framework and clear ideas about what is expected of them, and most teachers would not feel that they were adequately fulfilling their responsibilities if they did not provide both guidelines and a clear sense of direction. What is required, therefore, is some form of negotiation in which both pupils' and teachers' suggestions are given serious consideration.

Colin's teacher had devised what were called "choice books," in which the agenda of tasks to be completed was negotiated between the teacher and each individual pupil once each week. At the beginning of the school year, when the children were new to the class, the agenda consisted largely of activities suggested by the teacher. But, as the year progressed, the children began to add their own suggestions and, perhaps more important, to note when they had not yet completed a task satisfactorily or where they needed to make another attempt or gain further information or skill. Figure 6-1 shows a page from such a choice book.

However, not all teachers will feel comfortable with so much of the curriculum open for negotiation—at least, not initially. It is important to emphasize, therefore, that there is no one correct way to proceed. Indeed, different methods will probably work best for different teachers or for the same teachers with different classes of children. What is important is that, for at least a substantial part of the curriculum, there be genuine negotiation that enables pupils to feel that they have initiated some of their activities and have taken on others and made them their own. "Ownership" is the word that Donald Graves uses to make the same point about children's writing,[9] and it applies equally to other activities, right across the curriculum.

When children have a feeling of ownership and share the responsibility for the tasks that they engage in, teachers find that their relationships with the children change. Given responsibility, children behave responsibly and no longer have to be closely supervised every moment of the day. With an agreed agenda, they know what has to be achieved and spend their time productively, using resources appropriately, asking for the teacher's assistance only when other sources have proved inadequate, and moving on to a new task when the present one is completed. As a result, freed from the demands of managing resources, answering trivial questions about procedure, and continually monitoring classroom behavior, teachers are able to spend considerable periods of time with individual children, giving assistance when it is really needed and helping them to reflect on what they are doing and to see how to extend it in various directions.

This, then, is the goal, and these are some of the benefits that are likely to result. But how can it be achieved? Here again, there is no one formula for success, but classroom management—how time, space and other resources are allocated—is one important ingredient. Having the classroom divided into different areas appropriately organized for different activities is an essential preliminary, as is arranging re-

FIGURE 6-1   **A Page from a Child's Choice Book**

January 15th Toni 1) Weaving 2) Woodwork. Could you make a loom exactly the same size as ours? 3) Study stories. Please use the books to learn about the different types of stone. 4) Perhaps you and Mandy would like to make a book about our plants and seeds.	1) Work at improving your timing game. 2) Clay. The books show you different ways to make a cup. 3) Work at your sand village. 4) Story writing.
Wednesday January 17th To-day I done a Sand village with mandy and I made a cup and my hamdall came of and I done a StoryandWeaving. it was good. and my Story is going to be long and we tried to make a loom but it fell a prat	Can I do Clay I want to make a ashtray and avase. For my mum. and the Sand village and a dolls house.
January 22nd. 1) Try your loom again but with stronger wood. 2) Improve your timing game. Ask Kim about hers, it may give you some ideas. 3) Create your sand village or could you make a model of the school? 4) Begin to make a diary about things you have been doing.	1) Work on your story, so far I think it's promising. Please talk to me about it again. 2) Work with clay on Monday afternoon. I particularly want you to do your story today. Would you make our model display shelves beautiful. 3) Work on your house collage. 4) Shop.

Source: Reproduced from *Extending Literacy* (London: Centre for Language in Primary Education, Inner London Education Authority, 1980), p. 25.

sources—paper, glue, scissors, apparatus, reference books, etc.—so that children can gain access to them without disturbing each other or the teacher. Equally important is the organization of time. Children should have long periods of time to work on the same task, with as few interruptions as possible; and, as has already been implied, they should not all be expected to engage in the same activity at the same time. With individual agendas, there is little danger of this happening, but it will be necessary to ensure an equitable rotation of access to popular work areas and to scarce resources.

These are some of the organizational prerequisites. But perhaps the most difficult question is how to get started. From talking to teachers who have successfully changed their method of working, it is clear that there are many different starting points, ranging from encouraging individual children to pursue a topic that has particularly interested them to proposing a very general theme that individual children are invited to explore in a variety of different ways. Some teachers have made such a theme the center of all curricular activity over a period of one or two weeks; others have developed a theme in the area of social or environmental studies while maintaining their normal pattern of work in the rest of the curriculum. Some teachers have used a work of literature—a story, song, or poem—as the starting point for a wide range of individual activities; one first-grade teacher used the book *Watership Down* in this way, and a teacher of 10-year-olds started with the Prologue to Chaucer's *Canterbury Tales.*

The advantage of a broad theme within which all—or a majority—of the children choose topics to pursue is that there is an overall co-herence to the variety of their activities. This is reassuring to the teacher, as it reduces the feeling of being pulled in too many different directions at once. It also has advantages for the children, in that they can more readily work together in groups, collaborating with each other and learning from each other's efforts. Whole-class activities, too, such as visits, reading stories related to the theme, and—most important of all—sharing what each individual or group has created or discovered, have more significance when the theme is one in which all are equally involved.

To teach in this way—collaborating in the pupils' learning and negotiating the curriculum with them—is not easy, of course. It re-quires a considerable degree of flexibility and an ability and readiness to meet the demands for resources of information and materials that are called for by the interests that the children wish to pursue. It also demands a constant state of open receptiveness to children's ideas and a willingness to take them seriously, even when, from an adult point of view, they seem naive or immature. At the same time, it requires clear thinking and planning in relation to broad, long-term goals and imagination in finding specific themes, activities, and materials that will spark fresh interests and make connections between those that have already been developed.

Some teachers may feel that they are simply unable to meet such demands: that the breadth of their general knowledge is insufficient or that they lack some of the necessary skills. Such doubts are under-standable and very real, but they are probably also unnecessary. To teach collaboratively, it is not necessary to know all the answers to pupils' questions or to be already competent in all the skills that an open curriculum may call for. Indeed, a teacher who is universally knowledgeable and competent may actually make it more difficult for pupils to gain confidence in their ability to learn on their own. Learning is first and foremost a *process*—a continuous making and remaking of meanings in the lifelong enterprise of constructing a progressively more and more effective mental model of the world in which one lives. Learning is never complete. Furthermore, since this process is essentially interactive, it is more helpful for the apprentice learner to work with teachers who are themselves still actively engaged in learning and willing to engage with their pupils in doing so than it is to be instructed and evaluated by those who apparently no longer have the need to engage in such processes themselves.

It is important to emphasize, therefore, that there is no one correct way to proceed. The only really satisfactory solution is the one that each teacher works out for him- or herself, taking into account the particular children concerned, their parents, the school, and its resources and environment.[10]

Seven

DIFFERENCES BETWEEN CHILDREN IN LANGUAGE AND LEARNING

Up to this point, little has been said about the ways in which children differ from each other. Instead, the emphasis has been on the very great similarities between them in development and experience. But, as the comparisons between particular children have shown, there are substantial individual differences, and in this chapter we shall try to understand their significance—their nature, causes, and consequences.

No two children—and no two adults, for that matter—are identical. Each is unique as a result of his or her particular combination of genetic inheritance and individual experience. The recognition of this unique quality of every individual is essential, of course, as a basis for our personal dealings with them, but it does not help us very much in our attempts to understand the major factors that contribute to this variety, nor does it help policy makers to take appropriate action to alleviate disadvantageous influences. For both these purposes, it is necessary to look for common patterns—for characteristics that are related to each other in predictable ways as, for example, height and weight (other things being equal, taller people tend to weigh more than shorter people). In relation to language and learning, these sorts of studies are still very much in their infancy, so conclusions can only be drawn very tentatively. However, since important decisions are being made on the basis of the conclusions that have been reached, it is worth considering the evidence that is currently available.

■ THE LIMITATIONS OF TESTS AND ASSESSMENTS

On one matter there is almost unanimous agreement: as children grow older, their language ability generally increases and so does their ability to use their linguistic resources as a means of learning, problem solving, and the like. This is the assumption on which tests of almost every kind are based and, within certain limits, it is a reasonable assumption to make. If a child takes the same test under identical conditions at the beginning and end of the year, he or she will almost certainly, unless something disastrous has happened in the interval, obtain a higher score on the second occasion.

But even that straightforward statement needs to be qualified. First, can one be certain that the conditions on the two occasions are identical? Not only may the person administering the test be different, with the consequent possibility of a change in the interpersonal relationship between child and tester, but the child's understanding of the test itself and what is expected of him or her may have changed as a result of intervening experiences. And if these possibilities make it difficult to interpret the significance of the change in an individual child's performance from one occasion to the next, they make it even more difficult to compare large groups of children, either on the same occasion or between successive occasions.

This qualification does not only apply to formal tests, however, but to all kinds of assessment and, indeed, to the evaluation of any form of interaction. As we saw in the comparison between the two teachers who talked with Rosie (chapter 5), the child's "performance" does not depend on ability alone, but on the complex interrelationship between the participants, the task, and the context in which it is embedded. It is a difficult and risky business, therefore, to draw conclusions about an individual's ability from his or her behavior in any particular situation. So, to be comprehensive as well as valid, an assessment must be based on a number of observations made in a variety of situations. However, there has been very little research that has systematically investigated the important influence of situational factors on performance.[1]

A second, related qualification has to do with the fact that, in almost any form of interaction, all levels of linguistic ability are drawn upon simultaneously; yet the majority of tests and even of less formal methods of assessment tend to have a very narrow focus, concentrating exclusively on just one aspect of ability—range of vocabulary comprehended, control of syntax in production, functional uses made of language, and so on. If the assessment is to be truly adequate, all of these aspects of ability need to be included in some form of composite profile. Children do not necessarily develop evenly across the levels: to assess just one aspect is to risk forming a biased estimate of ability.

A still further qualification arises from this last point: that ability can never be observed or measured directly, it can only be estimated from a sample of actual performance or from a number of samples. For example, if two children differ in the frequency with which they are observed to use complex sentences, one using a wide variety of sentence types in several different contexts and the other using only a small number in the same range of contexts, is this the result of a real difference in ability or is it simply a difference in the sentence types that each chooses to use? Amongst educated adults, we would assume it was the latter. One might prefer William Faulkner to Ernest Hemingway, for example, but there would be little temptation to argue that Faulkner had greater linguistic ability simply on the grounds that his sentences were typically longer and more complex.

With young children, however, this is the assumption that is frequently made. Indeed, some writers have made the further assumption that more frequent use of complex structures of various kinds is evidence of a more advanced level of intellectual functioning. As yet, however, this claim has not been systematically investigated and, until a causal connection has been clearly demonstrated, it would be wise to be more cautious. The ability to express complex relationships fully and precisely in language is certainly an aid to effective communication; it may also facilitate thinking. However, the fact that a child does occasionally produce utterances of this kind is evidence that he or she *can* do so when he or she judges the situation to warrant it. How the frequency with which a child uses this linguistic ability relates to his or her habitual level of thinking is a question that is much less easily resolved.

A final qualification must be made about the significance of rate of development. The fact that some children develop earlier and faster than others has been clearly demonstrated. But, apart from those children whose retardation is the result of some physiological handicap, there is little firm evidence that slow developers cannot, under appropriately supportive conditions, eventually reach the same level as—or even overtake—their more rapidly developing peers. Indeed, as is well known, many people who have become successful in adult life did not begin to show their exceptional skills until many years after they left school. There is clearly more to achievement, therefore, than simply being an early or fast developer.

This point needs emphasizing because, in the competitive ethos that pervades our educational systems and our culture in general, we tend to attach an exaggerated importance to being faster or slower than average, particularly in the early stages. At school, considerable merit is attributed to the child who is at the top of the class and lack of it to the child who is at the bottom, despite the fact that, in Britain, the United States, and many other countries, children are allocated to grades almost entirely according to age. When comparing different varieties of plant, on the other hand, we tend to adopt very different criteria. The fact that variety A happened to flower and ripen earlier than variety B would not be considered important if variety B ultimately produced an equal yield of equally good tomatoes.

One of the dangers, therefore, of comparing children in terms of their rate of development is that it may lead us to make inappropriate inferences, which may still further exacerbate the problems of those who develop more slowly. Already at a disadvantage in being unable to do the same things as their more rapidly developing peers, they are further handicapped by being adversely labelled and by having attributed to them personal inadequacies for which there is often no justification. If such children do, in fact, in the long run fail to reach the same level of achievement as their age peers, the reason may have as much to do with the handicaps imposed on them by the reduced expectations and inappropriate treatment of those who assess them as with any intrinsic limitation in their potential ability.

For all these reasons, then, it is difficult to know just how important the differences are that have been found to exist between children in their language development. Progress is being made in describing their nature and origin; but it would be unwise, on the basis of present knowledge, to draw conclusions about their long-term consequences. This is particularly so when it comes to making predictions about the ultimate level of achievement that can be obtained by individual children.

In the Bristol Study we tried as far as possible to guard against the dangers just described by obtaining samples of naturally occurring conversation and by constructing a profile score from a wide variety of measures. This still does not completely avoid the risk of wrongly estimating the ability of an individual child; but, fortunately, we were never called upon to make an assessment in a context that might have had consequences for his or her later development. About the group as a whole, however, we did feel more confident in making general statements although, for all the reasons discussed above, even these must be treated with considerable caution.

■ INDIVIDUAL DIFFERENCES

Before going on to discuss the differences we observed in greater detail, however, I want to emphasize the very great achievement of *all* the children we studied. Indeed, in the population as a whole, all but a tiny minority of seriously handicapped children do succeed in acquiring functional competence in their native language. In the Bristol sample of 128 children, there was not a single child who had not mastered what might be called "basic English" by the age of five. Rosie was the least advanced child in the follow-up study and, as we have already seen, when she was talking with her mother and with Teacher B, she showed herself to be quite a competent communicator, drawing upon a variety of complex sentence types to achieve a range of conversational purposes. Furthermore, as was emphasized in chapter 3, all children, to a very large extent, follow the same sequence of development. Considered against this background of similarity in achievement, therefore, the differences that are observed between individuals in their rate of development are relatively small and may not be of any significance in terms of their ultimate achievement.

As with such physical milestones as beginning to walk, children vary quite considerably in the age at which they begin to use speech sounds with a recognizable intention to communicate. They also differ in the age at which they show that they have discovered the grammatical organization of language by producing their first two- and three-word combinations. In the Bristol Study, we found that a very small number of children had reached this latter stage by 15 months, while others were nearly 30 months old by the time they did so. At 3½ years, the difference between the most and least advanced was equivalent to almost three years. Generally speaking, children who started early tended to stay ahead, but late starters did not necessarily continue to lag behind. Even when they did, however, they continued to make progress, although at a slower rate.

The reasons for these differences are of two basic kinds: differences in the children themselves, and differences in their environments—in the opportunities that are provided for learning. In the first category, we can include such factors as personality, learning style, and general learning ability. Little is known in any detail about the contribution of these factors, but they are probably quite important. Just as people differ in their general ability to master new skills or ideas, so it seems likely that there are differences between children in their general ability to learn language, or at least in the speed at which they are able to do so. Such differences probably account for a considerable part of the variation observed in the children's rate of learning. But as constructing the language system and discovering how to use it appropriately involve different types of learning, it is possible that there are differences between children here as well. Some may be particularly quick and successful in mastering the sound system, others at forming and testing the hypotheses necessary for constructing grammar, and still others at acquiring control of the functional uses of language. In recent years a number of research studies have shown that young children may have different strategies for making sense of language or different preferences in what they attend to.[2] Some of these strategies or preferences may provide an easier entry than others or lead to more rapid mastery. However, the number of children investigated from this point of view is still too small for any firm conclusions to be drawn.

Personality differences also seem likely to be of considerable importance. Children certainly differ with respect to such traits as perseverance (sticking at a problem until it is solved as opposed to giving up rather quickly when difficulties are encountered) and risk taking (being satisfied with an approximation if it serves the immediate purpose as opposed to needing to get things absolutely right if they are to make the attempt at all), and such traits clearly influence the amount of helpful feedback they get from other speakers. Children also differ in such traits as sociability, curiosity, argumentativeness, and so on, all of which also affect the ways in which other people interact with them and, hence, the amount and kind of evidence about language that they obtain through conversation.

It is through a consideration of conversational experience that we can also best understand the influence on development of the factors that were referred to above as environmental. Parents too, like children, differ in personality; they also differ in their beliefs about how to bring up children and in the importance they attach to their own contribution to their children's development. As a result, they differ quite considerably in how often they engage in conversation with their children, in what contexts, and for what purposes. They therefore provide different models for their children concerning which they treat as the most important functions of language. Clearly, a child whose experience of conversation was largely limited to obtaining satisfaction of basic needs and being required to conform to an adult's definition of "good behavior" would be learning a rather different and more restricted potential for meaning than would a child whose experience also included discussion of things seen and events encountered outside as well as inside the home.[3]

In this respect, we have found that one of the more important differences between children is in the amount of conversation they have while engaged in shared activities with an adult—helping with the housework, cooking, playing together, watching television, looking at books, and so on. In such contexts, adults not only provide evidence of language in use, which is readily interpretable from the context, but they also tend to "scaffold" the activity to make it easy for the child to play his or her role within it.[4]

In the end, however, what is probably most important about the differences between parents and other adults in personality, beliefs, and attitudes is the effect these have on the characteristic style they adopt when interacting with the child. Do they, for most of the time, treat the child as an equal partner, sustaining and facilitating his or her attempts to communicate, or do they impose their own views and standards? Do they, for the most part, respond fully to the child's initiations, or do they generally limit conversation to the bare minimum? There is little doubt that it is experience of the first kind in each case that provides the most effective support for language learning.

If the parents' behavior influences the range and quality of the child's opportunities for learning, as it certainly does, it is also true that the child's behavior influences the parents'. Parents and other adults, when talking with young children, adjust not only to the age and developmental stage, but also to the particular characteristics of the individual child. Indeed this is particularly true of the most supportive parents. For all children, language learning involves an interaction between the child and his or her environment, but where parents are really responsive to the particular characteristics of individual children, it is hardly an exaggeration to say that it is the children who are teaching their parents how to interact with them in ways that provide them with opportunities to learn.

Not all children have such a facilitative experience, however. Some children, because of their own individual characteristics, do not provide such clear cues or such rewarding experiences for their parents, so they, in turn, experience conversation that is less well adjusted to help them to learn. This tends to be particularly the case for handicapped children whose speech development is markedly abnormal. But, while differences in the quality of environmental support owe something to the differences between children in the communicative behavior they elicit, the main responsibility for the variation must lie with the adults who interact with the children, since it is they who have the greater measure of control over when, why, and how to engage in conversation.[5]

■ SOCIAL DIFFERENCES IN LANGUAGE DEVELOPMENT

Because language is a social activity and is learned through interaction with other people, it is reasonable to expect that differences between children may be related to their membership in different social groups. At the level of individual families this is undoubtedly the case, though even here it is remarkable how different can be the developmental history of siblings growing up in the same home. Parents in our study often remarked on this when comparing the child we were studying with an older or younger brother or sister. What was surprising, however, was the fact that the same sorts of explanation were given for accelerated or delayed development, whether the child being described was the older or younger sibling. However, this bears out what was said earlier about the interactive nature of language learning: it may be either the younger or the older child who is the one who leads or follows, is outgoing or shy. A further factor that complicates the effect of the child's position in the family is the age gap between siblings and the child's preference for interacting with an older or a younger sibling. Overall, though, there was a slight tendency for only children or those without a sibling close in age to develop more rapidly, due most probably to the more frequent opportunities these children had for interaction with their parents on a one-to-one basis.

Possible differences due to the sex of the child have recently also come to be considered in terms of social rather than physiological causes. In fact, in the Bristol Study, no such differences were observed during the preschool years. There were no measures on which girls as a group were consistently ahead of boys, nor vice versa. Although this is consistent with the results of other recent studies, it is in marked contrast with the picture that emerged from earlier work, in which girls were found to develop more rapidly on a number of linguistic dimensions.[6] In retrospect, it seems likely that these results were due in part to the somewhat artificial conditions under which the assessments were made but even more to the rather different expectations that parents had concerning what was appropriate behavior for boys and girls. Boys were expected to be active and boisterous, little interested in quiet and reflective activities, whereas girls were expected to be quieter and more docile, interested in helping their mothers and playing with dolls. This is no doubt something of a caricature but, despite the much greater equality with which the two sexes are now treated, there is still some evidence from the Bristol Study that parents behave differently to their children, depending on whether they are boys or girls.

This came out clearly in the sorts of toys the parents bought for the children and their reasons for buying them, but it also emerged from an analysis of the situations in which they were more likely to engage in conversation with them. With boys, a greater proportion of speech occurred while they were playing with toys; with girls while they were helping with household tasks. However, over the preschool period as a whole, these differences were not very large and, as already stated, they did not lead to consistent differences between the sexes in their rate of development nor in their use of language.[7]

Of all the dimensions of social difference that have been investigated, however, there is no doubt that it is family background that has received the greatest attention.[8] As a result of a number of well-known studies, a rather simple account has been very widely accepted to the effect that middle-class children in general tend at any given age to be linguistically more advanced than their lower-class peers. In many of the early studies, children's class membership was based on the father's occupation alone; in more recent studies, level of education has been included as well and the scores used for assigning children to one social class rather than another have taken information from the mother into account as well.[9] But, despite these refinements, the message has remained the same: compared with middle-class children, children from a lower-class background develop more slowly and, in some formulations, tend towards the expression of a more restricted range of meanings and to the use of language for a narrower and less complex range of functions.[10]

Before reporting the results from the Bristol Study, several reservations need to be expressed concerning the way in which most previous studies obtained their evidence. First, social class has, for the most part, been treated as a dichotomy: a family belongs either to the middle class or to the lower class. Further distinctions might be made within these two classes—"lower" working class and "professional" middle class, for example—but the major split remains the same. In practice, however, the population is not really divided in this way, even in Britain. Quite apart from the considerable amount of movement that there has been in the past, as people have "worked themselves up" or "fallen in the world," there has, for a considerable time, been a gradual shift in the distribution of employment from heavy manual work to secondary industry and to service occupations generally. With this has also come a trend towards more extended education. Furthermore, at the level of individual families, there is a small but significant proportion in which the parents come from different sides of the notional divide (for example, Mr. and Mrs. Morel in D. H. Lawrence's Sons and Lovers). For all these reasons, it is clearly inappropriate to characterize individual families in terms of two crude stereotypes; class must be thought of as at least a continuum, and individual families recognized as being likely to change their position on the continuum over a limited time span.

A second problem with much of the research on language and class is that it has frequently been less interested in exploring the range of language use to be found in the population as a whole than concerned with demonstrating the existence of clear class differences. To this end, comparisons have been made between two groups, selected from near the extremes of the continuum, rather than in a manner that represents the actual class make-up of the population as a whole.[11]

In the light of these comments, it might be predicted that if one were to study a properly representative sample of children, a quite different—or at least a less stark—picture might emerge. And this is what the Bristol Study has shown. In selecting the 128 children, information about the education and occupation of both parents was taken into account, allowing each child to be given a score on a 12-point scale. This scale was then divided into four intervals, and an approximately equal number of children was chosen to represent each interval group. When the four groups were compared on a variety of language measures, the differences between them were not statistically significant. The reason for this is quite simple. All four family background groups contained children who were relatively advanced and others who were much less so, and these differences within the groups were much greater than the relatively small differences between the *averages* for each group. On the other hand, if we were to ask about the half dozen or so most advanced children, we should find that they did tend to come from the better-educated, professional homes. It was also true that the half dozen or so least advanced children came from homes where the parents were minimally educated and worked, or had worked, in unskilled or semiskilled occupations. But for the vast majority of the sample—representing about 90 percent of the population—there was no clear relationship between family background and level of language development attained. There is therefore little justification for continuing to appeal to simple class stereotypes when thinking about the oral language abilities of children at the point of entry to school.

In summary, all the dimensions of social difference that we investigated led to the same conclusion: stereotypes are not appropriate. Whatever the mode of grouping, whether it be position in the family, family status, sex, or social class, differences *between* groups in the conditions and experiences that have an influence on language development pale by comparison with the variety of individual circumstances found *within* each of the same groups.

■ DIFFERENCES IN EDUCATIONAL ACHIEVEMENT

One of the purposes of our study was to find out how far the differences we had observed in the preschool years would affect the children's success at school. Would differences in oral language ability at age 5 be as important as was often suggested in accounting for achievement at later ages?

To investigate this question we asked the teachers to make a comprehensive assessment of the children when they entered school, again at the end of the sixth term (at approximately age 7), and, finally, towards the end of their primary schooling, when they had reached the age of 10 years 3 months. At each of these points we also administered a number of tests: various aspects of readiness for school at age 5; reading and number work at age 7; and mathematics and spoken and written language at age 10.

As might be anticipated from what has already been said, the range in achievement at each age was wide. This emerged clearly both from the tests and from the teachers' assessments. What is more, there was relatively little change in the rank order of achievement over the whole of the period studied. Children who were ahead on entry to school tended to be the high achievers five years later, and those who were behind at age 5 were likely to be at the lower end of the rank order at age 10. Jonathan, for example, who was amongst the two or three highest scorers at age 5, was clearly the most advanced at the time of the last observation; and Rosie, who was the least advanced at age 5, maintained this unenviable position at each observation.

There is nothing very surprising about this outcome, and in itself it tells us little about the effectiveness of schooling. If the aim is equally well met in all schools of enabling children to profit to the best of their abilities from the opportunities that are offered, it must be expected that those who are most able will make the greatest progress. Indeed, there would be justifiable cause for alarm if the outcome were very different. However, what if there is an inbuilt bias in the educational system that makes it more difficult for some children than for others to progress at the rate that would be predicted by their early ability? Such is the claim that has been made about the experience of many lower-class children; and, certainly, the evidence suggests that, as a group, they do less well at school than it would be reasonable to expect, on the assumption that ability is fairly evenly distributed over the population as a whole.[12]

One way to investigate this question is to follow the progress of a representative sample of children from as early an age as possible to see whether there is a clear relationship between achievement and family background and, if there is, what bearing this has on schooling. In the Bristol Study, this was attempted for the 32 children who were observed over the full 9-year period. However, because of the original aims of the investigation, it was only linguistic achievement that was measured in the preschool years.

At first sight, the results of analyzing the data in this way are rather disconcerting. At the two points in the preschool years at which correlations were calculated between oral language achievement and family background (at ages 2 and 3½ years), only a weak relationship between achievement and family background was found, which was not statistically significant. However, as soon as the children were assessed at school, the strength of the relationship increased considerably and remained at approximately the same, statistically significant, level at all three ages of assessment (see Table 7-1).

What this seems to suggest is that, while there was little difference in achievement between children from different points on the continuum of family background during the preschool years (when the assessment was based on their spontaneous conversation in their own homes), there was something about the conditions under which they were assessed at school that put the children from the lower end of the family background continuum at a relative disadvantage. Before we can explore this possibility further, however, we need to look more closely at what it was that was assessed on each occasion.

TABLE 7-1   **Correlation between Achievement and Family Background at Successive Ages**

Age in Years	Correlation
2	.24
3½	.29
5	.66*
7	.58*
10¼	.59*

*Significant at the .01 percent level.

At ages 2 and 3½, as already explained, the assessment was concerned exclusively with oral language. The majority of the measures used were derived from analyses of the recordings of conversation and concerned the range of meanings expressed, the grammatical forms used to express them, and the functions for which speech was used. To these measures were added scores from two tests of comprehension, one of whole sentences and the other of isolated words (the English Picture Vocabulary Test, or EPVT).[13] This test was only given at age 3 years 3 months.

At age 5, the tests included the EPVT again, an oral comprehension test involving the acting out of a story, a test of hand-eye coordination, and a test of knowledge of literacy.[14] Neither at age 5 nor at age 7 was there any test of oral language production. At age 7, the EPVT was repeated and two other tests were given, the Neale Analysis of Reading[15] and a test of number concepts and operations of our own devising. At age 10, the Neale Analysis was repeated and two further tests were added: a test of reading comprehension and one of mathematics, both provided by the National Foundation for Educational Research. At this age, the assessment also included a number of writing tasks, and five tasks involving oral language: two of comprehension and three of production. At each age, the results of all measures and/or tests were combined to give an overall achievement score.

At each age, though, there were some measures that seemed to be particularly effective in predicting overall achievement at the next assessment. At age 2, it was the range of functions for which the child was able to use his or her linguistic resources; at age 3½ it was the range of different sentence types that he or she was able to use appropriately. From age 5 onwards, however, the measures based on oral language ability ceased to be so important as predictors. Instead, what became important were measures associated with control of written language: the Knowledge of Literacy Test at age 5, and Reading Comprehension at age 7. Since the last assessment was made at 10 years 3 months, we cannot yet look for predictions on to the secondary stage, although we hope, in due course, to be able to extend the study in this way. However, at this last assessment, performance on the reading tests still contributed substantially to overall achievement. Surprisingly, by contrast, oral language ability did not appear to make a significant contribution. However, this does not mean that the ability to speak effectively and listen with comprehension was not important for success at school, but rather that the majority of the children were able to cope with the oral language demands of the classroom, and that the differences between them in this respect did not contribute significantly to overall achievement.

These were the results that emerged from the analysis of the children's performances on the various tests. But perhaps tests do not accurately capture the differences that matter in the day-to-day work of the classroom. To discover whether this was so, we asked each child's teachers to complete detailed assessments at the same ages as those at which the tests were administered. Questions were asked about the development of social and physical skills as well as about linguistic and general intellectual achievements. In each of these areas, questions were followed by between three and five descriptions of behavior spanning the range of maturity that one might expect to find amongst children of the relevant age. By scoring the descriptions selected by the teachers for each of the children, it was possible to arrive at overall scores for the same areas of the curriculum as were assessed by the tests. The results were very similar. In the teachers' eyes, too, it was skill in reading and writing (particularly reading) and in mathematics that defined school achievement. Once again, differences between the children in oral language ability were not strongly related to the differences in the more highly valued areas.

It is not difficult to see why differences in the ability to read and write should figure so large in the overall assessment of achievement by means of tests, since successful performance on many of the tests actually requires the use of these skills. Perhaps, too, the need to be able to read and write effectively in many of the subject areas also explains why the teachers evidently rated these skills so highly as well. In addition, of course, throughout the elementary school years a great deal of time and effort is devoted to helping children acquire these skills and, as will be suggested in the following chapter, the acquisition of literacy and numeracy is associated with the development of more general intellectual skills that it is a central aim of schooling to foster.

However, this does not explain the much smaller importance attached to ability in using oral language. That result was quite unexpected. Even in the upper levels of the elementary school, a great deal of the content of the curriculum is still presented orally, and it might be expected that teachers would be particularly aware of their pupils' abilities, in discussion and in one-to-one dialogue, to understand and make use of the material they are being asked to learn.

Since there undoubtedly were differences between the children in their ability to express themselves coherently and fluently in speech in the oral tasks that they were asked to perform and also, to a lesser extent, in the teachers' assessments of various aspects of oral language ability, it can only be assumed that activities in which these skills are called upon do not contribute to what are seen as the more central areas of the curriculum. Or perhaps, as was suggested in chapter 5, exploratory and collaborative talk is not thought of as playing a significant part in learning. Whatever the explanation, it seems that a valuable resource is being insufficiently utilized, particularly as there are a number of children in almost every classroom who are able to work on new ideas more effectively in speech than in writing. If we are to match learning opportunities to individuals who differ in aptitude and learning style, this seems to be an issue that needs to be given a great deal more attention.

There is a further point that needs to be emphasized in all such discussions, and that is that achievement is not the same as progress. Measurements of achievement are almost always made with respect to a group of children of approximately the same age. They are therefore biased against slow developers who, by definition, achieve low scores relative to their age peers. However, it does not follow at all that because a child remains at the bottom of the class throughout a year or even several years that he or she has made less *progress* than the child who was consistently at the top of the same class. Progress is measured relative to an initial state and is concerned with the amount of knowledge or skill gained. Low achievers in a class may thus be making just as much progress as high achievers. In a highly competitive society, however, this is often treated as less important than the fact that they are slow developers. Always coming off worse in age-related comparisons of achievement, they may easily come to be seen and to see themselves as intrinsically less well able to learn and, as a result, cease to make the progress of which they are capable.

As with the other stereotypes, therefore, we must be on our guard against treating low achievers in any age group as necessarily less capable of ultimately reaching a satisfactory level of achievement than those who are currently high achievers. The important point to bear in mind is that achievement is the outcome of an interaction between potential ability and experience. Slow developers are often not less able but simply lacking in the relevant experience. When an effort is made to match the curriculum to the needs of individual children and these gaps in experience are filled, progress may be remarkable.

■ THEORIES OF LINGUISTIC DISADVANTAGE

The issue of the place of oral language ability in the classroom is particularly relevant when we come to consider the much-debated question as to whether children from the lower end of the continuum of family background are at a disadvantage, linguistically speaking, when they come to school. Many people have argued that they are and that this is a major cause of their low educational achievement. But there has been considerable disagreement as to the precise nature of the disadvantage.

Initially, the explanation was couched in terms of deficit: lower-class children simply had fewer linguistic resources than their middle-class peers and, for that reason, were less well able to participate in the largely linguistic activities of the classroom. In the view of the proponents of this theory, the obvious remedy was to provide a highly structured compensatory educational program that would equip these children with the skills that it was assumed they lacked and that were also assumed to be necessary for academic success.[16] Although this view emerged most strongly in the United States at the time of Operation Head Start in the mid-Sixties, it was also quite widely accepted in Britain and in other countries in which unskilled or semiskilled manual workers formed a substantial proportion of the population.

An altogether different explanation of linguistic disadvantage was proposed in Britain by Basil Bernstein.[17] According to this account, the educationally significant difference between children from middle- and lower-class homes was not to be found in their underlying linguistic abilities, but in the uses to which they habitually put them, and these they learned from their day-by-day experience of conversation in their homes. Because of their different relationships to the means of production in their roles at work, Bernstein argued, members of the two classes were likely to emphasize different types of relationships within the family and to enact these relationships through different selections from the linguistic resources that are in principle available to all of them as members of the larger language community. Lower-class families, he suggested, emphasized "positional" relationships and enacted them through a "restricted" linguistic code, in which much of the speaker's meaning was implicit—assumed to be already known and shared, or tied to the immediate context of activity. Middle-class families, by contrast, were said to emphasize "personal" relationships and, while meanings might on appropriate occasions be equally implicit, speakers would, where necessary, make their own personal point of view explicit and set it in a more universal context. This latter use of language was described as an "elaborated" code.

The significance of these two codes for children's achievement in school was that the habitual experience of one or other of them was said to orient children to different orders of meaning: the restricted code to context-bound, particularistic meanings and the elaborated code to more context-independent and universalistic meanings. And because education is concerned with the latter order of meanings, middle-class children, who were said to be already more familiar with the use of an elaborated code, adjusted relatively easily to the language demands of the classroom. The restricted code experience of lower-class children, by contrast, did not provide such a good preparation. Their disadvantage, therefore, was that their habitual experience of linguistic interaction at home did not match well with the expectations of the school.

There is, however, yet a third explanation, which has also been widely accepted. During his research on the different social dialects found in all urban centers, William Labov noticed how often lower-class children, particularly black children, appeared linguistically incompetent in classroom interactions with teachers and other adults. However, out in the playground with their peers or even in informal conversation with an adult, these children showed perfectly normal linguistic ability and often considerable expertise in the verbal activities valued by their friends. However, the dialect in which these verbal skills were displayed, like the dialect they spoke at home, was not Standard English, but a nonstandard dialect, black vernacular English (BVE), which differs systematically from standard English in a number of important ways. These children did not lack language, Labov argued; rather, their apparent incompetence was due to their lack of facility in situations in which they were required, or at least expected, to use Standard English. Their disadvantage, therefore, was that their dialect did not match the dialect used and valued by their teachers.[18]

As can be seen, these theoretical explanations of the linguistic disadvantage experienced by many lower-class pupils are very different in the value that they place upon the linguistic resources that these pupils have acquired at home and in what they consider should be the appropriate response of the school. At one extreme, the proponents of the deficit theory see the problem as residing almost entirely in the child and in his or her home environment. To them, the obvious remedy is to provide highly structured compensatory educational programs that would equip these children with the skills that it was assumed that they lacked and that were also assumed to be necessary for success at school: programs that involved much group responding to teachers' display questions; emphasizing answers in the form of grammatically complete sentences; and, as the children progressed, focusing on isolated sounds and letters as a preparation for the decoding of print.

At the other extreme, Labov argued that the children he studied were in no way linguistically deficient. What was necessary for their success at school was an adaptation on the part of teachers: an acceptance of the children's dialect and a proper valuing of the uses of language that they themselves valued.

Bernstein's position was somewhere in the middle. The fundamental problem, as he saw it, was in society as a whole—in the class-based inequalities of power and control. Schools needed to adjust to the different orientations to meaning that could be expected in children from different class backgrounds. At the same time, a determined effort needed to be made to give restricted code users experience of, and access to, the elaborated code.

These three theoretical approaches to an understanding of the linguistic disadvantage of lower-class children have all been extremely influential, both at the level of policy decisions about the best way to use available resources and also at the level of the classroom, through the initial and in-service education of teachers. All three of them have given rise to firm beliefs about the typical preschool conversational experience of children from different social backgrounds; they have also set up powerful, although somewhat different, expectations about the linguistic resources these children will have when they come to school. What is so dangerous about these beliefs and expectations, however, is that they have lacked any firm foundation in systematic empirical evidence.

As was pointed out at the beginning of this chapter, the aim of research has often been to demonstrate the existence of theoretically predicted differences, not to discover what is actually the case. In order to discover how far children's preschool linguistic experiences do in fact differ, it is necessary to select a representative sample of children and to observe the naturally occurring conversations in which they participate in a wide variety of contexts. Only when that has been done can one talk with any confidence about the linguistic resources that children have available and about the conversational experiences through which they have acquired them.

■ THE EVIDENCE FROM THE BRISTOL STUDY

One of the main aims of the Bristol Study was to obtain this sort of evidence, and every effort was made to ensure that, as far as it was possible to do so, the samples of conversation that were recorded were typical of the language that was used both by and with each child. We went to considerable lengths to ensure that the parents did not know precisely when the recorder was actually operating. If they were affected by the presence of the bug in their homes (although there was very little evidence that they were), the effect was presumably to bring their practice more into conformity with their beliefs which, according to the theories just discussed, would have tended to exaggerate any class-related differences. However, the parents' styles of conversation were never discussed with them during the course of the investigation; and, when we did ask, after the observations had been completed, the vast majority said they could not think of any ways in which their behavior had been changed by participating in the study. There is a strong reason to believe, therefore, that the evidence we obtained accurately represents the preschool linguistic experience of these children and of the population from which they were selected.

The most important finding has already been mentioned: up to the age of 5, there were no clear differences between the middle- and lower-class groups of children in their rate of development, in the range of meanings expressed, or in the range of functions for which language was used. Though it is true that the extremely fast and the extremely slow developers did show a marked tendency to be found at the upper and lower ends of the continuum of family background, these two groups together accounted for no more than 10 percent of the sample as a whole.

Essentially the same was true when we looked at the quality of the children's conversational experience. Certainly there was wide variation in the amount of conversation that occurred (from as few as 36 utterances to as many as 360 adult utterances addressed to different children in the eighteen 90-second samples that were analyzed at each observation). There was also wide variation in the quality of the conversation—in the extent to which parents sustained and extended their children's conversational contributions, as described in chapter 3. But in both quality and quantity, the differences were not significantly associated with family background. Neither were there obvious differences in style of child or adult speech that would tend to support the theory of strongly class-associated differences in code. In fact, in all homes the range and level of conversation was for the most part highly dependent on context and restricted to familiar, everyday experiences. Even when a detailed analysis was made of the frequency with which the parents' conversation with their children moved towards "disembedded" uses of language,[19] such as enunciating general principles and conclusions or encouraging their children to consider imaginary or hypothetical situations, such occasions were not significantly more likely to occur at the upper than at the lower end of the family background continuum.[20]

It is true we did not observe the families on visits outside the home—to the launderette, the doctor's consulting room, the park, or the museum. Examples claiming to show the difference between the two social classes in their styles of conversation are often taken from such settings, based on conversations that have been overheard. However, such comparisons are of dubious validity as a basis for more general statements, for two reasons. First, they represent only a very small proportion of any child's conversational experience; and second, such situations may lead parents to behave in uncharacteristic ways, which differ in a class-associated manner according to the degree of self-confidence that they feel when they are publicly on view and expected to keep their children under control.

On the basis of the evidence that we collected, therefore, there is no justification for continuing to hold the stereotyped belief that there are strongly class-associated differences in the ways in which parents talk with their children. Nor is there justification for forming expectations about children's oral language abilities on entry to school that are based solely on their parents' membership in a certain social class. Children differ, certainly, in the fluency and explicitness with which they habitually express themselves, but these differences do not necessarily correspond to their actual abilities, nor are they clearly associated with fathers' or mothers' occupations.

When children come to school, however, the picture apparently changes. There are class-related differences in their ability to cope with tests and testlike situations, and the teachers of the children in our study certainly perceived their oral language abilities to differ in ways that were quite strongly related to family background. However, we should not accept these results too readily at their face value. In the first place, the differences in test performance, although real, may reflect different degrees of familiarity with the conventions of testing rather than a real difference in ability in relation to the actual content of the tests.[21]

Second, it is highly probable that teacher expectations have some influence on the children's performances, and hence on the teachers' assessments of their linguistic abilities. Although, as already mentioned, there was no evidence that the teacher's perception of dialect—standard or nonstandard—had a significant relationship with subsequent achievement, there was no doubt that other cues, such as father's occupation or type of neighborhood, influenced the teachers' expectations. And these expectations, in turn, sometimes influenced the ways in which the teachers engaged in conversation with the children.[22] Where there were high expectations, teachers were more likely to encourage children to express their ideas spontaneously and to do so at length; conversely, low expectations led to a more strongly eliciting style of conversation on the part of the teacher, with few opportunities for the child to initiate or sustain a topic of conversation. (The example of Teacher A's interaction with Rosie in chapter 5 is an extreme example of this tendency.) The result is that, with different opportunities, children produce different performances, which merely serve to confirm the teachers' initial expectations. To some extent, therefore, without having any intention to do so—indeed even with clear intentions to foster a child's language development—a teacher can interact with a child in such a way that that child is caused to appear linguistically deficient or disadvantaged.

By age 10, however, the picture has changed. Differences between pupils in their performance on the oral tasks were not significantly associated with family background and the relationship, as far as the teachers' assessments of oral language ability were concerned, was barely significant. Since this result confirms the picture that we had obtained during the preschool years, it does tend to suggest that the association between oral language ability and class or family background on entry to school was more the result of differences between the children in the ease with which they adjusted to the linguistic demands of the classroom than of any more fundamental class-based difference in ability. However, we are still left with the very substantial association between family background and overall achievement to explain. To do this, we need to return to another of the tests that we gave to the children on entry to school: the test of knowledge of literacy.

This test, better than any other, predicted overall achievement at the age of 7; it was even a good predictor of achievement at age 10. Significantly, it was also the test that was most strongly associated with family background. In fact, at all ages, all the measures concerned with literacy—tests and teachers' assessments—were significantly associated with family background. In the light of these results, we decided to look more closely at the preschool observations and at the interviews with the parents when the children were age 3½ and 5 to see whether we could find an explanation.

From the interviews it emerged quite clearly that the children who obtained relatively higher scores on the knowledge-of-literacy test were likely to have parents who read more and owned more books; they were also likely to read more often to their children. This finding was confirmed by the number of times children were observed to have stories read to them during the recorded observations.[23] The children themselves were also more likely to show an interest in literacy, asking about the meanings of words and the significance of letter shapes; they were also more likely to spend considerable periods of time on activities associated with reading and writing. And, unlike the measures of oral language use by child or parent, all these literacy-related measures in the preschool years were significantly associated with family background.[24]

If some lower-class children did suffer from linguistic disadvantage, therefore, it was not in relation to their command or experience of oral language, but in the relatively low value placed on literacy by their parents, as shown by their own very limited use of these skills, by the absence of books—either children's or parents'—in the home, and by the infrequency with which they read to their children, if they ever did so at all. As a result, these children came to school with a

very limited understanding of the purposes of literacy and little knowledge of how to set about obtaining meaning from print.[25] Not surprisingly, therefore, they experienced considerably more difficulty in learning
to read and write; and, although they might acquire the mechanical
skills of decoding print to speech and forming letters, words, and sentences in writing, unless they discovered the value of these skills at
school, the children rarely achieved a level of independence by the age
of 10 sufficient to make reading and writing enjoyable and rewarding
activities. As a result, they tended to be less successful in other areas
of the curriculum as well, as was seen earlier when the components
of overall achievement were discussed.

However, lest we feel tempted to lay the blame for the plight of
these children on the inadequacies of their parents, we should consider
for a moment the larger social context in which both parents and
children find themselves caught up. Let us follow in imagination one
group of school entrants at the age of 5. Some of them are already
familiar with the activities of reading and writing and know how and
why to use books, even though they probably cannot yet read or write
for themselves. However, with such a good start, they quickly learn
the necessary skills and by age 7 or 8 have become independent readers
and writers. They are able to cope effectively with curricular tasks that
require these skills and continue to be able to do so throughout their
secondary schooling. At age 18 they continue into college or university
and, having acquired qualifications, go into some form of middle-class
occupation, in which they continue to use the skills of literacy. When
these young adults get married and have children of their own, their
regular work and leisure activities provide opportunities for their children to see the value of literacy, and they probably also share their
interests by reading and writing with them. Their children, in turn,
come to school already knowing about literacy and ready to follow the
successful educational careers of their parents.

By contrast, the children who come to school knowing little about
literacy frequently have difficulty in learning to read and write; and,
because these skills are given such importance at school, their relative
failure often leads them to lose confidence in their ability to learn. On
entry to the secondary school, they are placed in the lower streams,
or even in the remedial department and, unless they are very fortunate,
their lack of academic success—which is largely dependent on skills
in literacy—leads to disenchantment with the whole business of education. As a result, they leave school at the first possible opportunity
without qualifications and, when employment is available, they go
into lower-class occupations that require only minimal, if any, skills
in literacy. When these young adults marry and have children, they
too engage in many interesting and valuable activities with their children. But, because they do not enjoy reading and writing, they do not

engage in these activities themselves nor do they share them with their children. These children then come to school as disadvantaged, in their turn, as were their parents. In this way, the cycle of educational disadvantage is repeated: socially transmitted, as Bernstein suggested, through the characteristic patterns of activity and interaction that families of different social backgrounds engage in as a result of their own experiences as children and as pupils.

In my view, therefore, there is considerable validity in the theory of linguistic disadvantage, when this is understood as relative unfamiliarity with the significance of literacy and with its forms and functions. But it is important to recognize that this does not imply a general rejection of the rich oral language resources that all children have by the time they come to school, whatever the class or ethnic group to which they belong.[26] Nor does it imply that simply by knowing certain demographic information about a child's family, one can predict with any accuracy how much relevant preschool experience individual children will have had or how great is their potential for success in meeting the demands of the school. However, it does help to explain why, despite their evident command of spoken language, a significant proportion of children from those groups in society that do not belong to the educated, typically middle-class "mainstream" fail to benefit as much as they might from their formal education.[27]

Unfortunately, schools may inadvertently be helping to perpetuate this disadvantage by weighting assessment so strongly in favor of literacy at the expense of oracy. More use, I am convinced, could be made of the undoubted abilities that many lower-class pupils have to learn and to convey the fruits of their learning through spoken language. This is an area in which they are at much less of a disadvantage with respect to their middle-class peers. Yet, on the evidence of our study, they are not being given the opportunity and encouragement to make full use of these abilities. Talking to learn is just as important as reading and writing to learn, and we ought to plan so that both are given equal value as complementary modes of thinking and communicating in all areas of the curriculum.

At the same time, there can be no diminution in the efforts that we make to enable all children to become fully literate. However, this aim will not be served by delaying the start of learning to read and write in order to give such children so-called compensatory programs in oral language. This is doubly ineffective. In the first place, the children do not need them. They are quite able to speak in complete sentences when the occasion is appropriate and they are given the opportunity. But more important, what they do need, and need urgently, is experience of books and the pleasure that comes from being read to; they also need the opportunity to try to make meanings in written language for themselves. The reason that this is so important is the subject to be considered next.

Eight

THE CENTRALITY
OF LITERACY

Probably the most striking finding from the whole of the longitudinal study has been the very strong relationship between knowledge of literacy at age 5 and all later assessments of school achievement. In the previous chapter some suggestions were made as to why this test should have had such predictive power and why the differences between the children should have been associated with family background. In a sense, those suggestions already provide a denouement to the story, but they do not fully explain the underlying mechanism. Indeed, in some respects the test results, if taken at face value, might lead to some erroneous conclusions.

■ THE TEST OF KNOWLEDGE OF LITERACY

Let us look more carefully at the knowledge of literacy test itself.[1] It consists of two parts. In the first, the child is presented with an illustrated storybook called *Sand*. It is about a child going to the seaside, digging in the sand, making sand castles and so on. The items in this part of the test are designed to measure how much the child knows about how to cope with print. At the beginning of the test, the book is handed to the child upside down and back to front. The first item is scored according to whether or not he or she turns the book the right way around. The next item asks, "Which part tells the story?" and is scored according to whether the child points to the text or to the picture. The items increase in specificity regarding the child's concepts about print until, at the end of the test, the child is asked, "Can you show me a *word*?" and "Can you show me a *sentence*?"

The second part of the test is even more text-specific. The child is presented with a sheet of paper on which are displayed, in random order, all the letters of the alphabet in both upper- and lowercase form. The child is asked to name or sound as many as he or she can recognize.

Taken together, the two parts of the test provide a very reliable estimate of how much a child knows about the conventions of written language. And, as already noted, the score a child achieves is a very good indicator of how quickly and successfully he or she will acquire the skills of reading and writing and be able to use them in tackling work in other areas of the curriculum.[2]

But is the knowledge tapped by this test what is really crucial? Is it what explains the difference between those who quickly and easily learn how to read and write and those who do not? Or is it more a by-product of acquiring a different sort of knowledge about literacy that is of much greater fundamental importance? To put it differently, if we want to help children to become literate, is it here that we should start—by teaching the names or sounds of the letters and the operational definitions of terms like "word" and "sentence"?

There is no doubt that most readers do come to possess this knowledge, and it can be very useful as a means to further learning through instruction. But, as teaching methods that place the emphasis on what might be called "the mechanics of literacy" have shown, it is possible to be very successful in teaching children to operate on the surface appearance of print but to find that they still do not understand what they read and that they never voluntarily engage in this activity, either to obtain information or for the enjoyment it offers.

The point is perhaps made more clearly if we draw the comparison with spoken language. What use would it be for a child to know all the sounds of his or her language and the rules for combining them into words and sentences, if the child had not discovered that the whole point of this knowledge was that it was a resource for the exchange of meanings in the attainment of joint purposes of various kinds? The same is true, I believe, for an understanding of the mechanics of literacy. Important though this knowledge is for reading and writing, it is of little value if the child does not understand the purpose of these activities—if he or she does not know that written language conveys meaning and that it does so in ways that differ from those that apply in the use of spoken language.

■ LEARNING ABOUT LITERACY IN THE PRESCHOOL YEARS

How then might some of the children in our study have discovered something of the significance of written language before they came to school? To answer this question it is necessary to look more carefully at the sorts of activities that they engaged in, or observed, during the preschool years at home in order to see which of them might provide opportunities for the necessary learning. Two sources of evidence were available for this investigation: the parents' responses to questions asked during interviews with them and the transcripts of the actual recorded observations in the children's homes.

From the first source, it was obvious that the parents' own interest in literacy was important: the number of books they owned and how much they read and wrote in accomplishing their own purposes. In this, as in so many other areas, children learn from the model provided by adult behavior. This was particularly clearly shown with respect to the development of their writing. Children who, at age 9 or 10, were amongst the more accomplished writers were much more likely to have parents who themselves wrote frequently, particularly lists, memos, and notes for themselves. The reasons for this seem to be twofold: first, these forms of writing are likely to be particularly visible to children, since they occur in the course of other activities in which they may be involved, rather than in a secluded study or after the children have gone to bed. Second, because such occasions of writing occur as part of other, often shared, activities, their significance is quite readily appreciated by children and, indeed, may become a matter for actual discussion.

From the parental interviews, too, it was clear that the child's own interest in literacy was an important factor. This was measured not only by the number of books he or she personally owned, but by the general interest displayed in written language, in the form of signs, advertisements, labels, as well as the more conventional books and magazines. Some children more than others asked about words seen—their meaning and, in some cases, how to spell them. Even more important as an indicator of their interest in literacy was how absorbed they became in activities associated with literacy—how long, according to their parents' reports, they typically chose to spend on them.[3]

This last finding was the starting point for the next stage of the investigation, which involved a careful scrutiny of all the transcripts of the actual observations. If the extent of the child's own involvement in what we had generally labelled "literacy-related activities" was, of all the factors asked about in the interview, most strongly related to subsequent success in school, what were these activities, and were some of them more important than others?

Obviously, there are many activities that have the potential for helping the child to learn about literacy, but they are so specific and occur, relatively speaking, so rarely that we could not expect to capture them in our short and infrequent observations—such activities as spotting signs like "EXIT" or the names or logos of well-known brand names on goods or advertisements, watching Mother write a note for the milk- or breadman or reading the TV guide to find out when a favorite program is on. These are a few examples—and there are many others—where the use of reading or writing plays a small but significant part in the lives of the majority of families. In a literate society, all children begin to form hypotheses about the functions and organization of print from such experiences.[4] What may differ, however, is the extent to which the child is involved in these activities and how far he or she is encouraged to play an active role in them to the extent of his or her abilities.

There are other activities, however, that involve literacy much more centrally. These it did seem possible to investigate more systematically. Given the content of the knowledge of literacy test, on which the children had been so differently rated, one obvious place to start was with deliberate instruction on how to use a book and on the letters of the alphabet. However, although this no doubt took place in some homes, it was not a frequent occurrence in our recorded samples. If it was observed, it was nearly always incidental to some other activity, and so, as an independent activity, it was dropped from the investigation.

In the end, it was decided to search for occurrences of four activities. These were: looking at a picture book and talking about it; listening to a story; drawing and coloring; and writing—or pretending to write. Although not all the children had books of their own, there was no home without illustrated magazines and mail-order catalogues, and nearly all the children spent some time looking at or naming the pictures. Where an adult joined in this activity, this might provide a valuable preparation for learning to read, first because it involved handling a book or booklike object and, second, because looking at pictures and talking about the objects portrayed, their attributes, and the scenes in which they were involved might provide a valuable preparation for similar discussions at school—often an important part of a child's introduction to his or her first reading book. Listening to a story read aloud, on the other hand, provides a different sort of introduction to written language. Here what is encountered is continuous prose, in which meaning is built up cumulatively over many sentences and even chapters. Pictures occur in many storybooks, too, but in almost all cases as accompanying illustrations.

The inclusion of drawing and coloring was based on two rather different observations. In our visits to schools, we had noticed that it was a very common practice to ask each child to draw and color a picture and then to use the picture as the basis for the creation of a short written text. The child would talk about his or her picture and, with the teacher's help, compose a caption. This would then be traced over or copied and then finally read back to the teacher. Within such an instructional framework, therefore, drawing would be seen as intimately connected with reading and writing.

But drawing is also connected with writing in a different way. Both involve the attempt to give symbolic representation to what has been understood. As teachers and parents know, young children's spontaneous drawings are very far from realistic. Instead of drawing what they see, they try to represent what is essential about the subject as they have understood it. Indeed, Vygotsky has argued that this is an important step on the way to writing: first the child discovers that his or her understanding of objects can be represented directly, and at a somewhat later stage the child discovers that the speech in which those objects are referred to can also be represented.[5] For some children, therefore, we might expect to find occurrences of this fourth activity as, with pencil or crayon, they engage in "writing"—that is to say, in making marks of any kind that they themselves consider to represent a linguistic message.

Once it had been decided which activities to look for, all the transcripts were searched for evidence of their occurrence. Scores were given to each child, based on the number of occasions on which he or she was observed to engage in each activity. All the children were observed to look at picture books and to talk about them, although not equally often. "Writing," on the other hand, was observed only twice and by a different child on each occasion. In between came listening to stories and drawing and coloring, which were each observed in one or more transcripts of about half the children. The final step was to compare the frequency scores for each activity with the children's scores on the two later literacy measures: the knowledge of literacy test at age 5 and the test of reading comprehension administered after two years at school.

The results of this comparison were absolutely clear-cut. Of the three frequently occurring activities that had been considered as possibly helpful preparation for the acquisition of literacy, only one was significantly associated with the later test scores, and it was clearly associated with both of them. That activity was listening to stories.[6]

■ WHAT'S IN A STORY?

Why should listening to stories be so much more beneficial as a preparation for literacy than looking at books and magazines and talking about the pictures, or attempting to represent ideas graphically through drawing and coloring—worthwhile though these activities are for their own sake? There are, I believe, a number of reasons.

First, in listening to stories read aloud at the age of 2, 3, or 4—long before they can read themselves—children are already beginning to gain experience of the sustained meaning-building organization of written language and its characteristic rhythms and structures. So, when they come to read books for themselves, they will find the language familiar.

Second, through stories, children vicariously extend the range of their experience far beyond the limits of their immediate surroundings. In the process, they develop a much richer mental model of the world and a vocabulary with which to talk about it. As a result, as the content of the curriculum expands beyond what can be experienced firsthand in the classroom, children who have been read to find themselves at a considerable advantage. This is clearly apparent in the assessment made of our 10-year-olds by their teachers. Size of vocabulary was strongly related to overall educational achievement.[7]

Stories can also provide an excellent starting point for the sort of collaborative talk between children and parents that was described in chapter 3, as the parent helps the child to explore his or her own world in the light of what happens in the story and to use the child's own experience to understand the significance of the events that are recounted. Such talk and the stories that give rise to it also provide a validation for the child's own inner storying—that internal mode of meaning making which is probably as deeply rooted in human nature as is language itself.[8]

All these positive features of sharing a story can be seen in the following extract from a recording of David (age 3 years), who has chosen to have *The Giant Jam Sandwich*[9] read to him—obviously not for the first time. Notice how the mother leaves space for the child to offer comments and ask questions and how her contributions build on his, extending his understanding of both the matter of the story and the actual wording.

[*David is sitting next to Mother on the sofa so that he can see the book.*]
David: The Giant Sandwich
    [*4-second pause*]
Mother: Who's this here on the first page?
David: The wasps.
Mother: The wasps are coming. [*Turns the page*]
    Here's some more, look. Wow! [*Reads*]
        One hot summer in Itching Down
        Four million wasps flew into town.
David: I don't like wasps . . . flying into town.
Mother: Why's that?
David: Because they sting me.
Mother: Do they?
David: Mm. I don't like them.
Mother: They'll only sting you if they get angry. If you leave them alone

they won't sting you. But four million would be rather a lot, wouldn't it? They'd get rather in the way. [*Reads*]
> They drove the picknickers away ...

David: Mm.

Mother [*continuing to read*]:
> They chased the farmers from their hay
> They stung Lord Swell [chuckles] on his fat bald—

David: Pate.

Mother: D'you know what a pate is?

David: What?

Mother: What d'you think it is?

David: Hair.

Mother: Well—yes. It's where his hair **should** be. It's his head—look, his **bald** head. All his hair's gone.

David: Where is it?

Mother: Well, he's old, so it's dropped out. He's gone bald.

David: Where's—Is that his hat?

Mother: Mm. He's running, so his hat's fallen off. [*Reads*]
> They dived . and hummed . and buzzed . and ate

David: D'they eat him?

Mother [*laughs*]: I expect they might have tried to. I dunno. D'you think wasps eat people?

David: No.

Mother: What do they eat?

David [*with relish*]: They eat vegetables.

Mother [*laughing*]: Vegetables.

David: Yes.

Mother: What sort? What do they like?

David: They like [*5-second pause*] Um ...

Mother: What kind of vegetables were you thinking of?
[*Long pause*]

David [*looking at the illustration on the next page, which shows three male inhabitants of Itching Down, each attempting in his own way to get rid of the wasps*]: Is that a spray to shoo them away? Is that a spray to shoo them away?

Mother: Yes. It's probably some sort of insecticide . to get rid of them. And what's that net for, do you think? [*A butterfly net*]

David: It's for catching them with.

Mother: It doesn't seem to be much good though, does it?

David: No. They come out the holes.

Mother [*laughs*]: The holes are too big, aren't they? And what about this man? What's he got?

David: He's—What's he got?

Mother: What's that?

David: A note. What does the note say?

Mother: A note on a stick, is it? Is that what you think?

David: Actually it's a sound.

Mother: A what?

David: A sound. What's it called on the—on the stick? What is it? What's that man got?

Mother: Well you know, um—

David: Yes . . Sign.

Mother: You think it's a sign? Yes it looks very **like** a sign with writing on, doesn't it?

David: Yes.

Mother: But it isn't. It's like Mummy's—um—fish slice [slotted spatula].

David: What is it?

Mother: It's a swatter. He's going to hit the wasp with it.

David: How d'you hit wasps with . otters?

Mother [*checking*]: Swatters? Well, they're made of plastic usually—

David: Yes.

Mother: And they—you bang them down. See if you can squash the wasp. Looks very angry.
[*5-second pause*]

David: Is he hurt?

Mother: It looks as if he might be. He's making a funny face.

David: Why he making a funny face? Is that man—is that man shouting for them to go away?

Mother: Think so. He's got his mouth open, so he could be shouting.
[*5-second pause*]
Anyway—

David: Yes.

Mother [*reads*]:
> *They called a meeting in the village hall*
> *And Mayor Muddlenut asked them all,*
> *"What can we do?" And they said, "Good question,"*
> *But nobody had a good suggestion.*
>
> *Then Bap the baker leaped to his feet*
> *And cried, "What do wasps like <u>best</u> . to*

David: <u>best</u>

Mother: *eat?*
Strawberry

David: *jam.*

Mother: *Now wait a minute.*
If we made a giant sandwich,

David: Yes.

Mother: *We could trap them in it.*

What is particularly impressive about this last section is the timing. It is a truly shared recreation of the story, with David chiming in at exactly the right moment to fit the rhythm of the lines. It is also worth noticing David's interpretation of the picture of the man with the swatter: "a note on a stick." What power he attributes to written language. Even wasps can be vanquished by a sign with writing on it: "WASPS, GO AWAY!"

To understand the full significance of having stories read aloud from an early age, however, we need to look more closely at the relationship between language and experience that is found in stories—and in most extended uses of written language.

In ordinary conversation, which is every child's first and most frequent experience of language in use, the meanings that are communicated arise for the most part out of the context of ongoing activity or out of past or future events about which the participants have shared knowledge or expectations. To understand what is meant, therefore, they can use the context to help them interpret what is said. Indeed, as was suggested in chapter 3, this is what makes it possible for the child to construct his or her representation of language in the first place. In conversation, too, the participants are usually face to face and so can provide immediate feedback on the success of the communication and engage in negotiation if problems occur. At the same time they also have to manage their interpersonal relationship satisfactorily. All of which means that, in conversation, attention is only partly on what is said. In seeking to understand each other's intentions, participants make use of a variety of other cues, and the meaning that is finally constructed is the outcome of a collaborative and negotiated interaction, which owes as much to other sources of information as it does to the actual words spoken.

In written language, by contrast, the situation is usually very different. Because writer and reader are not in face-to-face contact, and indeed probably do not even know each other, there is no need for, or even possibility of, a moment-by-moment monitoring of the interpersonal relationship. For the same reason, the writer can make no more than very general assumptions about the knowledge that the reader will bring to the text, and there is no context to support the writer's meaning other than that created by the text itself and the form in which it is presented. All of this leads to a much greater focus on the text alone as the carrier of meaning and to a need for greater explicitness if the intended meaning is to be unambiguously communicated.

This is not to ignore, of course, what the reader brings by way of general expectations and personal experience to the task of constructing an interpretation of the text, nor to underestimate the importance of the cues that are available to the mature reader in the genre form in which the text is presented—verse, dramatic script, newspaper editorial, etc.—or to the novice reader in the form of illustrations. However, even these cues are text-dependent, in the sense that it is only by attending to the text that their significance is recognized. Even when a story is illustrated, as for example in the case of *The Giant Jam Sandwich*, it is the text that gives a precise significance to the illustrations rather than vice versa.[10]

In sum, the most important difference between typical instances of spoken and written language can be stated as follows. In conversation, and particularly in casual conversation around the home, what is said arises out of shared activity and only takes on its full meaning when considered in relation to that nonlinguistic context. The aim in conversational speech, therefore, is to make the *words fit the world*.[11] In most writing, on the other hand, there is no context in the external world to determine the interpretation of the text. The aim must therefore be to use *words* to *create a world* of meaning, which then provides the context in terms of which the text itself can be fully understood. To understand a story therefore—or any other written text—the child has to learn to give full attention to the linguistic message in order to build up a structure of meaning. For, insofar as the writer is able to provide cues for the reader's act of construction, he or she does so by means of the words and structures of the text alone.

What is so important about listening to stories, then, is that, through this experience, the child is beginning to discover the symbolic potential of language: its power to create possible or imaginary worlds through words—by representing experience in symbols that are independent of the objects, events, and relationships symbolized and that can be interpreted in contexts other than those in which the experience originally occurred, if indeed it ever occurred at all.

Compared with the longer-term effects of this discovery, it is easy to see why drawing, or matching names or sounds to the letters of the alphabet, although useful, is of much less significance for later progress at school. The same is true of the learning that takes place when looking at picture books or catalogues and discussing the names and attributes of the objects depicted. No doubt this activity helps children to enlarge their vocabularies—at least for those things that can be pictured. It also gives them practice in answering display questions of a limited kind, and this may well give them an initial advantage if they find themselves—as many do—in classrooms where such skills are emphasized. But it is a short-lived advantage and one that is, in the longer term, restricting. For ultimately—and ideally sooner rather than later—they will need to be able to answer (and also to ask) questions that go beyond naming and rote recall. They will need to follow and construct narrative and expository sequences, recognizing causes, anticipating consequences, and considering the motives and emotions that are inextricably bound up with all human actions and endeavors. In a word, they will need to be able to bring the full power of storying to bear on all the subject matter of the curriculum.

This interpretation of the connection between early experience of listening to stories and later educational achievement is confirmed by the final part of the investigation of children's preschool literacy-related activities. As well as comparing the frequency scores for the three activities—looking at picture books, listening to a story, and drawing and coloring—with subsequent scores on the tests of knowledge of literacy at age 5 and reading comprehension at age 7, we also compared them with the scores derived from the teachers' assessments of the children's oral language ability on entry to school.

Once again, the results were clear-cut. Only the frequency of listening to stories significantly predicted the teachers' assessment of oral language ability. And this was not simply the result of the children's having acquired a larger vocabulary. Children who had been read to were better able to narrate an event, describe a scene, and follow instructions. But perhaps what was most important in accounting for the teachers' higher assessment of these children's oral language abilities was the greater ease with which they appeared to be able to understand the teachers' use of language. This is not surprising when we consider how often the topics that teachers talk about—be it four-poster beds, children in other parts of the world, or sets in mathematics—are not physically present in the classroom. Even when speaking, therefore, the teacher tends to use a literate form of language and, to understand him or her, the child has to pay particular attention to the linguistic message and use that as the basis for reconstructing the teacher's intended meaning. That is to say, the child has to be able to exploit the symbolic potential of language.

This becomes increasingly important as the child moves up through the school and encounters more and more curriculum content that can only be brought into the classroom symbolically, through teacher talk and through books and other forms of symbolic representation. More than anything else, therefore, schools are concerned with the development of skills in symbol manipulation, first in "natural" language through talk and then in reading and writing and, later, in the symbol systems of mathematics, music, and science. (And to these we must now add the languages used in programming computers.) To understand the problems posed in the curricular tasks that children are given, and to succeed in finding solutions to them, children are more and more going to need to be able to "disembed" their thinking from the context of their own particular, taken-for-granted experience and to handle ideas of a more abstract kind, for which their own personal experience may provide only minimal support.

As Margaret Donaldson puts it:

> What is going to be required for success in our educational system is that [the child] should learn to turn language and thought in upon themselves. He must become able to direct his own thought processes in a thoughtful manner. He must become able not just to talk, but to choose what he will say, not just to interpret but to weigh possible interpretations. His conceptual system must expand in the direction of increasing ability to represent itself. He must become capable of manipulating symbols.[12]

This is what becoming literate really involves. And listening to stories and discussing them with adults in ways that lead children to reflect upon their own experience and encourage them to explore, through their imagination, the world created through the language of the text (as the extract from the reading of *The Giant Jam Sandwich* shows) are probably the experiences that most help young children to discover and begin to gain control of what Sapir called "the dynamo of language."

■ WHAT DOES THIS MEAN FOR ROSIE?

Rosie, it will be recalled, was the child who had the lowest score on all the tests we administered, including the test of knowledge of literacy. This can be largely attributed, I believe, to the fact that she never had stories read to her. According to both her mother's answer to the interview question and our observations, Rosie was not read to once before she started going to school. By comparison, Jonathan had something in the order of six thousand book and story experiences before starting school.

This difference in preschool experience was not limited to Rosie and Jonathan, however. There were other children in our sample whose experience differed in similar ways. And the same would be true in any large school or school system in any of the countries of the Western world. The question is: what can be done to help Rosie and children like her to catch up with their more fortunate peers?

It is sometimes argued that it is inappropriate to think in terms of compensating for experiences missed in the preschool years. Different cultures place different values on literacy, and schools should accept the fact that children will differ in the types of literacy event that they encounter in the years before they come to school and in the ways in which those events are interpreted in their communities.[13] However, while it is important to accept children as they are, this does not mean that steps should not be taken, when they come to school, to provide them with a firm foundation on which to acquire those skills of literacy and symbol manipulation that are so important for later success in all areas of the curriculum.

In our visits to schools, we observed a number of different strategies being adopted, with varying degrees of apparent success. In some, a language experience approach was adopted, in which children handled, observed, and talked about the objects and events in their environments and used this as a basis for drawing pictures and dictating captions, which were then traced or copied and later read back to the teacher. In others, a particular emphasis was given to what I have called the mechanics of literacy: time was spent on learning from flash cards the words in the first books in the reading scheme so that the children would be able to start working their way through the graded series of reading primers; considerable attention was also given to letter formation in writing, and to spelling and later to punctuating correctly. Sometimes both these approaches were used together.

Under these conditions, some children were learning quickly and most were making reasonable progress. But in almost every classroom there were some children whose progress was extremely slow; in a few the proportion of such children was disturbingly high. What was surprising, however, was that the strategies adopted seemed to bear little relation to the preschool experiences of the children, except that, in predominantly lower-class areas, more attention was given to activities intended to extend the children's oral language resources, on the assumption that this was the area in which they were most likely to be linguistically deprived.[14]

However, the evidence of our study suggests that, while some lower-class children, such as Rosie, would certainly benefit from increased opportunities to engage in collaborative, exploratory conversation with adults, children who have not already achieved sufficient command of their mother tongue to be introduced to books as soon as they come to school are extremely rare. If some children made little progress in learning to read and write, the problem, as we observed it, was not that they had insufficient oral language resources, but that they had not yet discovered the purpose of reading or writing or the enjoyment to be gained from these activities. (The predicament of children who are just starting to learn English as a second language is clearly different, but even they can enjoy books of an appropriate kind, even though they may not yet be able to read them.)

What children like Rosie need, I am convinced, is a personal introduction to literacy through stories. Listening to a story read to the whole class is no solution, for they have not yet learned to attend appropriately to written language under such impersonal conditions. For them, what is required is one-to-one interaction with an adult centered on a story. Such an experience provides not only an introduction to literacy but also an entry into a shared world that can be explored through the sort of collaborative talk that is the most effective way of facilitating children's learning and language development.

By the same token, picture storybooks, both those that are written for children and those that children create themselves, provide the best material for learning to read and write, once they have discovered the pleasure of sharing a story read aloud and acquired sufficient confidence to begin to join in the actual reading. There are now sufficient picture storybooks of varying levels of difficulty to enable a complete program to be based on books that children choose because they want to read them for themselves.[15]

■ COLLABORATION BETWEEN SCHOOL AND COMMUNITY

Many teachers would like to spend more time reading books with individual children or with groups of two or three. The problem is to find the time. This is an almost insoluble problem if the teacher has to meet all the needs of the children in the class single-handed. However, there are various ways in which other people can provide assistance, most importantly the children's parents.

There is little doubt that the great majority of parents recognize the importance of literacy—or at least of their children's learning to read and write. Typically, however, the responsibility for seeing that children acquire the skills of literacy is assumed to rest with the school, and all too often this assumption is reinforced by the advice that is given to parents by teachers. In interviews with parents of the children in our study, we were told more than once that they had been advised not to attempt to introduce their children to reading before they came to school, as the parents' approach might lead to the children's being confused when they began to be taught at school. No mention was made of the valuable contribution parents could make by reading stories with children; no advice was given on what would be the most suitable books to read or how to obtain them from the public library or the school. Instead parents were made to feel incompetent, and the mistaken impression was given that becoming literate is chiefly a matter of learning to decode letters to sounds, a skill that could be taught only by an expert.

Such an attitude on the part of teachers is doubly unfortunate. In the first place, it implies a denial of the spontaneous nature of children's interest in written language and of their ability actively to make sense of it for themselves if given the opportunity and encouragement.[16] Second, it undermines the confidence of the very people who are most likely to have both the time and the inclination to provide the conditions in which children can begin to become literate, namely by sharing books and stories with them in an enjoyable and unthreatening one-to-one interaction and by encouraging them to discover the possibilities of writing through the free exploration of the forms and uses of graphic symbols.

These are ways in which parents can and do help children to construct the foundations of literacy in the years before school. However, once children start going to school, supporting the continuing development of literacy should become a collaborative enterprise, in which the assistance of parents is positively encouraged. There are many ways in which this can be achieved. The Haringey experiment showed that parents regularly listening to their children read can significantly accelerate the children's progress.[17] This has been confirmed in other schools, where a similar practice has been adopted.[18] Along with help at home can go parental involvement in school, not only in listening to children read but also in reading to them. In one first-grade classroom in Toronto, all these ideas have been combined. Children take home not only books that they have chosen to read to their parents, but also books for their parents to read to them; in the morning, when the children are brought to school, parents who have time are invited to read to one child or to a small group of children a book that one of the children has chosen.[19]

Parents can help with writing, too. In some schools, parents help in the publication of the books that children have written. They also act, along with other members of the school and community, as sources of information whom the children consult on the topics about which they are preparing to write, as recipients of the children's written communications, and as readers of the children's books, once they are published.[20]

However, parents are not the only members of the community who can help to extend young children's experience of belonging to what Frank Smith has called "the literacy club."[21] In many schools, older children regularly read to children in first- and second-year classes and listen to them read. In some schools, these older children are also encouraged to write stories for their younger "buddies." Senior citizens, with time on their hands after they have retired, are often delighted to spend some of it in classrooms reading to children and talking with them about their interests. Outside the school, too, there are many opportunities for other members of the community to contribute as recipients of children's written communications and as respondents to their requests for information.

Once teachers recognize the support that is available to them from the wider community in promoting the value and enjoyment of literacy and are willing to enlist this support in various types of collaboration, their task in providing the sort of experiences that Rosie and children like her need does not appear so formidable. It may be difficult—and

perhaps even undesirable—to try to persuade all parents of the importance of providing the foundations of literacy by sharing stories with
their children in the years before school. But this should not mean that
their children are permanently deprived of this essential experience.
Means must be found to ensure that all children's first experiences of
reading and writing are purposeful and enjoyable. Only in this way
will they be drawn into applying their meaning-making strategies to
the task of making sense of written language. Only in this way will
they learn to exploit the full symbolic potential of language and so
become fully literate.

Nine

THE CHILDREN'S ACHIEVEMENTS AT AGE 10

Our study started by investigating the early stages of language learning. The questions we set out to answer were: how far do children show a common pattern of development, and in what ways is their development influenced by their environment? In the background, though, there were always further questions that we hoped to be able to answer about the educational significance of the differences between children that we had noticed from the very first observation. What effect did it have on later achievement at school whether children were early or late in learning to talk? How important were differences in oral language ability at the point of entry to school? Was there any evidence of class-related differences in language use in the home and, if so, did such differences provide an explanation for the class-related differences that had so often been reported in educational achievement?

The continuation of the study into the years of schooling gave us an opportunity to address these latter questions and, in general terms, the answers that we arrived at have already been reported in previous chapters. However, it is also interesting to look at these same questions from the perspective of case studies of individual children. In this chapter, therefore, we shall return to the six children who were introduced in chapter 1, in order to see how they fared over the period covered by our investigation.

At the same time, since literacy emerged as the major differentiating factor at school, we shall look in more detail at the shift in emphasis from speech to writing and consider some of the factors that are involved in making this transition. This will lead us into a reconsideration of the role of spoken language in the middle-school years (approximately ages 9 to 13) and, finally, to a plea for an integrated approach to language as the medium for learning across all the subjects of the curriculum.

■ LINGUISTIC INFLUENCES ON EDUCATIONAL ACHIEVEMENT

Rarely, if ever, has there been an opportunity to follow the same group of children from before they were able to speak until the end of the elementary stage of their education. The number of children that were involved throughout the duration of the Bristol Study may have been small but, given the uniqueness of the undertaking, the richness and variety of the information that was collected goes a long way towards compensating for the size of the sample. In particular, the comprehensive assessment of the children at the age of 10 has made it possible to look back over the preceding years in order to identify the major linguistic factors that were important in accounting for the differences in educational achievement observed at this age.

The age range studied naturally falls into two periods: before and after the beginning of schooling. In the preschool years our information is based largely on recordings of spontaneous conversation. During this period, irrespective of family background, the differences between children in their rate of development seemed to be largely due to an interaction between the intrinsic characteristics of the children themselves (their personalities and their general learning ability—though we have no direct measurements of these characteristics) and the quantity and quality of their conversational experience. To some extent, the differences in conversational experience were almost certainly the result of differences between the parents, which made some more willing and able than others to be responsive to their children's conversational initiations. Here, too, personality differences were involved and, to some extent, awareness of how best to provide a supportive and stimulating environment. In a few cases, there were external factors, such as poverty, overcrowding, or unhappy personal relationships, that made the parents' lives so stressful that they were too preoccupied to enjoy interacting with their children. But what was clear from listening to the recordings was that, although the parents were in most cases the more powerful influence on the quality of conversation, the actual conversations that occurred were always the outcome of an interaction to which both parent and child contributed, each influencing and being influenced by the other.

During these years, as already noted, the children all followed essentially the same sequence of development, although some made more rapid progress than others. In general, those who were early in beginning to speak were likely to be more advanced on entry to school, but there were a number of exceptions to this tendency. Almost certainly, slow beginners who caught up with their peers had benefited from a richer-than-average conversational experience, and the converse was probably also the case. Listening to stories was also a factor that contributed to differences between children in rate of progress.[1]

In the second period, from entry to school at age 5 until the time of the last assessment at age 10, there was much less change in the rank order of relative achievement. Children who entered school ahead, as estimated by the tests administered at that time and by the teachers' assessments, were very likely still to be ahead five years later, and the same was true for those lower in the rank order. As already described in chapter 7, the single most important factor in accounting for the differences between children in their subsequent achievement was how much they understood about literacy on entry to school. Other contributory factors were the amount of help that parents gave with schoolwork and the model they provided of the value of literacy in their own lives by the frequency with which they themselves engaged in reading and writing.

The relationships between the major factors to emerge from the analysis are shown in the form of a diagram in Figure 9-1. The numerical values inserted in the lines joining the various boxes are the correlations that were obtained. The values shown in bold type are the multiple correlations between the estimate of achievement at each point of assessment and the factors significantly influencing that achievement.

■ THE STORIES OF SIX CHILDREN

Figure 9-1 shows the main findings from the study in statistical terms. But what do these figures mean in terms of individual children? One way of answering this question is to present a number of case studies that illustrate the relationships identified by the statistical analysis. The children introduced in chapter 1—Rosie, Tony, Abigail, Gary, Penny, and Jonathan—were selected because they show the main trends particularly clearly.

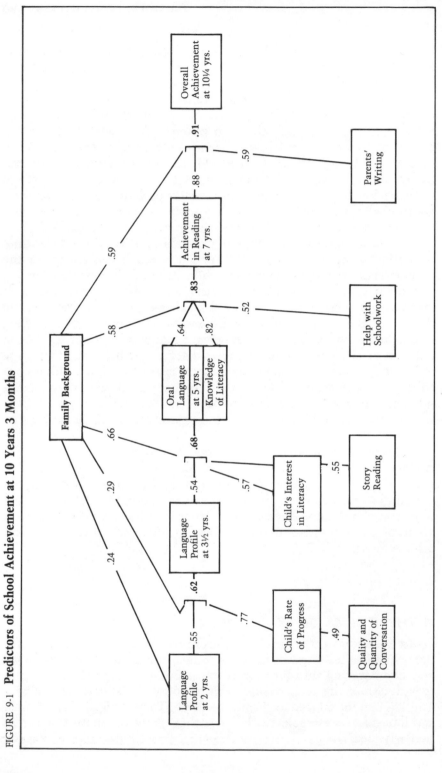

FIGURE 9-1 **Predictors of School Achievement at 10 Years 3 Months**

The six case studies that follow are based on three different sorts of evidence:

1. The scores that the children attained on the tests and other methods of assessment that were used. Rather than give the children's actual test scores, however, I have represented each score in terms of its corresponding position in the rank order of scores from all 32 children. Table 9-1 sets out the six children's ranks on some of the most significant measures discussed above.

2. Samples of their writing on two of the tasks that were set as part of the final assessment. The first of these required them to write a personal narrative with the title "The happiest day in my life." The second, also a narrative task, involved writing a story to fit a cartoon, in which a rather ineffectual-looking hunter was brought to bay with his dog at the edge of a cliff by a motley assortment of wild animals (see Figure 9-2). Both tasks were carried out without assistance from the teacher, and the children were given as much time as they needed to complete them.[2]

TABLE 9-1   **Six Children's Longitudinal Rank Profiles**

	Abigail	Anthony	Gary	Jonathan	Penny	Rosie
Language Profile at 2	8	32	30	2	1	14
Language Profile at 3½	7.5 =	23	7.5 =	1	3	29
Story Reading	5	13.5	13.5 =	1.5 =	26 =	32
Oral Language at 5	4 =	6	20.5 =	4 =	12.5 =	29
Knowledge of Literacy at 5	7.5 =	3	29	1.5 =	10	31.5 =
Child Interest in Literacy	4.5 =	15	27.5 =	4.5 =	12	31.5 =
Help with Schoolwork	24 =	3 =	17	3 =	17 =	24 =
Reading at 7	8	7	24.5 =	3	10	32
Oral Language at 10	2	11	6	1	8	32
Reading at 10	2	3	26	1	21.5 =	31.5 =
Writing at 10	3	4	22	1	11	32
Vocabulary at 10	2.5 =	2.5 =	22	2.5 =	5.5 =	30.5 =
Mathematics at 10	20	8.5 =	16	1	12.5 =	31.5 =
Parents' Writing	5	3	9	2	26	30 =
Overall Achievement at 10	2	3	22	1	13	32

Note: Equal sign ("=") indicates the fact that several children obtained identical scores and so obtained the same rank.

FIGURE 9-2 **The Cartoon Used for the Story-Writing Task**

3. Answers to questions that were asked in the interviews that were conducted with all the children at the end of the study.

The interviews were conducted in a very relaxed manner by the same interviewer in every case. He was already known to the children, as he had been involved in administering the tests, some of which had involved a considerable amount of interaction. The same basic questions were asked of each child, but the order in which they were asked was varied. At some point in each interview, however, the children were asked to describe a typical day at school. They were invited to answer in as much detail as they wished, but they were told that the interviewer would not interrupt them until they had finished. This was done in order to obtain a comparable sample of continuous speech from each child as one of the ways of assessing their oral language ability. (The other oral tasks involved listening to a Russian folktale and retelling it to a friend and learning to play a new board game and then explaining how to play it to a friend.)

Inevitably, however, despite the efforts taken to make the interview as relaxed and informal as possible, some of the children were less at ease than others. Nevertheless, according to the answers that they gave when they were asked if they had found it difficult to talk about themselves, none of them found the experience too daunting.

Rosie.   As may have been deduced from the discussion of Rosie's transition from home to school, she was chosen to be one of the case studies because, at least as far as educational achievement was concerned, she was the least successful child in the study. This estimate is confirmed by the information contained in Table 9-1. Nevertheless, as the interview clearly showed, she had many positive characteristics, and it was only in comparison with her age peers that she was seen to present a serious learning problem.

At age 2, Rosie was very slightly above average in her level of language development (rank 14). However, by age 3½, she had dropped very nearly to the bottom, having made very slow progress in the intervening 18 months. This can be accounted for largely in terms of the amount and quality of her conversational experience. For most of the children in the study, the average number of utterances produced in the 27 minutes of recorded time analyzed at each observation was around 120, about the same number of utterances was addressed to them in the same period of time. The figures for Rosie were very much lower: on average, somewhere between 30 and 40 each for Rosie and the other participants. Also, the conversation that did occur was very fragmentary; topics were rarely developed beyond two or three turns. Nevertheless, as the extract quoted in chapter 5 demonstrated, by age 5 Rosie had achieved a reasonable command of language and was developing in the same way as other children, although considerably more slowly. As far as we could tell, there was no deficiency in Rosie herself; what she lacked were the experiences necessary to nourish her intellectual and linguistic development.

Perhaps the most serious deficiency in Rosie's experience, at least with respect to her subsequent progress at school, was the complete absence of stories. Compared with the other children in the study, there was very little in her home environment to stimulate an interest in literacy, and on entry to school her score on the test of knowledge of literacy was at the bottom of the rank order. Not surprisingly, therefore, she made very slow progress in learning to read (rank 32 at age 7); and, despite a certain amount of help from her parents with schoolwork, she remained at the bottom of the rank order on all the measures obtained at age 10. As her teacher put it at the end of the final assessment: "Her present lack of reading ability is most likely to hold her back; other factors would be the home and its environment, also her lack of any real drive and initiative."

Rosie's writing was equally poorly developed. The following is her account of her happiest day.

at christmas my mun bought
Me a bioe &t chistmas my mun
bought Moea wircless
and a colouring Boon

In fact, this was quite an achievement for her, given the labor that was involved in the very act of producing a written text. However, with the difficulties she still had in forming the letters, spacing words, and achieving even a phonetically consistent spelling, she could give very little of her attention to the selection and shaping of her material to produce an overall effect.

Poor Rosie! Nothing seemed to work in her favor. From a materially impoverished and intellectually unstimulating home environment, she went first to a school where her homeroom teacher (Teacher A in chapter 5), despite her good intentions, did little to boost her confidence or to help her to become more actively interested in the new experiences of the classroom. No special effort was made to make up for her lack of stories at home—although it is only fair to the teacher to recognize that the majority of the children in Rosie's class were in need of the same individual story-sharing experience. By the time Rosie and her family were rehoused and Rosie transferred to a different school, she was seen to be in need of remedial teaching. So low was her achievement, in fact, that at around the age of 9, she was assessed by an educational psychologist, who recommended that she be sent to a school for children with special learning needs. At the time of our last assessment, however, she was still attending the local school.

Something of Rosie's own feelings about school can be gleaned from the following extract from her answer to the request to describe a typical day at school.

Rosie: When I goes to school . . I either gets told off . or gets smacked
[*laughs*] . . . or sometimes I gets . picked on by all the rest of them.
Or sometimes it's either me who's getting—or it's either me laughing
or it's either . . Sandy, the one who sits next to me . . sometimes Sandy
gets it.
I don't have dinners no more.
[*8-second pause*]
I used to get picked on in this class . . . .
When I used to go up—go somewhere for Miss, I used to go—I used to
go "Silly cow" . . 'cos I don't like our teacher. [*Laughs*]
I never like that teacher.

When asked whether she thought she was good at schoolwork, she first replied that she did not know; then, after a moment's reflection, she changed that to an emphatic "No." Despite all these negative feelings, however, she still preferred to be at school rather than at home.

Interviewer: D'you prefer being at home or at school?
Rosie: School.
Interviewer: Why's that?
Rosie: 'Cos you learns there. There's nothing to do when we're at home . . only just sit at the—sit down on the floor or on the sofa staring at the telly . . . . or help our mum wash up or . . . . and that's all, I think.

Given Rosie's accurate assessment of her lack of success in learning at school, one can only agree with her view of her probable future:

Interviewer: What d'you think you'll do when you grow up?
Rosie: [*after long pause*]: Dunno. Just walk around or get a job.
Interviewer: What sort of job would you get?
Rosie: Dunno.

Anthony.   Anthony shows almost the reverse pattern from Rosie. At age 2, he was the lowest in the rank order of language development. Slow to get started, he had caught up a little by age 3½, and by age 5 he was ranked sixth. Part of the explanation in Anthony's case is that he was an only child who, particularly as he got older and began to talk more fluently, enjoyed a great deal of conversation with his parents. Although only average in the interest he showed in activities associated with literacy and, according to our observations, not read to more than average, he scored high on the test of knowledge of literacy (rank 3) on entry to school and achieved consistently high rankings from then onwards. At age 7, when asked "What do you do when you read?", he replied: "You read it in your mind. Use your eyes ahead and read in your head." At age 10 he was ranked third in overall achievement. His teacher wrote about him, "A lively approach to life which makes the work he has to do enjoyable for him."

From the point of entry to school—and even before—Anthony's parents were determined that he should do well at school. Reading for information as well as for pleasure was emphasized; Anthony was also encouraged to write, and his parents provided a model in the range and frequency of their own writing (rank 3). At the interview when Anthony was age 7, in which the parents were asked about ways in which they helped with schoolwork, they replied that he no longer needed help with reading or with basic number work. However, they did make a point of taking him on visits to the museum and other places of interest, and they discussed the work he was doing in class. In the week before the interview, the mother remembered, they had spent more than an hour reading about the battle of Waterloo in the *Encyclopaedia Brittanica* in connection with a project that he was doing at school. From an educational point of view, Tony clearly enjoyed a very supportive home environment.

Two years before the final assessment, Tony transferred to the preparatory department of one of the prestigious local private schools. This was obviously an important event for the whole family, for it was about this that he chose to write when asked to describe the happiest day of his life.

THE HAPPIEST DAY OF MY LIFE

The happiest day of my life was a couple of
years ago. It was about May and I was just
collecting the post. One was for my dad and the other
one was also for Mum Dad. My Mum opened
a big brown one which had something for
my dad's office. After reading that. She opened the other
one and let out a yell and started hugging me
nearly crushing me. When I finaly got her sitting
down with a glass of water she told me that
I had passed the test for the * *
* and then she started ringing up every
realation saying that I had passed the exam.
She said that the last few days had been
hell not knowing whether I had passed because
a friend had told her that they were
saying who had passed and who had failed.
That was defintely my happiest day of my life.

Certainly Tony seemed to be enjoying school, as is clear from the following extract from the interview.

Interviewer: Which subjects do you like best at school?
Tony: Geography, because we're studying planets and the solar system. I'm enjoying history a lot. . . . English I enjoy quite a bit. In fact most lessons really.
Interviewer: What do you like about English?
Tony: [*after long pause*]: I think the imagination you can put into it.
Interviewer: Writing stories, that sort of thing?
Tony: Yes. Not comprehension, really.

Here is Tony's story about the hunter, showing just what he meant about imagination. It was certainly one of the most successful in its creation of a specific setting and in using that as a motive for the rest of the story. He had problems with the time sequence, though, perhaps because he felt he had to explain the situation depicted in the cartoon rather than simply tell a story about it.

THE TRAP

It was a plesant day in North Africa. Filthy Menasty
was making another trap to capture wild animals
He was doing this to make the biggest zoo in the
whole world. He had lead them all this way by
a dead carcus of a vison and a bowl of water.
The carcus was to get the lion, snake and vulture.
The water was to get the vegitirian animals. They have
stopped because they are suspicious about the ground
ahead which is a massive net covered with grass
so they would go over it The dog is scared because
Filthy treats animals awfully. Filthy also carries a
gun incase they charge at him. He is whistling because
he wants to get the animals to got to him and
fall in the net. The cliff edge is only a few
metres high and in a moment he will fall back
so the animals will go and look over the
edge but will fall in the net. The worm has
tunneled into the net and is warning the other
animals. But Filthy is at the wrong place and falls
to his death. The trap had failed.

Although, like Rosie, Tony preferred to be at school, he also had an interesting life outside school, which included reading, watching home videos, and learning to play golf, as well as making a collection of lapel badges. He also talked with enthusiam about the holidays that his parents had taken him on abroad. When asked about his future, he replied with some hesitation that, when he grew up, he thought he would be a dentist.

Gary. Gary provides a contrast of a different kind with Rosie. Initially, he was slow in starting to talk (rank 30 at age 2). But over the next year and a half he made rapid progress, reaching rank 7.5 = at age 3½, and this despite a slight stammer. In the interview, his parents said that they had very deliberately ignored the stammer, believing his speech would be most likely to improve if they concentrated on what he wanted to say rather than on how he said it. This policy was obviously successful, as there was no evidence of a speech problem in the final interview.

Several extracts from the recordings made when Gary was 5 were included in chapter 5. From these, one gets an impression both of Gary's competence as a speaker and of the quality of his conversational experience at home. It was a surprise, therefore, to find that, on entry to school, he was judged by his teacher to be below average in oral language ability. One wonders whether there were other factors that led to this low estimation, such as his nonstandard dialect or his somewhat aggressive enthusiasm. He had not shown much interest in activities associated with literacy at home, and this attitude continued at school, where he did not find it easy to settle down to tasks of an academic kind. His performance on the test of knowledge of literacy at age 5 was ranked almost the lowest and, despite an average amount of support at home, both in story reading in the preschool years and in help with schoolwork later, he remained in the lowest third of the rank order for reading and was ranked only slightly higher for writing. He was ranked 22 at the final assessment for overall achievement.

Here is an example of his writing: the account of his happiest day. It is full of detail, with its lists of presents and foods, and one can easily imagine his enjoyment of the Christmas holiday. But the obvious enthusiasm is also a liability, for it seems to have led Gary to neglect the need to shape his account to make a story out of what is at present only a sequence of events.

THE HAPPIEST DAY IN LIFE

dear
friend The happiest day in life was
        the Christmas just gone.
        I liked it because I had the
        things I wanted, and somethings
        I dident exspect like wakietalkies,
        powertrack, torches, radiocontarlecar
        and proper scrabling cloves.
        I played with them when my mum &
        DaD went to bed. I liked the TV
        programgs like exralong cartoons,
        the wondeful wizard of all
        and pinochio. After watching all that.
        My sister DAD ana I all
        went down my nans. I had
        Christmas cake, black pudding,
        and welsh cakes. The day after
        Christmas was boxing day. On
        the night all my famiely went back down
        my nans, and all the
        famiely were there. We all had
        a party. At fourteen oclock
        We Whent home and went to
        bed.

In other ways, though, Gary showed considerable talent. He was good at sports (he took part in a national archery competition just after the final assessment) and he played in the school football team. His particular passion at the time of the final assessment was motorbike scrambling (hence the reference to "scrabling cloves" among his Christmas presents), and he talked about it with great animation.

Gary: I want to be a professional scrambler. I go scrambling every Sunday. Me and my sister've got a bike—motorbike.

Interviewer: A small one?

Gary: No, a big one.

Interviewer: Can you ride it?

Gary: Yes—change gear on it. It's a six gear, mine is. We ride it on the common or at the airport [disused]. I goes on the grass—I used to go on the grass and now I goes on the proper bumpy track and out of our Dad's sight. He said "When you're ready—when you think you're ready, I'll let you go"—like wherever I want to go—like all the way round the track.

He returned to the same theme later in the interview when asked what he wanted to be when he grew up:

Gary: I wanted to be a farmer. But our Dad said: "No. You'll be an electrician and electronics—get a lot of money. It's the best job." If I gets a lot of money I'll buy myself a proper scrambler and just go practicing and that'll be my hobby—go weekends, go racing.

At the same time he also said he was going to take his Mum and Dad on holiday and buy them a video.

Asked about other activities he enjoyed at home, Gary mentioned reading—the newspaper and "war stories" borrowed from the library. He also gave the following interesting account of a (yet to be carried out) writing project:

Gary: Me and my sister are writing—like, um—say it was a court person. Like a policeman had to write a story about in court. And we writes horror stories. Me and my sister are going to discuss about writing a book and we're going to publish it and make a paperback. We're thinking of doing that.

Interviewer: And what'll that be about?

Gary: Um [*long pause*] "The Flowers in the Attic"—that might be the model. Or just make up a different story—any story, what we've done.

Interviewer: What? A story for children?

Gary: Yes, and adults if they want our—a paperback book.

Interviewer: How are you going to publish it?

Gary: My Dad—he's got a printing machine in his work and the proper paper. He's a mechanic and he can print it there. I don't know how I'm going to do it 'cos I'm not in charge. It's my sister. She's going to do it. It's up to her.

Throughout his time at school, Gary was popular with his peers and something of a leader. To some extent this was a handicap in the classroom, as he was likely to be at the center of any diversion, which did not endear him to his teachers—as Gary was well aware:

Interviewer: What do the teachers think about you?

Gary [*after long pause*]: Dunno . . . I reckon I'm an idiot.

[*A few minutes later*]

Interviewer: If you don't like them [your teachers], what are you usually upset about?

Gary: Like if you mutter to yourself you get lines. Like last week. Just 'cos I said, like, "Three times three equals nine," to myself, he says, "A thousand lines," 'cos he thinks you're talking to your partner.

In fact, it is tempting to argue that the teachers generally underestimated Gary's ability. For example, at the time of the final assessment, his teacher felt unable, for lack of information, to answer the question about Gary's ability to estimate lengths. At a follow-up visit to obtain an answer to this question, Gary was sent for by the teacher, presented with a sheet of paper on which a cross was marked, and asked to estimate a distance of 20 centimeters. When he had placed a second mark, the teacher measured the distance and showed considerable surprise that the estimate was within 0.5 centimeters of the distance required.

An area in which Gary certainly showed ability well above average was in the various oral language tasks in the final assessment (rank 6). In this, he contrasted quite markedly with Tony, whose oral language rank was considerably below the ranks that he achieved in reading and writing. What is significant about this comparison, however, is that in neither case did the level of oral language ability have a noticeable effect on rated overall achievement.

Abigail.   Like Tony, Abigail was another child who improved her position in the rank order after entry to school. Although certainly never a slow developer, she was somewhat overshadowed at home by her elder sisters and did not receive a very large share of her parents' undivided attention. Although she listened to stories more frequently than most, they weren't always read for her benefit alone. Nevertheless, she shared in her sisters' interest in reading and other activities associated with literacy so that, when she started school, she was very clear what books were about, even though she could not actually read.

This emerged very clearly at the first observation, when she had been at school about six weeks. Towards the end of the morning, the teacher asked her to fetch her reading book and read to her.

Abigail [*reading*]: They . . liked . the water . . Pat . likes . the water . . Pat likes—

After helping her to complete this sentence, the teacher told Abigail to put her book away and choose what she would do next. Abigail went to the book corner and, having chosen a book, she pretended to be the teacher, reading a story to two of her friends. Using the pictures as cues, she "read" a story, which started as follows:

Abigail: When me and Tom went upstairs to the attic we—Tom pretended
   to be a tiger.
   I found a jewel and inside the jewel was—inside the jewel was a—a bit
   of velvet, a picture and a old violin.
   And a cupboard full of—full of buttons: silver buttons and gold buttons
   and ordinary buttons.
   I found an umbrella there, but Tom got on the pile of books and looked
   out of the attic window.

The whole story was read with considerable verve and expression. It ended as follows:

Abigail: She gave her little daughter a purple fan and three beads. Then they
   sat downstairs and had their tea. Then Grandma said good-bye to me.

Although Abigail's parents did not themselves give her much specific help with schoolwork (rank 24 =), the home environment they provided was both stimulating and supportive, and the example of her sisters and their occasional help were sufficient to get her "hooked on books" and reading well by the time she was 7 (rank 8). From then on she was an enthusiastic reader and writer. In fact, when asked what she thought she might be when she grew up, she replied as follows:

Abigail: I might try to be an actor but not—but I think it's much too hard
   remembering all the things—the words. I don't think I'll ever get on
   television. A writer—poems and stories—really. For young people, not
   for old people—for infants really.
Interviewer: D'you do writing at home?
Abigail: I write stories and I've written a lot of poems. I write letters a lot
   to relatives and friends—pen-friends. I've got two pen-friends. One lives
   in America and one lives in Canada. I write to them about once every
   two weeks and then if I don't get a letter back in say the next two
   weeks, I'll write again.

Abigail was an adventurous writer, as can be seen from her way of tackling the task relating to the cartoon. The judges were strongly divided on its merits and in the end, despite its dramatic originality and its inventive exploitation of written form, it was ranked rather low on the grounds that it did not tell a story. The following is what she wrote:

HELP!

"He,s going to fall off the edge of the
cliff" murmured all the animals. "Serves
him right for almost killing us" said
Leo the lion. "I think he was quite
nice" sais mussels the monkey "you would"
said Ricky the rhinoceros "I don,t know
why you are called mussels your such a
softy". "Don,t be so mean Ricky" said
Avril the elephant "he used to be
very strong". "You lot ssstop nattering on
he,s going to fall" said silly snake.
Look he,s . . . . "Hellllp" . . . . . falling" said
Torpedo the tortoise.

Her account of her happiest moment, on the other hand, was much more conventional in form and, with its impressive control of the future-in-the-past tense and its careful shaping towards a climax, consciously literary in style. This piece was unanimously rated one of the most successful and, in its contrast with the previous piece, shows just how dangerous it is to judge a child's ability as a writer on a single text.

THE HAPPIEST MOMENT IN MY LIFE

We were going to go on a holiday
round a little bit of Europe.
Instead of going through France and into
Spain we were going round
through France into Germany then into
Austria where we would stay in a
small Austrian farm house for 4 days.
After that we would move on to Italy
there we stayed in a newly built
hotel with only 10 other people staying
there. Just across the road was a lake
where we could swim or hire a
surf sail or float or paddle in our
small rubber dingy it was absolutely
sensational just swimming in fresh
water. But the only sad thing there
was a thunder storm every evening in Italy.
But then we had to turn back to go
home such a sad thing when you
are having fun.

Abigail regularly went on holidays abroad. Indeed, her first memory was of a camping holiday in France: "I'm sure it's a strange thing to remember, but I remember doing the washing up in a bowl after we'd had chicken noodle soup. Just can't forget it." Even more vivid in the impression it gives of her is her memory of another, more recent outing:

Abigail: I like visiting places—old castles and old houses. My cousins came over one day and we went to Berkeley Castle and we looked round the gravestones and there was a very old grave where a jester whose master had died—he'd carved something on the side of it. A poem or something.

Abigail described herself as "a fun person." Her teacher wrote: "She responds well in class to what is offered, being an industrious child with a fairly serious approach to life generally. However, she is not without a sense of humor." Certainly both sides of her personality were revealed in the interview, which was one of the most interesting to listen to.

Like all children, Abigail enjoyed school for the opportunity it gave her to be with friends. But she also enjoyed (most of) the work that she was expected to do. In her account of a typical day at school, she referred to the project she was doing on "British life—our homes and our country" as "exciting" and, when asked if there was anything she did not like about school, she talked only about the things she did like, concluding "Without school I think I'd be very bored."

Not surprisingly, she was considered to be an excellent pupil and above average in potential. Her achievement at age 10 would certainly confirm this. She was ranked second in both oral language and in reading, and her vocabulary was judged by her teacher to be among the most extensive (four children tied for the first rank). In overall achievement, she was ranked 2.

Penny.   Somewhat like Gary, Penny is a child whose achievement at school did not fulfill the expectations that one might have formed on the basis of her oral language development in the preschool years. From most advanced at age 2, she dropped to rank 12.5 = on entry to school and then remained at about that level. Although she apparently rarely had stories read to her, Penny engaged with interest in a variety of other literacy-related activities (as was seen in chapter 5), entered school with a fairly good score on the knowledge of literacy test (rank 10), and was reading better than average at age 7. At age 10, however, her reading score was ranked considerably below average (21.5 =), well below her rank for oral language (8). On the other hand, her writing was above average (11), as was the teacher's estimate of the size and range of her vocabulary (5.5 =), and this was enough for her overall achievement to be ranked 13.

A vivacious child, Penny was described by her teacher as very skillful in games and other physical activities, although physically underdeveloped for her age. She herself listed swimming and cricket among her favorite activities and also playing games with large groups of friends. When asked about the things she liked doing at home, she mentioned helping her parents with jobs around the house (already apparent in the observation at age 2), but really became enthusiastic when talking about going out with her parents:

Penny: Sometimes we goes out Chew Valley Lake. My Dad and my Mum comes and the dog and we all runs around until it gets to about half past eight. Then we goes home. Then my mum says: "Go and have a wash and get ready for bed." And I goes and gets ready for bed while she makes my supper. And I goes up to bed, she tucks me in and says good night and she turns off the light.

The same enthusiasm comes across in her account of her happiest day, an event that she remembered in great detail. Like Abigail, Penny seems recently to have learned how to represent direct speech with conventional punctuation. The effect here is of an event recalled with pleasure in a good gossip.

SITUATION 1

The Happiset moment of my life was when I was
sevan years old. My uncle was getting Married
and I was asked to be a bridesmaid My uncle
said to me "Will you be a bridesmaid?" and I
answered him "What is that?" He told me and
I replied with a "yes." He said "We'll have you in
a long dress and white gloves socks and sandals." I went
with his fiance Mary. We went to a shop and
chose a hairdo She said to me "We won't
have you dressed yet as the wedding has
to be rehearsed so I left the shop and we
entered the florist and I chose a boquet. Net
we went to the dress shop and I chose an
off-white creme dress. She said "If it will go
with your shoes and socks you may have
that one." I replied "OK". Next of all I went
for my white shoes they were closed in and
lined with a gold strap. I put them on and
I chose them. Next we went in shops
for white glove I got a pair
a bit on the large side but it didn't
show so I had them and last of all
I chose a hairband which was white with
flowers and it had white ribbon. Mary put
all these neatly into a bag until I wanted
to see if it all went together she said you
chose it nicely. When the friday evening
came I went to the hairdressers and
I had my hair curly. When Saturday
came I drove to Marys and I

got dressed I put on my shoes and socks
after bathing and put on my dress I then
put on my belt, and Mary put my hairband
on I had my bouquet in my hand
and I turned round towards Mary
She said "You look splended"
And she put on her dress and we were
off to St. Barnabas church. When I walked
up the isle I felt happier than I had ever
felt before "I said to myself Why did
I say yes?" When we got out of
the church I said "I'm glad I did"
and We had pictures taken and it started
raining.

Despite her obvious enjoyment of life at home, Penny preferred to be at school because of the opportunities it provided for sports and for social contact with her friends. But, like Abigail, she also enjoyed the academic work at school and liked and was liked by her teachers. In fact, to be a teacher was her ambition for the future.

Academically, Penny was rated by her teacher to be above average in both achievement and potential. This was attributed both to her hard work and enthusiasm and to the influence of her home, which was described by her teacher as being "sensible and supportive." Certainly, this is the impression that emerges from her parents' answers in the interview with them and from the evidence of the preschool recordings (see chapter 5). Penny herself mentioned reading as one of her favorite activities at home, particularly in bed at night, and she also said that she wrote stories and poems at home and kept a "sort of diary." It is surprising, therefore, that her reading score was so low and that, when compared with the other children in the sample, her overall achievement did not rank more highly than just above average.

Jonathan.   In the whole sample, Jonathan is the child who most clearly demonstrates the connections that have been set out in the previous chapters. By age 3½, he had already reached the level of oral language development typical of the average 5-year-old and, as the extracts in chapter 2 show, he was capable of conversing on a wide variety of topics. An only child, Jonathan was also outgoing and, on occasions, even argumentative. As a result, he elicited a large amount of conversation from his parents, both of whom took his comments and questions seriously and attempted to respond in ways that would extend both his thinking and his means of expression.

Jonathan's interest in stories and in written language generally was already apparent by age 2 and over the following three years he had a rich diet of stories and of conversation about them. By the time he entered school, he already understood the principles of reading and writing and was quick to learn to read, being ranked 3 at age 7. From then on, he was ranked first or first equal on every measure and, as will be seen below, produced at age 10 by far the most mature pieces of writing.

Reading continued to be one of Jonathan's favorite occupations. At age 10, he had this to say:

Jonathan: I do quite a lot of reading. I'm very interested in books. Mum calls me a bookworm [*laughs*]. And I like mysteries. I like Enid Blyton, the Famous Five mysteries and the ones that she does in series, you know, with a group of people and she does, say, twelve mysteries on that. And the ones I liked best out of those were *Famous Five* and *The Five Find Out.* I like most mysteries. I'm not all that keen on fact books. I like fiction most. I read one by Julie Andrews, I think it was— someone like that. It was called *The Last of the Really Great Wandoogles.* They've got it in the library across there. It's awfully imaginative but it's very good. I like the ones like that, you know, where—It's way out. It couldn't happen but it's lovely.

Mysteries were not the only sort of books that Jonathan read, though. In describing a typical school day, he mentioned being read to by his teacher, specifically *The Lion, the Witch and the Wardrobe*—a book "which I'd read about ten times and knew nearly off by heart." He also regularly read the newspaper.

Jonathan: I read a few articles in it. I've been reading a lot about the Falklands lately because I like to see what's happening. They don't have that on there [television], the hue and cry's died down a bit. . . . I usually just read the headlines if they're interesting and I look at the jokes in the middle page.

However, Jonathan was not only a bookworm. He talked with enthusiasm about his bikes, of which he had two, and about swimming, which he took very seriously. He would have liked to pursue this in what he called a "sports school," but his Mum and Dad could not afford the fees. He also talked very knowledgeably about dog shows, to which he and his parents went with their own dog.

As might be expected, Jonathan enjoyed school.

Jonathan: It's a good place 'cos I got all my friends here. Most of my friends I got from school. I haven't really got many other people apart from at school. If it's at home for six weeks—I do sometimes get a bit bored during the summer holidays.

I like nearly everything except Geography. And I do get a bit bored with decimal points 'cos Miss does have a lot of it with us. I know how to do it—a lot of people don't—so I get a bit bored with that. . . . I like English, but not the punctuation and grammar, you know. I like the essays best of English—writing a nice long essay. Miss tries to make me do short ones, but I can't.

On the writing tasks that we set, however, both Jonathan's texts were short. Perhaps the challenge of writing to a topic of someone else's choosing was valuable discipline in his case for, although short, both display a level of maturity that is considerably beyond that achieved by any of the other children. Here is his account of his happiest moment.

THE HAPPIEST MOMENT OF MY LIFE

The happiest moment of my life
was as I bit into a rich, meaty
cornish pasty after a day's
weary travelling (at least that
was what it seemed like) and
a weeks holiday of golden sands,
ice creams and sun stretched
out before me. We were camping
on a quiet grassy hill; hill
especially. I felt that nothing
could be better. I was right.

As I read this text, the first thing that strikes me is the writer's control of his material in the long first sentence. His happiest moment is indeed a moment—the first bite into a pasty. However, this moment is itself presented as marking a divide, a pinnacle in time, from which the writer looks back down one side into the past to the weary travelling, and forward down the other to the holiday that "stretches out" before him. Perhaps this effect is fortuitous, however, and no more than a happy accident? I think not. For, as one reads on, one finds that the hill is a real one and the prospect from it is both literal and metaphorical. If further proof is needed of the deliberateness of the structure, one has only to note the contrast between the long first sentence and the two short final ones. In this context, the last sentence has a ring of assurance that convinces me that the writer is very conscious of the effect he is trying to achieve.

The second narrative is equally accomplished, but in a quite different way.

"WHERE'S THE ARK?"

Noah twisted his fingers awkwardly
behind his back as the animals
stared at him.
"But how *can* you forget to build
an ark?" asked the giraffe.
"I left a lovely field of juicy
worms to come here" chirped
a bird indignantly. "I demand
compensation!"
Meanwhile Noah was slowly
walking backwards, and eventually

fell off the cliff. Luckily he
fell on a wooden raft.
"Good old Noah!" yelled the
animals, and dived on with him.

There can be no doubt about the deliberate artistry here. It is to
be seen immediately in the way in which an atmosphere of tension is
created in the first sentence, and in such other details as the characterization of the bird and the use of italics on "can" to achieve the
tone of incredulity in the giraffe's question. But what is most remarkable is the confidence with which he assumes his reader's knowledge
of the biblical account of the building of the ark—a knowledge which
is essential for an appreciation of the humor of this version. For a child
of 10 to manage the allusion with such assurance is proof both of his
very considerable ability as a writer and of the richness of his personal
literary experience.

A year after the interview, in response to an open invitation to all
the children to send further examples of their writing, Jonathan showed
us what he meant by writing at length. He sent us a 37-page story—
another mystery—that he had written at school. It was in eight chapters
and was entitled *The Poisoned Griffin*.

It started in the local park, where two children happened one day
upon a griffin, who surprised them by being able to talk. He explained
that he had been poisoned by a witch and that he would die unless he
found the antidote to the poison. The children agreed to help him and,
towards the end of the search, they finally tracked down the old witch
who, they believed, still had the antidote.

CHAPTER VII   THE 'LITTLE OLD LADY'

Standing in the doorway was about the ugliest woman
imaginable. She had an egg-shaped bald head, one tooth,
bloodshot eyes and a nose that would make Pinnochio's look
like a pug's.
"Well", she hissed ungraciously, the vile stench of her
breath flooding over them, "What is it?"

It took Anthony some time to recover from the fumes, but
when he did, he spoke up.
"We were interested in the contents of a bottle you bought
at the bric-a-brac stall," he told her.
"What's that?" she screeched.
"WE ARE INTERESTED IN THE CONTENTS OF A BOTTLE YOU GOT
AT THE JUNK STALL!!!"
"What's contents?"
"The stuff inside!!!"
"Alright, I'm not deaf, you know," she wheezed.
"So they wants the compens, does they?" she muttered.

"Yus dearies, for ten gold peecis you can 'ave de condens
and welcome!"
"Done!"
"Oh, so dey's got the money, 'as dey? You can 'ave it for
twen'y gold pieces."
"We've only got fifteen," lied Clare.
"Yus? Well you c'n 'ave it for dat."

The lady grabbed the money from Anthony, shoved a bottle into
Clare's hands and slammed the door shut.

This is perhaps the most remarkable section of the story, with the
invention of the special representation of the witch's speech to convey
her ingratiating but untrustworthy character. But the rest of the story
is equally impressive in its control of style and its management of the
extremely complicated plot. Finally, after a day of nerve-racking sus-
pense, the antidote is found and the griffin is saved. Taking to their
magic carpet again, they reluctantly return to their home. The adven-
ture is over.

Griffin gave Clare a solitary wink, shimmered and disappeared.

Jonathan was not sure what he would do when he grew up. His
mother had suggested that he should be a vet, as this would be very
convenient in relation to their interest in dogs. He himself had thought
of being a doctor or of joining the police. But at the time of the interview
he was thinking of becoming a writer! Whatever his final decision, we
can predict with some confidence that he will be well prepared when
he completes his schooling to embark on the training for his chosen
career—whatever that may eventually be.

■ FROM ORAL TO WRITTEN LANGUAGE

Six children cannot in themselves provide the basis for drawing conclusions that have general applicability. Those claims must be based
on the results from the larger sample, which were summarized at the
beginning of this chapter. However, these six children are more than
isolated examples for, in many respects, they illustrate very effectively
the more general trends. At the same time, comparisons between them
give a sharpness to many of the issues that the study set out to investigate. One of these is the relationship between spoken and written
language in the achievement profiles of the different children.

The two sets of tasks on which the assessments were based have
already been described. In several important respects, they were fairly

similar, despite the difference in the mode of production. Both required the children to produce extended monologues, and both included tasks with differing communication purposes. It might have been expected, therefore, that there would be a strong relationship between individual children's spoken and written performances. However, this did not prove to be the case. Certainly, there were many children, such as Jonathan and Rosie, whose ranks, either high or low, were very similar. But there was also a substantial number whose ranks on the two sets of tasks were quite widely separated. Examples would be Gary and Tony and, to a lesser extent, Penny. The questions we need to investigate, then, are why some children show such a discrepancy between their performances in speech and writing and whether this discrepancy has consequences for their more general academic achievement.

In either speech or writing, creating a text involves managing two rather different types of processes. On the one hand there are the processes of composing (forming an overall plan, selecting the appropriate content, and organizing it to fit that plan). To a considerable extent, these processes are similar whether speaking or writing is involved. The second type of processes, on the other hand, is concerned with the physical production of the text (the encoding of the content in sentences and their expression according to the conventions of pronunciation or spelling and handwriting). Because these latter processes involve a temporal sequence of skilled physical activity, they tend to lag behind the processes of composing, particularly in writing, and as a result to constrain their operation. Whether spoken or written, texts also have to meet other constraints, arising from the purpose to be achieved, the audience to be addressed, and the genre selected. Once again, these constraints are more severe in the case of writing because written genres are more differentiated from one another than are their oral counterparts.

After many years of using oral language for a wide variety of purposes, the constraints involved in producing a spoken monologue cause children little difficulty, provided the topic is relatively familiar. The texts they produce, therefore, provide quite a reliable indication of the effectiveness of their composing processes.[3] On the other hand, for the majority of children, writing is still a relatively unfamiliar mode of linguistic communication and the constraints involved are much more daunting. As a result, the actual texts they produce may give a much less reliable indication of their composing ability.

For beginning writers, it is handwriting and spelling that provide the most serious constraints. They require so much attention that little can be spared for the task of composing or for attending to the demands of text production that are specific to writing. Typically, written texts are very short at this stage, and within this limitation, are not very different from the texts that are created in spoken monologue. Rosie is the clearest example of a child who is still at this stage.

Once some control has been gained over the means of production, however, children are freed to give more attention to the composing process and to meeting the constraints imposed by the audience and by the genre in which they are working—fictional narrative, personal narrative, argument, and so on. At this stage, their success as writers will depend to a large extent on how well they are able to manage the formal aspects of writing (choice of vocabulary and grammatical structure, control over the means for achieving explicitness and cohesion, and so on) and on their degree of familiarity with the characteristic organizing structures associated with the different genres. Jonathan is an example of a child who has acquired considerable ability to take these constraints into account in his composing: all the samples of his writing quoted above show that he can organize and encode his material in order to achieve a specific literary effect. Abigail and Tony have also both made considerable progress in the same direction.

Where children are relatively unfamiliar with these structures, however, or with the distinctive formal characteristics of written language, their tendency will be to fall back on the structures in which they might express the same content in spoken monologue. In such cases, even if the content is interesting and the conventions of grammar, spelling, and handwriting are observed satisfactorily, the resulting text will still not be very effective as writing. This is the problem faced by both Penny and Gary. Penny's personal narrative of the day she was a bridesmaid, for example, contains a great deal of interesting detail, but because it is organized in essentially the form of a spoken monologue, it was not judged to be a particularly effective piece of writing.

However, such children do not necessarily lack skills in composing when these are applied to the creation of a spoken text. This is very clearly the case for Gary. His account of a typical school day was one of the most successful in terms of its overall narrative organization and the way in which interest was maintained by a combination of general statements and illustrative examples. In the following extract, he is describing what follows a physical education period on a typical afternoon.

Gary: Then we comes in . . gets changed. We has three minutes, or four minutes, to get changed . . sitting down for it. You got to change in silence 'cos if you don't you just miss another P.E. Then we—um—does English. We're doing about um—what is it? Bristol . . Bristol. And when the—when the people go to camp, we're going to go to see, er—We're going to go from school to Bristol Bridge. Then we're going to have a walk round—going to do things as if we people had gone to camp—then go to the Lifeboat Museum, and then a coach back to school. That's er . after June the nineteenth, I think. Yeh. Umm—we does that till half past three. Then it's home time.

In meeting the requirements of the task and in its vigor and concern for accuracy as well as interest, this account was undoubtedly one of the most effective.

In the case of children like Gary, then, a low rank in writing does not indicate poor skills in composing or a limited command of language. The limitation is rather in *experience* of *written* language. It is perhaps significant that, whereas Abigail spoke of the poems and stories she wrote and of her correspondence with her pen-friends and Tony spoke of his enjoyment of English lessons because of the imagination he could put into writing stories, Gary described a project for writing a book that still had to be begun and, when asked about how the book might be published, he disclaimed responsibility: "It's my sister. She's going to do it. It's up to her."

Unlike Tony, whose strength was in writing rather than in speaking, Gary's interest was in spinning a good yarn to an interested audience. By comparison, he found writing both more difficult and less satisfying. For this situation to change, it would probably be necessary for him to become "hooked on books," both as reader and as writer.

■ THE STATUS OF ORAL LANGUAGE IN THE CLASSROOM

Such discrepancies between oral and written language ability, then, can arise from a number of causes. However, where there is strength in either mode, there is evidence both of a satisfactory command of language and an ability to use it to good effect. Now, if assessment of educational achievement took equal account of success in either mode, discrepancies such as those shown by Gary or Tony would not be a matter of great concern. Such a child could draw on his or her area of strength in tackling other curricular activities and simultaneously use it as a help in improving in the weaker language mode. However, this does not seem to be the case. From our results, it appears that it is only strength in written language that is valued, ability in oral language contributing little to the overall assessment of achievement. Despite his lower rank in relation to oral language (11), for example, Tony, with a rank of 4 on writing and 3 on reading, was still ranked 3 overall. Gary, on the other hand, with a rank of 6 on the oral tasks but 18 on writing and 26 on reading, did not achieve a better overall rank than 22.

Such unequal valuation of children's performances in speech and in writing must lead us to ask whether the spoken mode really is intrinsically less satisfactory than the written as a medium for learning. The answer may appear to have already been given in the previous chapter, where I referred to the "centrality" of literacy. However, that is only part of the answer. Certainly, our aim should remain that of helping all children to acquire the skills of reflective thinking that are so closely associated with effective use of written language. But, as already emphasized, such skills are not developed and used only when actually reading or writing. The oral-written dimension is a continuum, and there are uses of spoken language that engage many of the same intellectual processes as are called upon in writing. For many children who lack facility with written language, therefore, oral language could perhaps provide a viable route towards the goal of effective thinking and symbol manipulation.

In other research on children of this age, it has been shown that groups of children can work successfully through discussion to solve problems,[4] to explore alternative possible explanations,[5] and to make a discriminating response to literature.[6] Interestingly, all these researchers noted that pupils worked much more effectively when the teacher was *not* present. Unless such discussions are tape-recorded, however, as was the case in each of these projects, teachers are unlikely to be aware of just how much children can achieve in speech; and, unfortunately, if their concern is largely confined to writing, they are not likely to be interested in finding out.

When we look at the skills in oral language that are typically displayed for teachers to evaluate, we begin to see why, in assessing achievement, they are accorded a so-much-lower status than skills in reading and writing. Consider the following extract from a lesson with children of about the same age as those under consideration; it was chosen by John Sinclair and Malcolm Coulthard as typical of those that their research team observed.

Teacher: Now then, I've got some more things here that cut things that you've seen before, I think. Scissors. What do I cut with scissors?

Pupil: Paper, paper.

Teacher: Yes, paper. Somebody's shouting out at the back! And I've got some more cutters here. What's that cutter called?

Pupil: A knife.

Teacher: A knife, yes. What do I cut with a knife?

Pupil: Food.

Teacher: I cut food. What kind of food would you cut with a knife?

Pupil: Meat?

Teacher: **You** tell me.

Pupil: Fish.

Teacher: Fish, yes.

Pupil: Meat.

Teacher: Meat, yes.[7]

The lesson continued in this style for more than 104 exchanges, and at no point did a pupil utter more than an elliptical sentence fragment. However, this is not surprising, since this is exactly the sort of response that the teacher's questions called for. But what is more disturbing than the constraining effect of the teacher's questions on the pupil's contributions is the fact that the pupils did not share the teacher's understanding of the purpose of the questions. Even if they had been allowed to speak without first being questioned, they would not have known the basis on which to offer relevant contributions.

In these circumstances, the teacher gets a very biased view of the pupils' oral language abilities. And yet this is the evidence on which his or her judgments are likely to be based. The pupil who appears most able will be the one who is most successful at guessing the framework within which the teacher is operating—which is indeed a skill, but not one that is particularly relevant to the task in hand. What the teacher will not be able to discover, however, from interaction of this sort is how well individual pupils are able to use their oral language resources to narrate a story, to describe a scene or situation, or to formulate, explore, and attempt to resolve a problem that they have made their own, and then to communicate effectively with others in carrying out the task and reporting the outcome. Yet these are precisely the oral language abilities that can help to develop the sort of thinking skills that are most typically associated with written language. Generally speaking, these uses of spoken language do not occur because teachers are not sufficiently aware of the intellectual potential of genuinely collaborative and exploratory talk; so they make little or no provision for it to occur.

This is particularly unfortunate for children like Gary, who, for lack of experience with written language, do not find it easy to learn through that medium. Not only are they constantly brought up against their limitations, but they are also given little opportunity to make serious use of the linguistic skills that they *do* possess.

To reiterate, I do not wish to suggest that mastery of written language should be accorded less importance than is presently the case—though the means used to achieve this aim may well require considerable rethinking—but rather that it should be recognized that spoken and written language provide different but complementary resources for learning. However, for children who are slower in acquiring control of the written mode, spoken language can be exploited to enable them to develop and use some of the skills in symbol manipulation that are so essential for intellectual development.

At the same time, I also want to make a plea for a greater recognition of the educational value of spoken language more generally. Although in certain respects speech clearly has limitations—its transience, for example, and the consequent difficulty of reflecting on the verbal formulations of ideas that are produced—it also has compensating advantages. Writing and reading tend to be solitary activities and are all too often competitive. Talking and listening, on the other hand, are by definition social and, at least potentially, collaborative. They therefore provide an excellent means for fostering collaboration in learning through the pooling of ideas and the negotiation of points of view. These experiences are valuable for all pupils, of course, not simply for those whose written language skills are less well developed. But for this latter type of pupil they are likely to provide a particularly effective means of learning.

Ten

THE SENSE OF STORY

What has emerged in the preceding chapters as the major determinant of educational achievement is the extent of a child's mastery of literacy. As children progress through the primary years, the content of the curriculum comes increasingly to be presented symbolically through uses of language that are more characteristic of writing than of conversation. Without the ability to cope with this literate form of language, therefore—that is to say, with the linguistic representation of ideas that are disembedded from a context of specific personal experience—children become progressively less able to meet the demands of an academic curriculum and, whether justly or not, are judged to be intellectually limited.

This is not a new discovery, of course, but what has become increasingly clear from our longitudinal study is just how early these crucial differences between children begin to be established. By the time they came to school, the rank order of the children in our study was already fairly firmly established. This is not to say that school made no difference. Indeed, all the children made considerable progress during the five years of school through which we followed them. But, because the schools provided rather similar learning environments, individual children did not change their relative position in the rank order very much. Several gained or lost a few places, it is true, and there is good reason to believe that this was partly due to the quality of the teaching they received.[1] However, there is little doubt that, in accounting for the *differences* between children, the major influence was that of the home, particularly during the preschool years and the first year or two at school.

There are many ways in which parents foster their children's development in these years, not least through the quality of their conversation with them. But what this study clearly demonstrates is that it is growing up in a literate family environment, in which reading and writing are naturally occurring, daily activities, that gives children a particular advantage when they start their formal education. And of all the activities that were characteristic of such homes, it was the sharing of stories that we found to be most important.

On the surface, this may not appear remarkable. We have always known that reading stories to children is a worthwhile activity. However, as I thought about our results, I began to wonder whether there was not more to stories than was suggested by the simple relationship between reading stories and learning to read. At the same time, I began to read some of the work that had been carried out on stories from other perspectives. Gradually, the various findings from our study began to fit together for me, forming a pattern around the concept of storying. This chapter is a first attempt to sketch out that pattern.

What I want to suggest is that stories have a role in education that goes far beyond their contribution to the acquisition of literacy. Constructing stories in the mind—or *storying*, as it has been called—is one of the most fundamental means of making meaning; as such, it is an activity that pervades all aspects of learning. When storying becomes overt and is given expression in words, the resulting stories are one of the most effective ways of making one's own interpretation of events and ideas available to others. Through the exchange of stories, therefore, teachers and students can share their understandings of a topic and bring their mental models of the world into closer alignment. In this sense, stories and storying are relevant in all areas of the curriculum.

■ MAKING SENSE THROUGH STORIES

There has probably never been a human society in which people did not tell stories. Many of them went unrecorded, of course; but, as is still the case in nonliterate societies, the most important were preserved in oral form and handed down from one generation to the next. These formed the culture's heritage of myths and legends: stories that attempted to explain and give coherence to the otherwise inexplicable. This continues to be, at least in part, the function of literature in literate societies, in which a sizeable proportion of the population have both the ability and the time to read. There are, of course, important differences between the essentially social conditions under which stories are created and recreated in an oral culture and the much more solitary conditions under which most written literature is created and interpreted. But the underlying purpose is the same: to provide a cultural interpretation of those aspects of human experience that are of fundamental and abiding concern.

Such public stories, however, are only the most highly developed and polished instances of a form of human behavior that is both universal and ubiquitous. Whenever people come together socially, they begin to exchange stories—personal narratives, anecdotes, or just snippets of gossip. James Britton refers to such stories as language used "in the spectator role," and he contrasts this with the use that is made of language when we are involved as "participants" in getting things done. Freed from the demands that are made on us when we are actually engaged in practical events, we are able as spectators to adopt a more reflective attitude—to look for their inner consistency and structure and to express it in the stories of everyday conversation and later, perhaps, in writing.[2]

Such stories do not only offer a personal interpretation of experience, however. Because they occur in the context of social interaction and are produced in conversation, they, like all other conversational meanings, are jointly constructed and require collaboration and negotiation for their achievement. In this way, members of a culture create a shared interpretation of experience, each confirming, modifying, and elaborating on the story of the other. Whether at home or at work, in the playground or in the club, it is very largely through such impromptu exchanging of stories that each one of us is inducted into our culture and comes to take on its beliefs and values as our own.

Even this, however, does not take us to the heart of the pervasive significance of stories. For what is done socially and verbally in conversation has its roots in the perceptual and cognitive processes through which, as individuals, we make sense of all of our experience. Each act of recognition, whether it be of objects in the external world perceived through our senses or of a conceptual relationship "seen" through an act of the mind, involves a sort of inner storying. This is how we make sense of it.

Rarely, if ever, do we have all the necessary visual or other sensory information to decide unambiguously what it is we are seeing, hearing, or touching. Instead we draw on our mental model of the world to construct a story that would be plausible in the context and use that to check the data of sense against the predictions that the story makes possible.[3]

Waking in the middle of the night, for example, I creep downstairs without switching on the light to get a cool drink from the refrigerator. But as I pass the table in the dining room, I decide to have an apple instead and reach out my hand to the fruit bowl, which I know is in the middle of the table. To my surprise, however, the object that I touch, although spherical and apple-sized, is furry and slightly springy. It does not match my expectations at all. At this point, processes that had been going on unattended now become the focus of my attention. I search for a story that will enable me to make sense of my sensations and finally I recall an episode earlier in the afternoon when my son had found a tennis ball in the garden and asked what he should do with it. I had suggested putting it in the fruit bowl so that we would remember to give it back to our neighbors. So now, with this story, I am able to interpret my sensation: what I am grasping is not an apple but a misplaced tennis ball.

This example concerns an occasion unusual enough for the task of finding an interpretative story to require conscious attention. However, it illustrates rather clearly the processes whereby, in every act of perception, the world "out there" is interpreted in relation to the inner mental model in terms of which that world is represented. Making sense of an experience is thus to a very great extent being able to construct a plausible story about it.

Stories in this sense surround the infant from the moment of birth. Even before they can talk, infants begin to construct a mental model of their world, based on the regularities in their experience, and in due course this model plays a major part in helping them to make sense of their linguistic experience and so to learn the language of their community. By reference to it they construct mental stories about the shared context—Mummy preparing dinner, the birds eating berries—and use them to predict the meanings of the utterances that are addressed to them. At the same time, stories provide the framework within which their own behaviors are interpreted; and, as children begin to speak and understand the speech of others, their view of the world is strongly influenced by the stories that other people offer them, as they interpret their experience for them and recount the stories of other people's experiences. In this way, stories are woven into the tapestry of a child's inner representations, producing the patterns that give it significance.

Thus, although storying may have its roots in the biologically given human predisposition to construct mental stories in order to make sense of perceptual information, it very quickly becomes the means whereby we enter into a shared world, which is continually broadened and enriched by the exchange of stories with others. In this sense, the reality each one of us inhabits is to a very great extent a distillation of the stories that we have shared: not only the narratives that we have heard and told, read, or seen enacted in drama or news on television, but also the anecdotes, explanations, and conjectures that are drawn upon in everyday conversation, in our perpetual attempts to understand the world in which we live and our experiences in it.

■ THE DEVELOPMENT OF NARRATIVE

What has just been suggested is that storying is one of the most fundamental means whereby human beings gain control over the world around them. In Barbara Hardy's words, it is "a primary act of mind."[4] In its beginnings, therefore, storying is not a conscious and deliberate activity, but the way in which the mind itself works.

At a later stage, however, there does begin to be a conscious shaping. To narrate a story—to tell it in words—necessarily involves a selecting and ordering of the elements to be brought together. This is true even of 2-year-olds, though to begin with they may require considerable assistance from an adult if the original impulse to link events in a narrative structure is to come to fruition. In the following example, Mark provides the embryonic outline of a narrative structure as he makes the connection between his observation that the man has gone and the shop that he himself had visited in the past; his mother helps him to extend the structure with her questioning prompts.

[*Mark has been watching a man making a bonfire in his garden (see p. 24).*]

Mark: Where man gone? Where man gone!

Mother: I don't know. I expect he's gone inside because it's snowing.

　　[*A brief silence*]

Mark: Where man gone?

Mother: In the house.

Mark: Uh?

Mother: Into his house.

Mark: No. No. Gone to shop, Mummy. [The local shop is close to Mark's house.]

Mother: Gone where?

Mark: Gone shop.

Mother: To the shop?

Mark: Yeh.

Mother: What's he going to buy?

Mark: Er—biscuits.

Mother: Biscuits, mm. What else?

Mark: Er—meat.

Mother: Mm.

Mark: Meat and . . sweeties. Buy a big bag of sweets.

Mother: Buy sweets?

Mark: Yeh. M—er—man buy sweets.

Mother: Will he?

Mark: Yeh. Daddy buy sweets. Daddy buy sweets.

Mother: Why?

Mark: Oh er—uh shop. Mark do buy some sweeties. Mark buy some—um—
Mark buy some—um—I did.

By age 4 or 5, children are often able to manage the narration by themselves, although the causal relationships are frequently left implicit in the ubiquitous use of "and" or "and then."[5] However, by this age we also begin to see another dimension of stories, in the form of dramatic or imaginative play. Here the function of the narrative is not reflective—to give significance to events recalled or anticipated—but rather to create a framework that will guide subsequent action and allow it to be interpreted by the other participants so that their activities may be coordinated.

[*Lee (age 5) and Robert (age 6) are playing cops and robbers.*]
Robert: Right. I'm Starsky. You're Hutch.
Lee: Hello. I'm Hutch.
Robert: You don't need to go in there [imaginary building].
Lee: I'm going in.
Robert: Come out.
   [*Lee makes car noises.*]
   I drive. Starsky drives. [*He pretends to drive.*]
Lee: No. I've got to take my car.
Robert: No. They have—have only got one car.

One of the striking characteristics of such play is how much of the time is spent negotiating roles and appropriate actions, with the result—in some cases—that there is no time left actually to put the decisions into effect! When such play is successful, though, one clearly sees the important structuring role of the story, enabling the participants to integrate their imaginary worlds.

In the following example, Sam, John, and David, all aged 5, are playing with a variety of play-people and animals. David has a cardboard box: this is his base. Sam also has his own territory, a wooden boat, on which he has a family of lions. All around them is the sea—the playroom carpet. At this point in their play, John, who also has a boat and an assortment of play people, is torn between joining David on his base or Sam on his boat. The problem is that neither base nor boat has sufficient room for all John's people. As each child contributes from his own imaginary world, it is the jointly constructed narrative line that enables them to integrate those worlds in a collaborative manner and to manage the interpersonal conflicts that so often arise in the course of play. (*Note:* in the following dialogue, utterances in italics are spoken in "play" voices appropriate to the characters concerned.)

Sam [*to John, to take his play-people somewhere else*]: Now you have to live on your boat.

David [*to self*]: 'Tend it was put down like that [*arranging his base*].

John [*to Sam*]: Why? Why do we?

Sam. 'Cus there was no room for you [on his boat]

[*David puts people, furniture, etc. into his base.*]

John: Pretend we was sending trials back [*moves Sam's boat with the lions on*].

Sam: [*speaking as lions*]: No, that's our boat. That's our boat.

John: No, but pretend we was sav—saving them back so people could get, um—[*to David, who has got in the way*] That was your fault.

Sam: O.K., we're living on here [on the boat].
Oh, we'll die.

[*John begins to put his people on David's base.*]

David: We—we've got all the luggage. *I'm going to sleep.* [*Pretends to cry.*] All our luggage is—is— One of, er—one of our boyfriends is crying in a corner [*pretends to cry*]. Pretend one of the—the—their children was crying in a corner [*pretends to cry*].

Sam: Why was that?

David: It was because they didn't like being on the— [*pretends to cry*]

Sam: They didn't like being on land.

David: —all squashed up, did they?

Sam: No, they didn't like being—

David: They went outside, didn't they?

Sam: Yeh, and they had to go out. And it was poison on the sea and they had to die, didn't they?

John: No, they didn't. They got on this boat [the lion's boat]. They jumped on to there. They was good jumpers.

Although the reader of this extract probably has some difficulty in following the thread, the children clearly had none. Even when their suggestions were in conflict, they listened to each other's contributions to the jointly constructed story and modified their actions in ways that were mutually acceptable. One interesting feature of this particular example is the use of the past tense in those utterances which develop the narrative. It is as if they know that, to be recounted, the actions must already have happened, and it is tempting to see in this the influence of the stories they have heard, for all three boys were frequently read to. It seems likely that being read to is also the source of their much greater sophistication in making the narrative structure explicit. Certainly their experience of stories enriches the range of their imaginative play—the roles they take on and the understanding they show of their characters' thoughts and feelings in the predicaments in which they set them.

As many writers have argued, this sort of dramatic play can have particular significance in enabling children to explore and work through emotions that are too urgent to cope with in the actual world and too frightening in the world of inner reality. Play provides a relatively safe area, in many ways complementary to the imaginary worlds created by the fairy tales and other powerful stories that children hear, in which the narrative structure serves to contain and make intelligible feelings that might otherwise remain violent but inarticulate.[6]

■ THROUGH STORIES INTO READING AND WRITING

In the previous section, I have traced the early development of storying and considered the interpretative power of stories in a number of interpersonal situations: narratives and anecdotes in conversation, stories told or read aloud from books, stories explored in talk,[7] and stories created in dramatic play. In all these settings, children are able to come to a greater understanding of their own experience through relating it to the experience of others, whether real or imaginary. At the same time, through interacting with others in the creation and interpretation of stories, their own inner storying is sustained and enriched and its effectiveness as a means of making sense of experience confirmed. And since stories can only be shared with others through language, children have also been led to discover, albeit unconsciously, the enormously facilitating power that language has, as a symbolic mode of representation, in organizing and shaping the thoughts and feelings that are garnered from experience.

With this in mind, I think we can now see more clearly why the early experience of listening to stories is such a good preparation for learning to read and write. In conversation, children discover the forms of oral language that correspond to their inner storying. But in listening to stories read aloud they not only extend the range of experience they are able to understand but also begin to assimilate the more powerful and more abstract mode of representing experience that is made available by written language. Then, having already discovered one of the chief functions of reading and writing—that of conveying stories—they are prepared for the task of mastering this new medium and the conventions and skills that this involves.

What is needed at this stage, I am convinced, is opportunities to discover how meaning and graphic representation are related, through activities involving reading and writing that have purpose and significance in their own right. As in learning to talk, children have to construct their own understanding of written language and how to use it, and the best way of helping them to do so is by enabling them to approach the tasks of reading and writing as means of communicating meaning. Guidance will certainly be necessary but, as in conversation, it will be most helpful if it is responsive to the connections that children are making between their own meaning intentions and expectations and the written language forms of the texts that they are creating or interpreting.

What this implies is that reading and writing should be treated as complementary activities, work on one informing and enhancing the other. In some schools, the practice is to concentrate first on reading and to introduce writing only when a sight vocabulary of a certain size has been acquired. Not only is this artifical—it would be odd to suggest that children should only learn to talk when they had reached a fair degree of competence in comprehending the speech of others—but it is also counterproductive. Children who already know enough about the functions of written language to be able to embark on learning to read also know enough to be able to begin to write. This has been amply demonstrated recently by a variety of experimental and observational studies of children's spontaneous learning about literacy.[8]

What all these studies show is that, by the time they enter school, almost all children are able to write—at least in a rudimentary way—and that they gain a great deal of satisfaction from doing so and from having what they have written read by other people. In the early stages it may well be necessary to provide a transcription service—typing what the child has composed so that it can be read by other children and by the child him- or herself on a later occasion. The important thing, however, is that children make the discovery that they have experiences to share, stories to tell that others find interesting; that they belong to the fraternity of writers.

At the same time, in order to write, they must necessarily also learn to read, so that they can later interpret what they have written. For, if what a child has experienced is sufficiently significant to write about, it is likely to prove equally meaningful as material to read. An additional advantage of giving equal attention to writing in the early stages, moreover, is that writing requires a focus on the graphic display with an attention to detail that is more concentrated than in reading. An emphasis on writing as composing can thus also be a powerful spur to the development of reading.[9]

The range of situations in which children may find it meaningful to read and write is extremely wide, ranging from organizing routines around the classroom (such as feeding the hamsters or recording the stages in the development of tadpoles) to corresponding with parents and other people outside the classroom. But it is likely that for the majority of children it will be stories that assume the greatest importance.

The arguments for using picture storybooks as the staple for learning to read were set out in chapter 8. Similar arguments apply to stories as the form in which most children will find it easiest and most meaningful to learn to write. As will be clear by now, this does not only mean imaginary stories—though some children find their greatest satisfaction in creating stories about exciting worlds of princesses and dragons, monsters and space ships. Stories arise equally appropriately out of personal experience, at home or in the classroom, or from reading, watching television, or visiting places outside the school. One of David's earliest achievements as a writer, for example, was a book about insects, some of which he had encountered personally while others he had only met in picture reference books or through watching television. Whether based in reality or in fantasy, what is important is that what children write should be their own stories, not ones that are written to someone else's design. "Ownership" is vital if the child is to make a real commitment of time and effort to the task of learning the craft of writing.[10]

But perhaps the most important reason for advocating a strong emphasis on writing right from the beginning is its potential as a tool for learning. Once some proficiency in composing in this new medium has been acquired, writing provides a means of recording what has been observed or discovered through talking, listening, and reading and through reflection on those observations and discoveries. And because what has been written remains, it can form the basis for further discovery as the text that has been created is reread in order to launch off anew or engage in the process of revision. If, as Margaret Donaldson suggests, one of the prime aims of schooling is to become able to direct one's thought processes in a thoughtful manner, this is most effectively learned through writing.[11] Writing is, par excellence, the activity in which we consciously wrestle with thoughts and words in order to discover what we mean. "The process itself unfolds the truths which the mind then learns. Writing informs the mind, it is not the other way round."[12]

These suggestions for facilitating children's entry into literacy are based on the assumption that they have already had a wealth of experience of creating and responding to stories in a variety of interpersonal situations. Where such is the case, the transition to the more private activity of making meaning in writing, with all the new processes that this involves, is likely to be made without undue difficulty. But, as we have seen, there is a substantial proportion of children who come to school without this advantage. It is not that they lack stories to tell or write, it is rather that they lack familiarity with the way in which stories are constructed and given expression in writing.

For these children it is even more important that the emphasis should not be placed on the conventions and associated skills *in dissociation* from the purposes of reading and writing. Learning the sounds and names of the letters of the alphabet is clearly essential if they are to take possession of this new and exciting medium, but without an equal emphasis on the purpose and meaning of reading and writing *for them*, the mechanical skills may eventually be acquired, but the children will have no personal commitment to using them. On the other hand, what better way could there be to help these children achieve this commitment than through experiences that involve the creation, interpretation, and discussion of stories, first in speech and then also in writing?

For *all* children, then, stories continue to provide one of the most enriching contexts for the development of language, both spoken and written. As has been emphasized, facility in using language is a means to achieving communicative purposes, not an end in itself. For the most part, it is best achieved by attending to the purposes for which language is used, rather than to the linguistic form itself. Stories provide a real purpose for extending control over language, all the more effective because they also tap one of the child's most powerful ways of understanding, enlarging, and working on experience. In listening to, telling, reading, and writing stories, children simultaneously enrich and reorganize that experience and extend their linguistic resources the better to allow them to do so.

■ STORIES ARE FOR UNDERSTANDING

Having gained this enhanced understanding of the significance of stories and storying as a fundamental way of making meaning, I began to look at their place in education more generally. What I found was that, beyond the early years, they received little official recognition, except in the literature lesson and in "creative writing" sessions. School, it appears, is for learning about the "real" world and, for most teachers, a concern with stories seems frivolous and pupils' personal anecdotes an annoying and irrelevant interruption of the official matter of the curriculum. Stories are all very well for preschoolers and for learning to read and write. But, once the skills of literacy have been acquired, the emphasis should shift to facts—to real-world knowledge and the subject disciplines in terms of which that knowledge is organized. However, in the light of what we now understand about the fundamental significance of storying, I believe that such a view is inappropriate and the assumptions upon which it is based are mistaken.

The first mistake is in assuming that the imaginative and affective response to experience is of less value than the practical and analytic—or, indeed, in thinking that they are in competition. The education of the whole person, which is the declared aim of probably every school system, can only be achieved if there are opportunities to explore feelings and values in specific real or imagined situations as well as lessons devoted to the consideration of general principles. Indeed, as pupils get older, it is probably more rather than less important to help them to recognize that the knowledge that they encounter in the various subjects of the curriculum is arrived at as the result of the activities of specific individuals and that it has implications for the lives and actions of other individuals in the future. Inevitably, therefore, knowledge has moral and aesthetic dimensions as well as practical and conceptual ones, and a fully mature response is one that achieves a balance between them.

Such issues are raised, for example, when studying history, by the consequences of European conquest and settlement for the indigenous populations of all the other continents; in geography, by the exploitation of the earth's resources; in biology, by the possibilities of birth control or genetic engineering. But the same need for a balanced response to knowledge applies equally in other subject areas; and, in all areas, stories have a major role to play in achieving this, in the form of biographies, historical novels, newspaper and magazine feature articles and, of course, the stories that students bring in speech or writing from their own experience.

The second mistaken assumption concerns the simple opposition that is often made between fact and fiction: facts are true while stories, if not false, are certainly less accurate or reliable. Quite apart from the difficulty involved in deciding what is a fact, such a simple dichotomy fails to do justice to the interpenetration of fact and fiction in all branches of human knowledge.

All fiction—novels, plays, even fairy tales and science fiction—is firmly based in fact, in the sense that it is about recognizable people acting in recognizable ways, but in a "possible world" that differs in certain ways from any that has actually existed. To read or write fiction is not to abandon the search for truth, therefore, but to search for the truth within the world created by the imagination rather than the truth provided by documentary evidence, measurement, and so on.

However, if fiction is rooted in fact, so are facts embedded in something very similar to fiction. Isolated facts—items of information—only take on significance when they are related to other facts, and connections of various kinds made between them. Such coherent assemblages of related facts may then appear to correspond in a direct way to the reality that forms the background to our existence. Knowledge just is: given and unquestionable. Certainly, this is the impression that is created by many textbooks and works of reference. However, such a view is seriously misleading. As Richard Gregory showed in the article referred to above, the facts in any academic discipline are only facts within the framework of some theory, and theories share many of the imaginative "as if" characteristics of fiction. Moreover, as theories change through radical reconceptions of the subject matter with which they deal, so do the facts they underpin.

This point is put in a somewhat more humorous vein by Harold Rosen, when he writes:

A few days ago my son passed on to me a paper of his. It was sufficiently opaque for the title itself to be, for me, completely opaque. If I have understood the drift of one part of his argument, it is that if you aspire to becoming an invertebrate paleontologist you must be someone given to storytelling. What is geology but a vast story which geologists have been composing and revising throughout the existence of their subject? Indeed what has the recent brouhaha about evolution been but two stories competing for the right to be the authorized version, the authentic story, a macronarrative? There are stories wherever we turn. How do we understand foetal development except as a fundamental story in which sperm and ovum triumph at the denouement of parturition? Every chemical reaction is a story compressed into the straitjacket of an equation. Every car speeds down the road by virtue of that well-known engineer's yarn called the Otto cycle.[13]

If theories are "macro-narratives," similar in many respects to the stories we class as fictions, what about the way in which theories are constructed and knowledge built up? Does that not too form a story, in the succession of contributions of different thinkers to a particular discipline (for example, the progression in physics from Galileo to Newton to Einstein)? Equally, if we were to study the way in which intellectual and scientific advances are made by any one of these individual thinkers, would we not find that, at a rather abstract level, it involved a form of storying, as alternative hypothetical worlds were considered in order to decide which made the best sense of the available evidence?

On closer inspection, then, thinking—even advanced thinking—involves imagination as well as logical reasoning. To use Gregory's words:

By neither being tied to fact nor quite separate, fiction is a tool, necessary for thought and intelligence, and for considering and planning possibilities. Fiction is vitally important—indeed we may live more by fiction than fact.[14]

This is equally true for the developing thinker as well. Very young children, it is readily accepted, find it easier to assimilate new ideas when they are presented within the framework of a story. Only gradually do they learn to move from the particularized example to the general principle and from a narrative mode of expression to an expository or argumentative one. However, even older students find that illustrative anecdotes make general principles easier to grasp and, given the opportunity, will frequently look for such anecdotal examples in their own experience, as they work at new ideas in speech or writing in the attempt to assimilate the new material to what they already know. As students of all ages encounter new ideas, therefore, it is helpful to illustrate these ideas with stories—with particular contextualized examples—and to support their inner storying by encouraging them to work through the story mode themselves on the way to the expression of a more abstract formulation.

In the end, of course, it is important that students should be able to deal with abstractions and generalizations and to express them in the appropriate modes of discourse. But if, as has been suggested, storying is the most fundamental way of grappling with new experience, the best path to this achievement is likely, both developmentally and in the tackling of each new problem, to take them through the domain of stories, their own and other people's. Stories provide a major route to understanding.

■ STORIES ACROSS THE CURRICULUM

If these arguments are correct, we should expect to see stories continuing to occur in all subjects of the curriculum, in both speech and writing. Of course, the major function of stories will vary from one subject to another. In English or Language Arts, for example, there will be a concern with stories, along with plays and poems, for their own sake as works of verbal art. In science or humanities subjects, on the other hand, stories may have a much more incidental role—as a way of considering particular instances on the way to a more abstract understanding of a general principle or as illustration once that principle has been formulated. But, underpinning this diversity, we should expect to find a recognition that, in both speech and writing, a story drawn from experience can be an essential step on the route to more differentiated modes of knowing and of working on what is known.

Unfortunately, observations in classrooms suggest that this is rarely the case. In secondary schools, except in the English lesson, there is little opportunity for stories of any kind, particularly in the written mode.[15] When a student does proffer a story from personal experience, as in the example quoted from Barnes in chapter 5, it is often cut short as an irrelevant departure from the point of the lesson. Even in many elementary classrooms, the importance of stories is only recognized within the narrow confines of creative writing; and, if stories are read by the teacher or by individual pupils, it is often only as a way of filling odd moments when the "serious" work has been completed.

There are classrooms, however, at both elementary and secondary levels, where the curriculum is not fragmented in this way—where activities in one area are planned to lead into activities in another and where each is enriched by connections made with the others. In such classrooms, too, pupils are encouraged to collaborate on the tasks they undertake and, as a result, they learn from each other and discover the value of their own knowledge by having it accepted and validated by their peers. Not surprisingly, perhaps, when pupils are given the freedom and the responsibility to work in this way, there is ample evidence that it is indeed their natural impulse to tell and write stories as a means of achieving understanding and of making connections between what they are learning and what they already know.

Since this more integrated approach to learning is still not particularly common, I should like to describe in some detail one particular class of 10-year-olds who were working in this way. All the activities to be described took place in the course of a single day in a longer period during which this class was being recorded.[16]

The school, which was in southwest London, was celebrating its centenary, and this occasion provided the starting point for the greater part of the curriculum for most of a term. Within the theme of "Life a Hundred Years Ago," small groups of children, twos or threes, undertook individual projects in which they explored, through reading, writing, drama, painting, practical work, and discussion, some aspect of late-nineteenth-century life.

Not all the time was spent in these small groups, though. On the day in question, the teacher brought the whole class together to listen to the next chapter of *Journey into Yesterday*, a sort of science fiction story in which two children were carried back into the past and met a boy who was bedridden with pneumonia. In talking with him, they found themselves having to explain such technical matters as the working of a television set, motorcars and flight in the Concorde—matters which up till then they had taken for granted. As the teacher stopped reading at the end of the chapter, discussion spontaneously broke out among the pupils as they considered how they would try to give explanations. The following extract will give a taste of this discussion. One of the boys had just described the appearance of a car.

Teacher: How does it go, though?
Pupils: The engine—By engine.
Pupil 1: He might not know what an engine is.
Chad: Miss, he would know what an engine was because of a—er—steam engine.
Pupil 1: Oh, that's different though.
Pupil 2: Yeh. That doesn't work on steam, does it?
Pupil 3: It's different.
Pupil 4: It might be a different engine though, mightn't it?
Pupil 1: More technology.

Syena: Mind you—
Teacher: Sh! Let's hear.
Syena: Because it works differently. The steam engine works by fire and
   coal and um—the um—car—
Pupil 5: Yeh.
Pupil 6: Steam.
Syena: —works by petrol.

After some 15 minutes, during which the teacher intervened only
occasionally to assign speaking turns when several children were trying
to speak at once, she posed the more general question:

Teacher: Could you actually explain something about this to somebody—
Pupils: No.
Teacher: —who really didn't know anything at all about the type of things
   that you had?
Pupil 6: I'd ask him what their things are like.
Teacher: Yes, and then?
Pupil 7: Miss, if, um—the sort of things in those days were the same like
   today—well—it could be, you know—he could explain a bit easier.
Syena: It could be—you could compare it together in a way and see, er—Say
   you see some things the same as ours—say it works like that but it's
   different.

In the light of the discussion of facilitative conversation in chapter 3,
these answers seem remarkably perceptive.

Following this spontaneous discussion, the teacher called on two
of the girls, Syena and Niki. They had been finding out about schools
a hundred years ago and had chosen to present the results of their
research in the form of two related stories about a particular school.
The following is a transcription of the dramatic presentation of Syena's
version.

Syena: It's a story, um, about a Dame School and I'm the dame and Niki's
   the child. But I'm going to read **my** story. [*Reads*] The morning started
   when the children came in. When I thought everybody was here, I got
   one piece of paper—it was the only piece of paper that I had. On it was
   all the names in the class.
   "Susan?" "Yes, Miss Dame."
   "Abigail?" "Yes, Miss Dame."
   "Nicolette?"
   "Nicolette? Nicolette?"
   Then I looked up and saw Nicolette sleeping and said, "Susan, go and
   get the cane." So Susan got the cane and brought it to me. I walked
   slowly to the place where Nicolette was sleeping and I tapped the back
   of her neck. She suddenly woke up. I said, "Why were you sleeping in
   class? Stand up!" She got up—she got up and bent down. She knew
   what was going to happen. I got off the shelf a metal top which fitted

onto the cane. Then I took Nicky—that is what we called her for short—by the ear and I took the cane and hit her two times on her bottom. In a way I felt a little sorry for her. Then I asked her why—then I asked her why she was sleeping in class. She said:

Niki: "Miss Dame, I am very sorry but, er—but my mother and father had to work in the shop and because it was very busy I had to work too. So I went to bed very late. And I had to get up very early and clean the shop."

Syena: In the afternoon, I did some—we did some sums and Nicky got hers wrong. I hit her on the hand with the cane and put a dunce cap on her. The next day we did our chanting out. I found that Nicky could not sit down on her bottom for a long time. She did not look at me for a long time.

Teacher: Start that bit again.

Syena: So I said, "Nicky, tell me your letters, A to Z, and don't get them wrong or else!"

Niki: "A,B,C,D,E,F,G,H,I,M,N—"

Syena: "Stop! Stop!" I cried. "You've done it wrong. Why don't you learn them at home? Oh, I've forgotten, you have to work at your mother's and father's shop. I will come to your shop and see your mother and father and talk to them about your sums and letters." So after school I went with Nicky to her house and talked to her mother and father. In the morning, Nicky came to school on time. I asked her, "Tell me your five times table."

Niki: "One five is five. Two fives are . .

Syena [*whispering*]: Ten.

Niki: "Ten. Three fives are . . fif—er, sixteen."

Syena: "Sixteen is not in the five times table. I thought I told your mother and father you had to learn your letters and sums."

The other children were clearly appreciative of the story. But they also saw it, and its authors, as a source of information. Several questions followed about the school and its organization, with one of the other girls showing a particular interest in the dunce cap.

The teacher indicated that these questions should be addressed to the authors, the experts on this subject. And indeed their story does give a very accurate picture of a dame school, with its emphasis on rote learning and the use of corporal punishment for minor misdemeanors. It also captures another aspect of Victorian life—the exploitation of child labor. But what is equally impressive is the quality of the writing: the dramatic conception, the characterization, and such features as the aside, "that is what we called her for short," and the dame's moment of empathy, "In a way I felt a little sorry for her." Given the chance to choose a dramatic narrative form, these two girls have been able to convey what they have learned in a way that their classmates are obviously able to understand and appreciate.

However, the discussion did not stop at the historical content of the story. One of the children drew attention to the dame's apparent cruelty to Nicolette, and Syena replied at first in terms of her conception of the character of the dame. But as the discussion proceeded, the children began to explore some of the more complex issues involved, such as the difference between manner (tone of voice) and actions and the difficulty of capturing this in writing.

Syena: I didn't like her at all. And I was very cruel anyway, and I'd hit her for anything.

Eduardo: It gives you an example of, um . . how it was back in the past. It was like an example.

Teacher: Good.

Kurt: But the way Syena talked, she sounded quite nice.

Teacher: Do you think she sounded nice?

Theresa: Miss, she sounded like wicked.

Teacher: You thought she sounded wicked?

Theresa: Yeh.

Pupil: —like she was a wicked teacher.

Syena: I think really I had to. I don't think she sounded very wicked but— 'cos in the playground we sort of play . . um . . games when *I'm* a child in a dame school and she's the teacher. And she sort of is wicked when we're in the playground.

Niki: She shouts a lot.

Syena: But it's easier to act it than to write it down, I think.

William: Miss, it's like the words are wicked but her voice—she doesn't do the right examples of being wicked. It's just the words.

Teacher: What's William trying to say? [*5-second pause*] What's he saying, Kurt?

Kurt: He's, um, trying to say that the voice—you have to say it like the voice—like, um, you say things.

William: When she was about to hit her, she should have said, "Come here!" and had a kind of croaky voice, isn't it?

Patty: Miss, when we play in the playground the game of um, . . .

Teacher: Dame school?

Patty: Yeah, the dame school, Syena be the dame. Then she has a sister. Her sister bes kind. She bes wicked and they have a fight at the end. They kill each other.

Kurt: Miss, Syena didn't like Nicky very much in the story. But I don't understand really, because she said that she felt a little bit sorry for her.

Syena: Well, I did it because . . I like—I don't like—I didn't like her. But like, er, in the playground, if I hit someone or something, I feel sorry inside me, and it's—I think it's the same as if I were a teacher.

The story has obviously become more than a piece of schoolwork for these girls; it has also been assimilated to the perennial childhood game of "goodies and baddies." But for Syena, in addition, it has provided an opportunity for a growth in moral understanding, as she recognizes that, although they are in positions of power and authority, teachers, like her, may have feelings of shame or regret when they cause suffering to others.

Later the same day, the children were at work again on their group projects. Two were painting pictures of miners at work, others were reading and writing; a group of girls was discussing a story they had read, and another mixed group was engaged in weaving on a hand loom. The teacher went to join two boys, who were using a variety of books and other source material to find out about markets. After some discussion about what they had discovered from their reading, the teacher invited Chad to read aloud the story he had written and beautifully illustrated, about an escapade in a market. After he had finished, the teacher turned to Eduardo, who had spent his early life in Portugal.

Teacher: Is that kind of market very similar to the market you would have in Portugal, Eduardo?

Eduardo: No.

Teacher: Can you tell us something about a Portuguese market?

Eduardo: Well, it would be much busier and it have more things to sell. More—um, fruit and meat and, um— It did—doesn't have quite a lot of shops. It has more stalls. And it would be much busier than here. Because it would be more full of, um—fruit and meat and things. It would be much bigger and—

Chad: You mean it would be more crowded than the Portobello Market on a Saturday?

Eduardo: Yes. And it's, um—it's not very long, er, it's quite wide—wider.

Chad: You mean . . . it's a wide road?

Eduardo: Yes.

Chad: It's very wide?

Eduardo: Yes.

Teacher: Would it be a road?

Eduardo: No.

Teacher: What would it be?

Eduardo: Like, um—

Chad: A park or something? * * * .

Eduardo: It has a lot of pavements that are quite big.

Chad: Like a courtyard?

Eduardo: It's like a swimming pool, um—but very big—bigger than that . . .

Teacher: When was the last time you saw a Portuguese market?

Eduardo: Er—

Teacher: Was it years ago?

Eduardo: Yes. . . . It's going to have all these chickens and . . rabbits and, er—

Teacher: Livestock?

Eduardo: Yes, livestock.

Chad: In the country, er—in Sussex—there used to be a—by the station there used to be a kind of . . . things where cows and chickens and stuff went to and there were kind of—fair for judging—for judging the, er— best cow.

Teacher: Yes?

Eduardo: Do they still do that?

Chad: No, but no, no—in the country. They don't any more. They're going to turn it into a car park, I think.

Teacher: That's a shame, isn't it?

There are several characteristics of this discussion that are worth remarking on. Perhaps most important is the relaxed and easy atmosphere. Each is listening carefully in order to understand the others' intentions. This comes over very clearly in Chad's questions. As well as expressing some surprise at the claim that any market could be busier than Portobello Market on a Saturday, he is obviously trying to help Eduardo to make his meaning clear. As for Eduardo, offered the opportunity to take on the role of expert, he rises to the challenge and, although still somewhat uncertain in his command of English, he successfully manages to convey something of the appearance and atmosphere of a market in his homeland.

This sort of collaboration between pupils is, unfortunately, all too rare. However, as a result of the teacher's example, in this classroom it was the norm. And, watching the videotape, I was able to see how, on this occasion, it was achieved. Sitting between the two boys, she had been turning first to one and then to the other as the discussion prior to this extract proceeded. However, when she invited Eduardo to speak, she leaned back, so that he was speaking directly to Chad. This unobtrusive gesture, so effective in its message, makes one realize just how important teachers' nonverbal behavior is in indicating how pupils are expected to relate to them and also to each other.

Although clearly interested in the pupils' ideas and skilled in helping them to extend those ideas, this teacher also had her own suggestions to make. Shortly after the extract quoted above, she brought the discussion back to the subject of the Portobello Market and produced some street plans of the area, which she had photocopied from the records at the public library. These had been selected from different chronological points in the development of the area and, with her help, the boys discovered how to interpret them, bringing these records of the past into relation with their firsthand knowledge of the present layout of the area. Together, they discussed some of the changes that had taken place over the previous century, as the area had become progressively urbanized. And, from this, the decision arose quite naturally that the boys should extend their project on markets to include an investigation of the way in which the Portobello Market had developed.

At this point the teacher left them, having spent more than 25 minutes with them. But at the end of that time, enthusiastic about the topic, they were ready to continue on their own, collecting and sifting information in preparation for the presentation of their work, in writing, diagram, and illustration, to the rest of the class.

These few extracts from the observation made on a single day cannot do justice, of course, to the range and depth of the learning that was taking place in this classroom. But they will perhaps have served to give the feel of the place and an indication of the type of purposeful activity in which the children were engaged. They will also have conveyed an impression of the collaborative spirit in which pupils from a wide range of ethnic backgrounds were learning from each other as well as from the teacher. All the extracts show a concern for language but, both in speech and writing, the concern is with using language to learn about the topics that have been chosen and to communicate what has been learned, rather than with the development or practice of language skills for their own sake.

This classroom thus illustrates, probably as well as any could, what have been some of the main themes of this book, in particular the way in which meaning is negotiated and the collaborative quality of teacher-pupil interaction that enables pupils to make knowledge their own. In the context of this chapter, however, what is particularly striking is the central place of stories: stories read to the class by the teacher; stories read by pupils individually and in small groups; and, most obviously, stories told and written by pupils.

It also provides a fitting end to my story of the development of the making of meaning. Let me end this more personal chapter, then, with another quotation from Harold Rosen, for it is from him and from the other writers quoted in this chapter that I have learned the value of stories for my own work as a researcher and as a reporter of that research to others:

We are in error if we believe narrative . . . stands in complete contrast to other kinds of discourse. In fact it is an explicit resource in *all* intellectual activity.[17]

Eleven

———

RELATING PRACTICE
TO THEORY

Two main claims have been repeated at intervals throughout this book, like the refrain in a ballad or traditional story. They are that children are active meaning makers and that the best way in which adults can help them to learn is by giving them evidence, guidance, and encouragement. The first claim is based on the evidence that we collected in our longitudinal study, and I have tried to give it more immediacy by quoting at length from the recordings, writings, and interviews of a small number of children. The second claim is a corollary of the first, and it too has been supported by quotations from parents and teachers who have intuitively understood its correctness and tried to find ways of relating to the children in their care in such a way as to facilitate this development.

■ THE NATURE OF CONVERSATION

Thus far, then, I have placed the emphasis on the empirical evidence for these claims. But there are also grounds for accepting them of a different kind: namely, the nature of conversation itself.[1]

In talking about conversation, we often use such phrases as "sharing ideas" or "exchanging opinions" as if, through what he or she says, a speaker were able to cause another person to have the very same thoughts or feelings as were in his or her own mind. We are all aware, of course, of occasions when this is patently not the case—when a misunderstanding occurs for any of a variety of reasons—but we still continue to act as if this were the exception rather than the rule, believing that, if we say things clearly enough, our listeners will "know what we mean." Taken literally, such phrases express an optimism which is, I believe, mistaken, as I think will be clear from a closer examination of the processes that are involved in any instance of linguistic communication.

When I communicate with other people, whether it be to inform, request, or persuade, what I have in mind is an idea—an event, action, or outcome—that I intend they should understand. However, this idea arises from my mental model of the world, which is itself the product of my unique personal biography. Nobody else has exactly the same mental model of the world, since nobody else has had exactly the same experience. It follows, therefore, that nobody can have exactly the same ideas as I have.

Even if my listener were able to form the same ideas as I have, however, I still am not able to transmit my ideas directly to him or her in all their simultaneity and multifaceted particularity, since language, the most effective means of communication available, requires that I select and arrange what I mean in an ordered sequence that is compatible with the temporally organized possibilities of syntax and vocabulary. Furthermore, while my ideas are personal and particular, the categories of language, in terms of which I now have to represent them, are public and general. It is simply not possible, therefore, to convey the ideas that I have in mind in a form that does full justice to their simultaneous complexity and specificity.

However, this is still not the end of the problem for, in order to reach my intended audience, my message must be further re-encoded into a stream of vocally produced sounds—or, if writing, into a sequence of marks on a page—that has only an arbitrary but conventional relationship to the meanings that I intend. All that is available to the receiver, therefore, is a patterned sequence of vocal sound, or a graphic display, which in itself is totally meaningless. This is immediately apparent if we listen to a speaker of an unknown language or attempt to interpret a text in an unknown script, as was forcibly brought home to me on a visit to Yugoslavia some years ago, when I found that the menu in the hotel where I was staying was completely impenetrable. Unable to recognize the letters of the Cyrillic alphabet, I could not even begin to decipher the words that were written there, let alone work out what they might mean.

Even to a listener/reader who knows the code, however, the task of reconstructing the intended meaning is not simply a matter of working "from the bottom up"—of decoding the sequence of sound into a pattern of words in a syntactic structure and then reading off the cor-responding meaning. In the first place, as anyone who has tried to transcribe recorded speech will know, one cannot even hear the sounds until one knows their meaning;[2] and, second, even if one can decipher the words and structures, they only make sense when one can give them a specific interpretation in the light of one's own previous knowl-edge or experience.[3] Interpreting another person's message, therefore, requires that one also have expectations, based on prior knowledge or information derived from the situational context. Comprehension is the result of an act of meaning construction by the receiver. It occurs only when the meaning derived from a decoding of the linguistic mes-sage fits with the meaning that the receiver predicts from an interpre-tation of the context in the light of the relevant aspects of his or her mental model of the world.

What all this leads to is a recognition that one never *knows* what other people mean by what they say or write. One can only make an informed guess, taking into account all the cues that are available: from the communication context, from one's own relevant experience, and from the actual linguistic signal. To put it differently, I cannot know what idea is in your mind as you speak or write. I can only know what ideas I would have had in mind if I had produced the same lexico-grammatical sequence as I believe you to have produced in the context that I think you think we currently share.

In normal conversation between mature adult members of the same culture, however, this does not normally cause a problem. Their past experience, both of language and of the world to which it refers, is sufficiently similar for there to be a considerable overlap between them in the ideas they might wish to communicate. Furthermore, in speech at least, there are strategies available for negotiating over the intended meaning if a mismatch is suspected. Finally, where conver-sational meaning is jointly constructed over successive turns, there are opportunities to amplify or modify what one has said in the light of the feedback received in subsequent contributions. Although partici-pants in a conversation never know for sure what the other meant by a particular utterance, over the conversation as a whole there are suf-ficient opportunities for each to calibrate his or her interpretation of what is meant against that of the other for a consensus to be reached that is usually adequate for most of the purposes for which people communicate with each other.

On the other hand, where the conversational participants come from different cultural backgrounds, or where they differ greatly in their level of cognitive and linguistic maturity—as is the case in in-teractions between children and their parents or teachers—the possi-bility of misunderstanding is both substantial and ever-present. And unless they—or at least the more mature of the participants—take the necessary steps, the meanings that they construct on the basis of their differing mental models and linguistic resources are likely to become increasingly divergent.

What these steps are has already been dealt with at some length when considering the ways in which adults can facilitate their children's language development (p. 50). The four principles that were suggested were:

- To treat what the child has to say as worthy of careful attention.
- To do one's best to understand what he or she means.
- To take the child's meaning as the basis for what one says next.
- In selecting and encoding one's message, to take account of the child's ability to understand—that is, to construct an appropriate interpretation.

However, where these principles are followed by both participants, it *is* possible for minds to make contact—even when they are separated by wide differences in maturity and experience. Although it may not be possible literally to share the thoughts of another person, it is possible, through the collaborative construction of conversational meaning, to extend and modify one's own thoughts in response to the cues provided by the other and, in turn, to provide cues that enable the other to estimate how close one has come to the ideas that he or she originally had in mind.

Conversation may not be perfect as a means of information exchange, therefore, but when engaged in collaboratively, it can be an effective medium for learning and teaching. In any case, since there is no better alternative, we must do the best we can.

■ THE GUIDED REINVENTION OF KNOWLEDGE

If the argument of the previous section is correct, together with the evidence from our own study, as I have interpreted it, it follows that the conception of teaching as "transmission" must be a mistaken one. First, it is not possible, simply by telling, to cause students to come to have the knowledge that is in the mind of the teacher. Knowledge cannot be transmitted. It has to be constructed afresh by each individual knower on the basis of what is already known and by means of strategies developed over the whole of that individual's life, both outside and inside the classroom. On both these counts there are bound to be substantial differences between the individuals in any class of students and, hence, a wide variation in the interpretations that are put upon the teacher's words. Unless students are given opportunities to formulate the sense they make of new topics in their own way, using their own words, an important means of gaining understanding is lost. In addition, the teacher loses the opportunity to discover what meanings the students bring to the topic and so is unable to make his or her contributions contingently responsive.

Second, a unilateral definition of what is to count as worthwhile knowledge and of how it is to be constructed undervalues the contributions that students can make in terms of their own experience, interests, and methods of inquiry, thereby impoverishing the learning experience. Furthermore, to override their natural predisposition to attempt to construct their own knowledge is to force them into a relatively passive role, with a consequent reduction in their commitment to the endeavor and an increase in the likelihood that what is learned will not be integrated into their action-oriented model of the world and so will soon be forgotten.

In sum, what is wrong with the transmission model is that it places the teacher or textbook at the center of the educational enterprise and focuses almost exclusively on the input, in the mistaken belief that, to obtain the desired outcomes, what is most important is to ensure that the input is well selected, sequenced, and presented in terms of the educated adult's understanding of what is to be learned.

However, once we give due recognition to the fact that knowledge can only be constructed by individual knowers and that this occurs most effectively when they have an active engagement in all the processes involved, it becomes clear that a different model of education is required—one that is based on a *partnership* between students and teachers, in which the responsibility for selecting and organizing the tasks to be engaged in is shared.

To urge that classrooms should be places in which the curriculum is negotiated—where students are encouraged to take the role of expert when they are able to do so, and where they have a part in determining the goals to be aimed for and the procedures to be followed—may seem to be reducing the importance of the role of the teacher. However, this is very far from being the case. What is required, though, is a different conception of the relationship between teacher and students—one in which the teacher aims to facilitate learning rather than to direct it. This is not to deny the teacher's greater expertise and experience, but to argue that it will be of much greater value to students if it is offered collaboratively rather than being imposed.

Nor am I suggesting that the teacher should relinquish the overall responsibility for setting directions, proposing specific content, or evaluating achievement. On the contrary, final decisions on these matters require informed judgment that can only be gained through professional training and experience. Nevertheless, in fulfilling these responsibilities, the teacher should explain the criteria on which decisions are based so that, within the limits of their capabilities, students can share in the day-to-day planning of learning activities to an increasing degree. The aim, therefore, should be to foster the development of students' ability to take control of their own learning so that eventually they can assume these responsibilities for themselves.

Following these principles, teaching can no longer be seen as the imparting of information to relatively passive recipients and then checking to see that they can correctly reproduce it. Instead, it is more appropriately characterized as a partnership in learning. The tasks of the partners are necessarily different as a result of their differing levels of expertise, but the goal is the same for students and teacher alike. Without too much exaggeration, it can be described as *the guided reinvention of knowledge.*

■ FROM PRACTICE TO THEORY—AND BACK AGAIN

Abstract theory is all very well, I suspect some readers are saying, but what does it amount to in practice? Or, if those readers are teachers, their question is probably more specifically, "What should I do in my particular situation?"

This is a very important question, and one that is urgently in need of an answer. However, it would be inappropriate for me to attempt to provide a detailed response because there is not *one* but *many* answers. Furthermore, the only valid answers are the ones that individual teachers construct in the light of their knowledge of themselves, their students, and the setting—colleagues, school system, and community—in which they work.

Nevertheless, it is possible to offer a number of general suggestions, and this I have attempted to do in the preceding chapters. More important, I have described and quoted from work in classrooms in which teachers have found their own specific and practical answers, which are appropriate to their own particular circumstances.

In practical terms, what is common to them is that they have arranged the daily program so that a variety of activities is going on simultaneously. This has made it relatively easy for them to allow individual children to follow different patterns within the total curriculum so that, at any time, they can give help where it is most needed. And from there to allowing the child to share the responsibility for designing and implementing his or her own individual curriculum is a small and relatively easy step to take. Some teachers are happy for the greater part of each child's work to be carried out individually, but others feel that there is much to be gained by encouraging collaborative group work. Where this is the case, there is much to be said for starting with a broad theme, with the expectation that small groups will choose their own specific aspect to work on, as in the example reported in the previous chapter, where the broad theme of life one hundred years ago allowed for a wide variety of topics to be investigated, using a variety of methods of inquiry and subsequent presentation. By guiding individual or group choices of topic, the teacher can ensure that, over a reasonable length of time, each child is tackling topics across the range of the curriculum

For those who find this too large a change to make—at least at first—a similar strategy might be adopted for just one part of the day, for example in social studies or in project work. The "writing workshop" described by Donald Graves[4] is another possible starting point, but this would need to be linked to some other major area of learning if the strategies developed in the workshop were to permeate the curriculum more widely.[5]

What these examples show is that the best source of suggestions is to be found in other teachers. What is needed, therefore, is more, and more frequent, opportunities for teachers to meet together to pool their ideas and experiences—putting together, for example, a list of themes that have proved successful starting points and compiling a central pool of resources of various kinds that could be drawn upon in exploring these themes. There are already schools where the staff meet together regularly in this way, and the encouragement and support that this provides for individual teachers is out of all proportion to the initial difficulty of finding a time in the lunch hour or at the end of the working day when all the staff can meet on a regular basis. In other cases, support groups have got together on a wider front, involving teachers in a group of neighboring schools or in an area served by a teachers' center.[6]

Clearly principals and head and advisory teachers have an important leadership role to play in facilitating the functioning of such groups. But it is important that they do not take on too directive a role. If teachers are to discover effective ways of helping their students to take some of the responsibility for their own learning, they must themselves have the opportunity to learn in the same way. The same is true of more formally provided teacher education, whether at the level of initial training, in-service courses, or programs leading to higher degrees. Unless teachers' experiences as students are of this kind, they can hardly be expected to take easily to working in this way with their own students.

Every teacher needs to become his or her own theory-builder, but a builder of theory that grows out of practice and has as its aim to improve the quality of practice. For too long, "experts" from outside the classroom have told teachers what to think and what to do. They have even designed programs and materials that are "teacher-proof" in an attempt to bypass teacher involvement in the same way that so many teachers have bypassed student involvement. Such programs must be rejected for exactly the same reasons as were given above for rejecting a transmission model of classroom teaching. At every level, students must be encouraged actively to take responsibility for their own learning, and this applies as much to teachers as learners as it does to the students that they teach.

■ CONCLUSION

We are the meaning makers—every one of us: children, parents, and teachers. To try to make sense, to construct stories, and to share them with others in speech and in writing is an essential part of being human. For those of us who are more knowledgeable and more mature—parents and teachers—the responsibility is clear: to interact with those in our care in such a way as to foster and enrich *their* meaning making.

NOTES

■ CHAPTER ONE. THE CHILDREN AND THEIR FAMILIES

[1] Some of the extracts from the recordings contain words and grammatical structures that are features of the local dialect. Although these may be unfamiliar to some readers, I have retained them in order to preserve the authenticity of the material.

[2] A number of categories of children were excluded, including those with any known handicap, those in full-time care, and those whose parents' first language was not English. In all, these categories amounted to less than 10% of the initial random sample.

[3] In calculating the index of family background, information was used concerning the status of occupation (using the Registrar-General's classification) and the extent of full-time education of both parents.

[4] The recordings were made by means of a radio-microphone worn by the child. This was left at the child's home on the day before the observation and collected on the day following. During the actual observation, there was no observer present, as we did not want in any way to interfere with the spontaneity of the family's normal activities. In order to obtain information about the contexts in which the short samples of speech were recorded, the person who was to transcribe the tape called at the child's home in the evening, after the observation was finished, and asked questions about each of the recorded samples to find out who had been present, where they had been, and what they had been doing. Questions were also asked about any utterances that were unclear or in other ways difficult to understand, and any other information was noted that would make it easier to understand the conversation.

[5] Derek Edwards explores this idea in some depth in "Social relations and early language" in A. J. Lock, ed., *Action, Gesture and Symbol* (New York: Academic Press, 1978).

■ CHAPTER TWO. LEARNING TO TALK: THE PATTERN OF DEVELOPMENT

[1] The existence of substantial cultural variation in beliefs about how children learn to talk and in the associated child-rearing practices is now well established. (See, for example, Elinor Ochs, "Cultural dimensions of language acquisition," in E. Ochs and B. B. Schieffelin, *Acquiring Conversational Competence* [London: Routledge and Ke-

gan Paul, 1983]. See also Bambi Schieffelin, *How Kaluli Children Learn What to Say, What to Do and How to Feel* [Cambridge: Cambridge University Press, in press].) However, these differences do not in themselves rule out the possibility of a universal answer. Whether or not this is possible will depend on the role of the environment in language learning. This issue is discussed in chapter 3.

[2] Such a study is already being carried out at the University of California at Berkeley by Dan Slobin in collaboration with researchers from many other parts of the world. For some of the results, see D. I. Slobin (ed.), *The Cross-Linguistic Study of Language Acquisition* (Hillsdale, NJ: Lawrence Erlbaum, 1985).

[3] Lenneberg provides what is probably the best-known argument for the universality of the developmental sequence at this level of generality in *The Biological Foundations of Language* (New York: John Wiley & Sons, 1967).

[4] But see the references to Brown and to Crystal *et al.*, below.

[5] A more detailed account of this method, together with a rationale for its use, can be found in the full account of the research project. See C. G. Wells, *Language Development in the Pre-School Years* (Cambridge: Cambridge University Press, 1985).

[6] A much fuller account of the sequence of development can be found in my *Language Development in the Pre-School Years*. In addition, Roger Brown provides a very detailed discussion of the early stages from a semantic point of view in *A First Language* (Cambridge, MA: Harvard University Press, 1973); David Crystal, Paul Fletcher, and Michael Garman describe the complete age span from a grammatical perspective in *The Grammatical Analysis of Language Disability* (London: Arnold, 1976). For convenience, I will use the stage labels I through V suggested by Brown, since they are also used somewhat similarly by Crystal, Fletcher, and Garman.

[7] Michael Halliday observed essentially the same first functions in the speech of his own son; see *Learning How to Mean* (London: Arnold, 1975). However, he made rather more distinctions—for example, subdividing Want into Instrumental and Regulatory.

[8] Interestingly, many children don't at first include any relative pronoun in this structure. Those that do are, like Mark, more likely to use "what" than "that."

[9] Surprisingly, after the very early stages, there has been much less interest in the developing structure of the lexicon (but see John Macnamara's *Names for Things* [Cambridge, MA: The MIT Press, 1982] and the chapters by Susan Carey and Eve Clark in *Language Acquisition: The State of the Art*, edited by E. Wanner and L. R. Gleitman [New York: Cambridge University Press, 1982]). We hope to be able to say something about this topic in the future, when we have completed our analysis of the lexical content of the transcripts.

[10] That not all the basic grammar has been learned by age 5 is clear from, for example, the detailed study of Carol Chomsky (*The Acquisition of Syntax from 5 to 10* [Cambridge, MA: MIT Press, 1969]) and Annette Karmiloff-Smith (*A Functional Approach to Child Language* [Cambridge: Cambridge University Press, 1979]).

■ CHAPTER THREE. LEARNING TO TALK: THE CONSTRUCTION OF LANGUAGE

[1] Chomsky sees the problem to be that of discovering the relationship between sounds and meanings. But that ignores a logically prior discovery—namely, that there is a relationship to be discovered.

[2] Jonathan Bennett, the philosopher, offers an account of the way in which human language might have evolved in terms of just such a purposeful use of the available nonverbal channels of communication in *Linguistic Behaviour* (Cambridge: Cambridge University Press, 1976).

[3] See Tom Bower, *Development in Infancy* (San Francisco: W. H. Freeman, 1974).

4 Colwyn Trevarthen makes this claim at the conclusion of a detailed description of this aspect of human development in "Communication and cooperation in early infancy" in M. Bullowa (ed.), *Before Speech: The Beginnings of Interpersonal Communication* (Cambridge: Cambridge University Press, 1979).

5 John Newson makes this point very clearly in "Dialogue and development" in A. Lock (ed.), *Action, Gesture and Symbol: The Emergence of Language* (New York: Academic Press, 1978). Catherine Snow similarly points out that the responsiveness of other human beings allows babies to discover that they can affect their environment long before they are able to receive feedback from their actions on the physical world. See "Social interaction and language acquisition" in P. S. Dale and D. Ingram (eds.), *Child Language—An International Perspective* (Baltimore, MD: University Park Press, 1981)

6 Colwyn Trevarthen describes the development of this relationship in great detail in a chapter entitled "Primary Intersubjectivity" in Lock (1978). Daniel Stern gives a similar account based on his own research in *The First Relationship: Infant and Mother* (London: Open Books, 1977).

7 See Maureen Shields, "The child as psychologist: constructing the social world," in Lock (1978).

8 J. S. Bruner, "From communication to language—a psychological perspective," *Cognition* 3 (1975): 255–87.

9 In addition to Halliday's work, which was mentioned in chapter 2, there are interesting studies by Elizabeth Bates and her colleagues L. Camaioni and V. Volterra ("The acquisition of performatives prior to speech," *Merrill-Palmer Quarterly* 21, no. 3 [1975]: 205–26) and Ann Carter ("Prespeech meaning relations: an outline of one infant's sensori-motor morpheme development," in P. Fletcher and M. Garman [eds.], *Language Acquisition* [Cambridge: Cambridge University Press, 1979]) on the development from gestures to words, and by John Dore on the earliest speech acts ("Holophrases, speech acts and language universals," *Journal of Child Language* 2 [1975]: 21–40), all of which assume a functional continuity from preverbal to verbal communication.

10 This stage is described in detail by Anat Ninio and Jerome Bruner ("The achievement and antecedents of labelling," *Journal of Child Language* 5 [1978]: 5–15) and by John McShane (*Learning to Talk* [Cambridge: Cambridge University Press, 1980]).

11 Jean Piaget and Barbel Inhelder, *The Psychology of the Child* (London: Routledge and Kegan Paul, 1969), p. 13.

12 Eve Clark discusses this aspect of language development in "Building a vocabulary: words for objects, actions and relations" in P. Fletcher and M. Garman (eds.), *Language Acquisition* (Cambridge: Cambridge University Press, 1979).

13 These two explanations are often described as *behaviorist* and *nativist*, respectively. The former, or something rather similar, is proposed by B. F. Skinner in *Verbal Behavior* (New York: Appleton-Century-Crofts, 1957). The latter, or various versions of it, has been proposed by Noam Chomsky in *Aspects of the Theory of Syntax* (Cambridge, MA: The MIT Press, 1965) and *Reflections on Language* (London: Fontana, 1976). The continuing debate is well represented in two recent collections of papers: W. Deutsch (ed.), *The Child's Construction of Language* (New York: Academic Press, 1981) and E. Wanner and L. Gleitman (eds.), *Language Acquisition: The State of the Art* (Cambridge: Cambridge University Press, 1982).

14 Ruth Clark, "Performing without competence," *Journal of Child Language* 1 [1974]: 1–10. See also Ann Peters, *The Units of Language Acquisition* (Cambridge: Cambridge University Press, 1973).

15 Essentially the same conclusion seemed to emerge from our investigation of the relationship between the sequence of development and the differential complexity of what had to be learned. For the four linguisitic systems investigated—pronouns, auxiliary verbs, sentence meaning relations, and functions—the items within each system were ranked according to their cognitive and linguistic complexity. The rank orders were then compared with the order of development within each system. In every case the match between the two rank orders was extremely close, which led us to conclude

that of the various explanations considered, this was the most satisfactory. For further details, see Wells, *Language Development in the Pre-School Years*, chapter 9.

16 This is certainly true for children in Western cultures. However, some caution is needed in interpreting this finding more generally. In cultures where children and caregivers rarely take part in such activities together, children still successfully learn to talk (see the references cited in note 1 of chapter 2). However, at the present time, there is no evidence to show whether they develop at the same rate or not.

17 Jerome Bruner refers to this type of facilitation as "scaffolding" in *Child's Talk* (New York: Norton, 1983). As with all scaffolding, however, once the purpose for which it was erected has been achieved and the child is able to play his or her role in the conversation, it is gradually dismantled.

18 For details, see R. Ellis and G. Wells, "Enabling factors in adult-child discourse," *First Language* 1 (1980), 46–62; and S. Barnes, M. Gutfreund, D. Satterly, and G. Wells, "Characteristics of adult speech which predict children's language development," *Journal of Child Language* 10 (1983): 65–84.

19 Catherine Snow provides a summary of many of the early studies in her chapter, "Mothers' speech research: from input to interaction," in *Talking to Children: From Input to Acquisition*, C. Snow and C. Ferguson (eds.) (Cambridge: Cambridge University Press, 1977). A more recent review can be found in G. Wells and P. Robinson, "The role of adult speech in language development" in C. Fraser and K. Scherer (eds.), *Advances in the Social Psychology of Language* (Cambridge: Cambridge University Press, 1982).

20 I am grateful to Margaret MacLure for this example.

21 Roger Brown, "Introduction," in C. Snow and C. Ferguson (eds.) *Talking to Children: From Input to Acquisition* (Cambridge: Cambridge University Press, 1977).

22 Andrew Lock, *The Guided Reinvention of Language* (London: Academic Press, 1980).

■ CHAPTER FOUR. TALKING TO LEARN

1 Peter Robinson and Susan Rackstraw, *A Question of Answers*, 2 vols. (London: Routledge and Kegan Paul, 1972).

2 Barbara Tizard and Martin Hughes, *Young Children Learning* (London: Fontana, 1984). Their study involved 30 girls, half from middle-class and half from working-class families, in a comparison of the language experienced in the two settings of home and nursery class. As this is the topic of chapter 5, I shall refer to their study in greater detail there.

3 Probably the greater part of our general knowledge is acquired in this incidental way, as we respond to the interests expressed by others and they respond to ours. Certainly, children learn a great deal in this way before they begin to receive more systematic instruction at school. P. L. Berger and T. Luckman refer to this sort of learning through spontaneous interaction as *the social construction of reality* (Garden City, NY: Doubleday, 1966).

4 Reading is potentially of particular importance and will be discussed in more detail in chapter 8.

■ CHAPTER FIVE. FROM HOME TO SCHOOL

1 Describing the adult's contribution to such conversations, Roger Brown sees two major functions: "It serves as a running check on the child's progress in building an apperceptive mass shared with his family—his psycholinguistic socialization as it were. At the same time, the adult tries to add a pebble to the pile." (See "The maintenance of conversation," in D. Olson (ed.), *The Social Foundations of Language and Thought* (New York: Norton, 1980).

2 Margaret Donaldson refers to this more reflective thinking and use of language as "disembedded" and links it very closely with the acquisition of literacy. (See *Children's Minds*, London: Fontana, 1978). Carl Bereiter and Marlene Scardamalia emphasize the importance of children's deliberately taking responsibility for their own learning. See "Schooling and the growth of intentional cognition: Helping children take charge of their own minds" in Z. Lamm (ed.), *New Trends in Education* (Tel Aviv: Yachdev United Publishing Company, 1983).

3 This issue is discussed in more detail in chapter 7.

4 When their dialect use at age 7 was compared with their eventual level of attainment, however, a significant correlation was found. Interpretation of these apparently contradictory findings is not straightforward and must therefore be extremely tentative. At neither age did nonstandardness of dialect or accent cause a problem for teacher-pupil communication, so it is unlikely that it was in any direct manner a cause of the later associated lower attainment. It seems, therefore, that, rather than nonstandardness of dialect and accent being a source of difficulty that results from a child having learned in the preschool years a variety of language that impedes successful communication at school, it is, instead, a mark of group identity that is adopted or exaggerated after entering school, perhaps in response to a growing perception of low attainment. Although this is different from Labov's account (W. Labov, "The logic of non-standard English" in F. Williams [ed.], *Language and Poverty* [Chicago: Markham Publishing, 1970]), it is not altogether incompatible with it.

5 Of the children's requests, 67.9% were indirect at home and 83.2% in the classroom.

6 The conclusion that there is little difference in the actual forms and functions of language found in homes and classrooms may seem to be at odds with reports of other research, particularly in the United States (cf. Courtney Cazden, "Classroom discourse," in M. C. Wittrock [ed.], *Handbook of Research on Teaching*, 3rd edition [New York: Macmillan, in press]; Hugh Mehan, *Learning Lessons* [Cambridge, MA: Harvard University Press, 1979]); but there have been few direct comparisons between recordings of naturally occurring interaction obtained in the two settings. Where such comparisons have been made, as, for example, in the study by Tizard and Hughes (1984), similar results have been obtained (see notes 9 and 10 below). A further possible reason for the discrepancy in results is that the American work has frequently investigated situations in which there is a major ethnic and cultural discontinuity between the school and the community that it serves (e.g., Susan Philips, "Participant structures and communicative competence: Warm Springs children in community and classroom," in C. B. Cazden, V. P. John, and D. Hymes [eds.], *Functions of Language in the Classroom* [New York: Teachers College Press, 1972]). This was not the case for any of the schools or social groups in the present study.

It is not being claimed, however, that the overall pattern of language use is the same—or even similar—in the two settings, but rather that it is not a lack of the necessary linguistic resources that accounts for the ineptitude that some children display in the classroom. With Shirley Brice Heath and others who have carried out ethnographic studies in the two settings, we agree that for all social groups, but for the less "literacy-oriented" in particular, it is the role that language habitually plays in the construction of shared meanings that most differs between home and school. This is the problem, not the children's language resources. See also M. MacLure and P. French, "A comparison of talk at home and at school," in C. G. Wells, *Learning Through Interaction* (Cambridge: Cambridge University Press, 1981).

7 Because in several cases one or even two of the samples were recorded when the child's microphone was out of range of the radio receiver (for example, when the child was going with the mother to fetch a sibling from school), only 8 of the samples were transcribed, and only 7 (the largest number that was found to be in range in every recording) were used for the quantitative analysis reported in Table 5-1. In some cases, the radio-microphone was not put on the child at home until somewhat later than was planned. When this happened, the time-based sampling was simply delayed. In one case, however, owing to a machine malfunction, the whole recording had to be carried out in the afternoon.

8 For a full account of the procedure and of the results obtained, see C. G. Wells, "The

language experience of five-year-old children at home and at school," in Jenny Cook-Gumperz (ed.), *Literacy, Language and Schooling* (Cambridge: Cambridge University Press, in press).

9 B. Tizard, H. Carmichael, M. Hughes, and G. Pinkerton, "Four year olds talking to mothers and teachers," in Hersov *et al.*, *Language and Language Disorders in Childhood* (Oxford: Pergamon, 1980), p. 68. The study is reported in more detail in B. Tizard and M. Hughes, *Young Children Learning: Talking and Thinking at Home and at School* (London: Fontana, 1984).

10 D. Wood, L. McMahon, and Y. Cranstoun, *Working with Under Fives* (London: Grant McIntyre, 1980), p. 65.

11 Elementary education in England is organized in two stages. The first stage, from 5 to 7 years, is called the Infant School. The second stage, from 8 to 11 years, is called the Junior School. In the majority of cases, the two schools that a child attends between 5 and 11 years are independent institutions, each having its own Head Teacher.

12 Douglas Barnes, *Language, the Learner and the School*, rev. ed. (Harmondsworth, Middlesex: Penguin, 1971), p. 28.

■ CHAPTER SIX. HELPING CHILDREN TO MAKE KNOWLEDGE THEIR OWN

1 C. Rosen and H. Rosen, *The Language of Primary School Children* (Harmondsworth, Middlesex: Penguin, 1973), pp. 43–51.

2 Ibid., p. 51.

3 This material was recorded under the direction of Moira McKenzie, Warden of the Centre for Language in Primary Education in the Inner London Education Authority, for use in a series of video programs entitled *Extending Literacy*. I am grateful for her permission to reproduce this and the other examples from these programs, which are quoted here and in chapter 10.

4 Edward Sapir, *Language* (New York: Harcourt Brace, 1921), p. 14.

5 Lev Vygotsky, *Thought and Language* (Cambridge, MA: The MIT Press, 1962).

6 In the study carried out by David Wood and colleagues referred to in chapter 5, it was found that as much as 44% of teacher talk was concerned with management (Wood, McMahon, and Cranstoun, *Working with the Under Fives*); and in another piece of research involving 7- to 9-year-olds, the length of most interactions with an individual pupil was 30 seconds or less—barely time for more than a summary evaluation of work carried out or for brief instructions on what to do next. Of course, there were longer episodes, but these were balanced by many more that were much shorter. (Vera Southgate, Helen Arnold, and Sandra Johnson, *Extending Beginning Reading* [London: Heinemann Educational Books, 1981]).

7 Douglas Barnes, *From Communication to Curriculum* (Harmondsworth, Middlesex: Penguin, 1976).

8 I recently heard two educators talking about "tooling up the curriculum" for the following year. Presumably the school was the factory in which the new precision-engineered curriculum was to be installed, with teachers the skilled work-force to operate it and the children the raw material to be processed into acceptably educated members of society.

9 Donald Graves, *Writing: Teachers and Children at Work* (Portsmouth, NH: Heinemann Educational Books, 1982).

10 Most of the ideas presented in this chapter are not new. They can be found in the writings of many of the major educational thinkers of this and previous centuries and in the practice of teachers in the present and the past. Particularly important in the development of my own thinking has been the work of John Dewey who, more than

80 years ago, was putting these ideas into practice in his experimental school at the University of Chicago. His books still have relevance today, particularly *The Child and the Curriculum* and *The School and Society*, published in one volume (Chicago: University of Chicago Press, 1956).

■ CHAPTER SEVEN. DIFFERENCES BETWEEN CHILDREN IN LANGUAGE AND LEARNING

[1] This point was made as long ago as 1970 by Courtney Cazden in "The neglected situation in child language research and education," *Journal of Social Issues* 25: 35–60.

[2] See, for example, Ann Peters, *The Units of Language Acquisition* (Cambridge: Cambridge University Press, 1983), in which it is suggested that some children may adopt a holistic approach in the early stages, learning and producing unanalyzed "chunks" of language, while others are more analytic in their approach, breaking down sentences and phrases into their constituent parts and then recombining them in the production of their own utterances. Both Lois Bloom (L. Bloom, P. Lightbown, and L. Hood, *Structure and Variation in Child Language* [Chicago: University of Chicago Press, Society for Research in Child Development Monographs, 40, 1975]) and Diana Horgan ("Nouns, love 'em or leave 'em" in V. Teller and S. White [eds.], *Studies in Child Language and Multilingualism. Annals of the New York Academy of Sciences*, 345 [1980]) have suggested that there may also be a difference between children in their preference for using nouns or pronouns in their referring expressions.

[3] Katharine Nelson, "Individual differences in language development: implications for development and language," *Developmental Psychology*, 17 (1981): 170–87.

[4] Rod Ellis and Gordon Wells ("Enabling factors in adult child discourse," *First Language* 1 [1980]: 46–82) found that amount of talk (in the context of helping with household tasks, in particular) was associated with the children's rate of development in the early stages. See also Jerome Bruner, *Child's Talk: Learning to Use Language* (New York: Norton, 1983) and Courtney Cazden, "Adult assistance to language development: scaffolds, models and direct instruction" in R. P. Parker and F. A. Davis (eds.), *Developing Literacy: Young Children's Use of Language* (Newark, DE: International Reading Association, 1983) on the issue of scaffolding.

[5] David Wood and Susan Gregory of the University of Nottingham Department of Psychology have reported in unpublished papers that, when the didactic quality of their speech is pointed out to the parents of deaf children, they can be helped to modify their interaction to make it more contingently responsive. This appears to have beneficial results for their children.

[6] For a review of the issue of sex differences in language development, see Louise Cherry and Michael Lewis, "Differential socialization of girls and boys: implications for sex differences in language development," in N. Waterson and C. Snow (eds.), *The Development of Communication* (Chichester: John Wiley & Sons, 1978).

[7] For futher details, see C. G. Wells, *Language Development in the Pre-School Years*, chapter 8.

[8] I use this term quite deliberately to avoid the specific interpretations given to alternative terms such as "social class" or "socioeconomic status" in different parts of the world. However, since much of the research on this issue has been carried out in Britain and in other parts of Europe, where the the terms "middle class" and "lower class" are fairly well understood, I shall use these terms where it would be too cumbersome to refer to the upper and lower range of the continuum (or, more precisely, cluster of associated continua) of family background.

[9] See, for example, the index used by Bernstein in his empirical studies of the relationship between class and code (W. Brandis and D. Henderson, *Social Class, Language and Communication* [London: Routledge and Kegan Paul, 1970]).

¹⁰ For examples of British work in which such conclusions are drawn, see Peter Hawkins, "Social class, the nominal group and reference," *Language and Speech*, 12 (1969): 125–35, and Joan Tough, *The Development of Meaning* (London: Allen and Unwin, 1977). In the United States, the early study by R. Hess and V. Shipman ("Early experience and the socialization of cognitive modes in children," *Child Development*, 36 [1965]: 869–86) arrived at very much the same conclusions; more recently, perhaps because of the growing recognition of the importance of cultural as well as socioeconomic differences between different social groups, there is much less tendency to draw such sweeping conclusions.

¹¹ See, for example, the work of Joan Tough, cited above.

¹² There is also the possibility that a similar bias operates against the slow developer. However, for the lack of appropriate longitudinal evidence, this possibility must for the moment remain in the realm of unproven conjecture.

¹³ A. Brimer and L. Dunn, *English Picture Vocabulary Test* (Windsor, Berks.: National Foundation for Educational Research, 1963).

¹⁴ The term *knowledge of literacy* is used to denote the summed, weighted scores from two tests by Marie Clay: Concepts about Print and Letter Identification. They are published in *The Early Detection of Reading Difficulties: A Diagnostic Survey* (London: Heinemann Educational Books, 1972).

¹⁵ M. Neale, *Neale Analysis of Reading Ability*, 2nd ed. (Basingstoke, Hants: Macmillan Education, 1969).

¹⁶ See, for example, Carl Bereiter and Siegfried Engelman, *Teaching Disadvantaged Children in the Preschool* (Englewood Cliffs, NJ: Prentice-Hall, 1966).

¹⁷ Bernstein's theory was developed over a considerable period of time and went through a number of versions. Many of his more important papers are collected in *Class, Codes and Control*, Vol. 1 (London: Routledge and Kegan Paul, 1971). One of the clearest and most recent statements of the theory is to be found in the Introduction to Diana Adlam's report, *Code in Context* (London: Routledge and Kegan Paul, 1977). However, the version that was most influential amongst educators was an earlier one, which did not give much importance to the effect of the specific context of interaction. Partly because of the surface inconsistencies among his ideas as they developed over time and partly because of the oversimple dichotomizations in his theory that were too readily seized upon by those in search of a simple political solution to a complex social problem, Bernstein has been much misunderstood and, in recent years, in my opinion, inappropriately rejected. The insight at the heart of his theory—that educational inequality is socially transmitted from generation to generation through the different values that are enacted and given expression in the linguistic interaction experienced by different groups of children at home and at school—is one that all those concerned with the care and education of children would do well to take seriously.

¹⁸ Labov's sociolinguistic studies are reported in *Language in the Inner City* (Philadelphia: University of Pennsylvania Press, 1972); his most influential article, however, is "The logic of non-standard English," which has been reprinted in a variety of books, including F. Williams (ed.), *Language and Poverty* (Chicago: Markham Publishing Co., 1970).

¹⁹ This term, which more accurately describes the relationship between language and specific personal experience than the more commonly used term "context-independent," is used by Margaret Donaldson in *Children's Minds* (London: Fontana, 1976). The explanation of linguistic disadvantage that is suggested here, in terms of lack of experience of literacy, owes much to her clear and insightful account of children's intellectual development.

²⁰ For further details, see C. G. Wells, "Some antecedents of early educational attainment," *British Journal of Sociology of Education*, 2 (1981): 181–200.

²¹ See A. V. Cicourel *et al.*, *Language Use and School Performance* (New York: Academic Press, 1974).

²² In conversations with the class and head teachers, a child's performance in school was frequently commented on as surprising or not surprising, "considering the background

[he or she] comes from." Such comments were made far more often about children at the lower end of the continuum of family background than about those at the opposite end.

²³ This varied from a minimum of 4 stories a day in the case of Jonathan to no stories at all in the case of Rosie. Simple arithmetic allows one to compute the magnitude of this difference: 4 stories a day for each of the 365 days in the year over the period from one to five years given a total of nearly 6,000 story reading experiences for Jonathan; for Rosie the total, which was confirmed in the interview with her mother, was 0.

²⁴ For further details, see C. G. Wells, "Pre-school literacy related activities and success in school," in D. Olson, A. Hildyard, and N. Torrance (eds.), *Literacy, Language and Learning* (Cambridge: Cambridge University Press, 1985).

²⁵ This finding in no way contradicts the results of recent research, for example by Emilia Ferreiro and Anna Teberosky (*Literacy Before Schooling*, Portsmouth, NH: Heinemann Educational Books, 1982), which shows that, in a literate society, all children develop progressively more adultlike hypotheses about the organization of written language from the print in their environment. What is at issue here is what some children were discovering in addition. That is to say, it was not whether the children had acquired *any* knowledge about literacy that predicted their later achievement, but the differences between them in *how much* they had acquired and how closely that knowledge was related to the functions of literacy that are important in education. Shirley Brice Heath has suggested from her research that the differences are qualitative rather than quantitative: in different subcultures, literacy is used in different ways and valued for different purposes (*Ways with Words* [Cambridge: Cambridge University Press, 1983]). This may have been true to some extent of the different social groups in our study, but the more obvious difference was in the frequency with which they engaged in any of the uses of literacy.

²⁶ One aspect of oral language development that does suffer from a low valuation of literacy in the home is vocabulary. Children who are read to regularly and whose parents themselves read are exposed to, and acquire, a much more varied and extended vocabulary. It is for this reason that vocabulary tests, such as the English Picture Vocabulary Test (see note 13 above), are significantly associated with both family background and subsequent educational achievement.

²⁷ It is important to note that it is not class or ethnic group membership as such that is important in explaining the processes whereby some children come to be linguistically disadvantaged with respect to the opportunities provided by formal education. Rather it is the actual practices that families engage in with respect to literacy events in the home and the different values that they give to them. This is richly documented by Shirley Brice Heath in her comparative study of three communities in the southeastern United States, which was referred to in note 25.

■ CHAPTER EIGHT. THE CENTRALITY OF LITERACY

¹ This test was designed by Marie Clay. With a parallel form, it is published as *The Early Detection of Reading Difficulties: A Diagnostic Survey* (London: Heinemann Educational Books, 1972).

² In both this and the earlier follow-up study (Gordon Wells and Bridie Rabon, *Children Learning to Read*, Final Report to the Social Science Research Council [U.K.], 1978) the correlation obtained between scores on the two parts of this test combined and reading attainment at 7 years, as measured by the Neale Analysis of Reading (see chapter 7, note 15) was $r = 0.79$. In the present follow-up study, the correlation between the test of knowledge of literacy and reading at age 10, as measured by the NFER test, was again $r = 0.79$.

³ The correlation between this variable and the test of knowledge of literacy was $r = 0.65$. Its correlation with overall educational attainment at age 10 was $r = 0.63$.

⁴ See chapter 7, note 25.

⁵ L. S. Vygotsky, *Mind in Society* (Cambridge, MA: Harvard University Press, 1978).

⁶ For a fuller account, see Wells, "Pre-school literacy-related activities and success in school" (chapter 7, note 24).

⁷ On the relationship between size of vocabulary and educational achievement, see also Donald Hayes, "On measuring the richness of children's natural language environments: conversation, books and television" (San Francisco: American Sociological Association, September 1982).

⁸ I owe this insight to Margaret Spencer, who discusses this aspect of children's stories in "Stories are for telling," *English in Education* 10 (1976): 16–23. This idea is further developed in chapter 10.

⁹ *The Giant Jam Sandwich*, story and pictures by J. V. Lord with verses by J. Burroway (Piccolo Picture Books, 1974).

¹⁰ I certainly do not want to deny the importance of intertextuality—the fact that, for both writer and reader, "a story only exists as a story by virtue of the existence of other stories" (Harold Rosen, "Narratology and the teacher," *Stories and Meanings* [National Association for the Teaching of English, 1984]). But for the current story to be related to other stories, the cues must be present in the text.

Although emphasizing the work carried out by the reader, Terry Eagleton makes a related point when he writes that, as readers, "we are all the time engaged in constructing hypotheses about the meaning of the text . . . drawing on a tacit knowledge of the world in general and of literary conventions in particular. The text itself is really no more than a series of "cues" to the reader, invitations to construct a piece of language into meaning." *Literary Theory: An Introduction* (Oxford: Blackwell, 1983), p. 76.

¹¹ I have borrowed this terminology from John Searle, who contrasts different classes of speech acts in terms of the direction of fit between words and world (J. R. Searle, "A classification of illocutionary acts," *Language in Society* 5 [1977]: 1–23).

¹² Margaret Donaldson, *Children's Minds* (London: Fontana, 1978), pp. 88–89.

¹³ The differing attitudes to literacy and the differing ways in which people engage in literacy events, even in the same broad linguistic community, are clearly brought out in Shirley Brice Heath's study of three cultural groups in a single city in the southeastern United States. In all three communities, there were certain types of literacy event that were considered important, but it was only in the "mainstream," educated group that children had the sort of experience of literacy that prepared them for the approaches to reading and writing that they would be expected to adopt at school. (*Ways with Words* [Cambridge: Cambridge University Press, 1983]).

¹⁴ In one such school, this policy was taken to such lengths that almost no attention was paid to written language in the first few months at school, the emphasis being placed almost entirely on remedial oral language work. The children were not allowed to have a reading book nor to borrow books from the library because they could not read; and they were not learning to read because, being judged by definition not ready, they were not allowed access to books. It was hardly surprising, therefore, that at the end of the first year these children were severely retarded in reading and writing.

¹⁵ For assistance in selecting and organizing books for such a program, see Jill Bennett, *Learning to Read with Picture Books*, 2d ed. (South Woodchester, Stroud, Glos., The Thimble Press, 1982); also Cliff Moon, *Individual Reading* (Centre for the Teaching of Reading, University of Reading, revised annually). A similar source of information about available picture storybooks in North America is being prepared by Linda Hart-Hewins and Jan Wells for the Toronto Board of Education.

¹⁶ For evidence of the nature and extent of children's spontaneous construction of understanding about written language, see Ferreiro and Teberosky's book referred to above (chapter 7, note 25); also Marie Clay, *What Did I Write?* (London: Heinemann Educational Books, 1975); Yetta Goodman, "The roots of literacy," *Claremont Reading Conference Yearbook* 44 (1980), 1–12; Jerome C. Harste, Virginia A. Woodward, and Carolyn L. Burke, *Language Stories & Literacy Lessons* (Portsmouth, NH: Heinemann

Eudcational Books, 1984); and Don Holdaway, *The Foundations of Literacy* (Sydney, Australia: Ashton Scholastic, 1979).

[17] J. Hewison and J. Tizard, "Parental involvement and reading attainment," *British Journal of Educational Psychology* 50 (1980), 209–15.

[18] See, for example, Angela Jackson and Peter Hannon, *The Bellfield Reading Project* (Rochdale, Lancashire: Bellfield Community Council, n.d.).

[19] Linda Hart-Hewins and Una Villiers, "Please will you read me a story!", unpublished paper, Ontario Institute for Studies in Education, 1984.

[20] Donald Graves gives many helpful suggestions as to how parents and other adults besides the teacher can contribute to the classroom "writing workshop" in *Writing: Teachers and Children at Work* (Portsmouth, NH: Heinemann Educational Books, 1982).

[21] Frank Smith has suggested this way of thinking about helping children to become literate in a paper to be published in the proceedings of the International Writing Convention, University of East Anglia, April 1985.

■ CHAPTER NINE. THE CHILDREN'S ACHIEVEMENTS AT AGE 10

[1] The data on which these findings are based are reported in detail in chapters 8 and 9 of C. G. Wells, *Language Development in the Pre-School Years* and in "Some antecedents of early educational attainment," *British Journal of Sociology of Education* 2 (1981): 181–200. The full retrospective analysis is reported in *Linguistic Influences on Educational Attainment*, the (unpublished) Final Report to the Department of Education and Science, December 1984.

[2] The children were all asked to write on the same topics in order to allow comparisons to be made between them. We were aware that this was not an ideal situation, as there is no guarantee that a topic of someone else's choosing will call forth an equal commitment from every child. We hoped, though, by asking them to write on a number of different topics, that we would obtain an overall estimate of their writing ability that would not be biased in favor of, or against, any particular individual. In retrospect, however, we are not convinced that this expectation was appropriate. It might have been better if we had been able to collect samples of the writing that they did in the course of their normal classroom activities. However, this too would have caused problems, as the frequency and type of writing that they undertook was in most cases strongly influenced by the teacher and varied considerably from one class to another. There does not seem to be any really satisfactory solution to this dilemma.

The tasks themselves were designed by Barry Kroll for use in an earlier follow-up study of some of the children in the older half of the Bristol sample. The results of his analysis of the samples of writing that were collected in that study can be found in "Antecedents of individual differences in children's writing attainment," in B. M. Kroll and C. G. Wells (eds.), *Explorations in the Development of Writing* (Chichester: John Wiley & Sons, 1983).

[3] Other things being equal, of course. A speech impediment, for example, or a serious lack of self-confidence could cause a different sort of constraint that would effectively mask ability in composing.

[4] Terry Phillips, "Talk among yourselves: it's not my style," in *Language and Learning: An Interactional Perspective*, C. G. Wells and J. C. Nicholls (eds.) (Philadelphia: Taylor and Francis, 1985).

[5] Douglas Barnes and Frankie Todd, *Communication and Learning in Small Groups*, (London: Routledge and Kegan Paul, 1977).

[6] Jeremy Mulford, "Reading," *English in Education* 5, no. 3 (1971).

7 Quoted by J. McH. Sinclair and M. Coulthard in *Towards an Analysis of Discourse: The English Used by Teachers and Pupils* (Oxford: Oxford University Press, 1975), pp. 94–95.

■ CHAPTER TEN.   THE SENSE OF STORY

1 In the first follow-up study, a significant relationship was found between the amount of progress children made in their first two years at school and the subjectively assessed quality of the teaching that we observed them to receive. This suggests that, with better teaching, many more children could make better progress at school, though this would not necessarily lead to a significant change in the rank order, since this is largely determined by factors outside the school's control. (Gordon Wells and Bridie Raban, *Children Learning to Read*, Final Report to the Social Science Research Council [U.K.], 1978).

2 James Britton, "Writing and the story world," in B. M. Kroll and C. G. Wells (eds.), *Explorations in the Development of Writing* (Chichester, Sussex: Wiley, 1983). As Britton acknowledges, this distinction was first made by D. W. Harding in "The role of the onlooker," *Scrutiny* 6 (1937): 247–58.

3 Richard Gregory, in an article entitled "Psychology: towards a science of fiction" (*New Society*, 23 May 1974), refers to such stories as "brain fictions." He goes on to argue that essentially the same processes are involved when, in more formal contexts, we make sense of the evidence obtained through scientific observations or through other forms of research.

4 Barbara Hardy, "Towards a poetic of fiction: an approach through narrative," in *Novel: A Forum on Fiction* (Providence, RI: Brown University, 1968).

5 See, for example, the stories told by Josh and recorded by his mother, quoted in Margaret Meek's chapter, "Imagination and language—play and paradoxes: some considerations of imagination and language," in C. G. Wells and J. C. Nicholls (eds.), *Language and Learning: An Interactional Perspective* (Philadelphia: Taylor and Francis, 1985).

6 See, for example, James Britton, "The role of fantasy," in *Prospect and Retrospect: Selected Essays of James Britton* (Montclair, NJ: Boynton/Cook, 1982); Margaret Spencer, "Stories are for telling," *English in Education* 10 (1976), 16–23; and Bruno Bettelheim, *The Uses of Enchantment: The Meaning and Importance of Fairy Tales* (New York: Knopf, 1976). See also M. Meek, A. Warlow, and G. Barton (eds.), *The Cool Web* (New York: Atheneum, 1978) for a very comprehensive and helpful discussion of children's literature.

7 See the example of David and *The Giant Jam Sandwich* quoted in chapter 8. To this list should also be added the stories that children see on television. Certainly these stories have a powerful influence on the content of their dramatic play.

8 See, for example, chapter 8, note 13.

9 This point is made more fully by Marie Clay in "Getting a theory of writing," in B. M. Kroll and C. G. Wells (eds.), *Explorations in the Development of Writing* (Chichester: Wiley, 1983).

10 This is one of a number of very important points about learning to write that is made by Donald Graves in *Writing: Teachers and Children at Work* (Portsmouth, NH: Heinemann Educational Books, 1982). Another very helpful suggestion that Graves makes concerns the importance of individual "conferencing" at various stages in the process of writing. As I understand this proposal, it is a particularly clear instance of the contingent responsiveness that I have suggested should characterize the guidance that the teacher gives to help children develop their mastery of this or any other craft or area of knowledge.

11 See reference in chapter 8, note 12.

12 I have been unable to trace the source of this quotation, but I would not wish to claim the credit for phrasing this insight so aptly.

[13] Harold Rosen, "The nurture of narrative," *Stories and Meanings* (National Association for the Teaching of English, 1984), p. 16.

[14] Richard Gregory, "Psychology: towards a science of fiction," *New Society*, 23 May 1974, pp. 439–41.

[15] See, for example, the results of the studies of writing by the "Writing across the Curriculum" group (N. Martin, P. D'Arcy, B. Newton, and R. Parker, *Writing and Learning across the Curriculum* [London: Ward Lock Educational, 1976], 11–16), of reading, by the Schools Council Project (E. Lunzer and K. Gardner, *The Effective Use of Reading* [London: Heinemann Educational Books, 1979]) and of the ORACLE study of the primary school (M. Galton, B. Simon, and P. Croll, *Inside the Primary Classroom* [London: Routledge and Kegan Paul, 1980]).

[16] This material comes from the video program *Extending Literacy*. See chapter 6, note 2. For descriptions of similar secondary school classrooms, see Mike Torbe and Peter Medway, *The Climate for Learning* (Montclair, NJ: Boynton/Cook, 1981).

[17] Rosen, "The nurture of narrative," p. 15. My emphasis.

■ CHAPTER ELEVEN. RELATING PRACTICE TO THEORY

[1] The same arguments, or at least very similar ones, also apply to written communication. However, this has been much more readily accepted for written rather than for spoken language, particularly in recent literary critical theory. As yet, though, the implications do not seem to have been much considered by writers of textbooks.

[2] In most passages of recorded speech, I have found, there are utterances that are, initially, completely unintelligible. Even after several replayings, I am simply not able to "hear" them. However, it has been my frequent experience that, on replaying them on a later occasion in a different context, the problem disappears. With a different set of expectations, I am able to reconstruct a meaning; and, when I have an interpretation, the speech signal itself immediately becomes clear.

[3] This is demonstrated very clearly in a number of experiments reported by Bransford and McCarrell. One of their examples involves the sentence "The notes were sour because the seams had split." This initially uninterpretable message becomes clear when one knows that the reference was to music played on the bagpipes—at least if one has any knowledge of the construction of that instrument. (J. D. Bransford and N. S. McCarrell, "A sketch of a cognitive approach to comprehension," in W. B. Weiner and D. S. Palermo (eds.), *Cognition and the Symbolic Processes* [Hillsdale, NJ: Lawrence Erlbaum, 1974].)

[4] See reference in chapter 10, note 10.

[5] This point is made by Lucy Calkins on the basis of her observations as a member of Graves's team. *Lessons from a Child* (Portsmouth, NH: Heinemann Educational Books, 1984).

[6] See, for example, the report of teachers in Coventry secondary schools edited by Mike Torbe, *Language Policies in Action* (London: Ward Lock Educational, 1980) or the various publications of the CEL (Child-Centred, Experienced-Based Learning) Group in Winnipeg.